TRAINING FOR TRANSFORMATION

BOOK IV

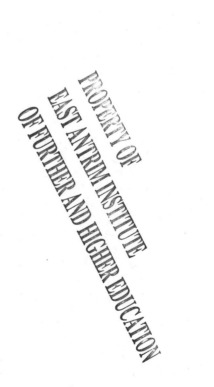

Training for Transformation

A handbook for community workers

Book IV

ANNE HOPE
and
SALLY TIMMEL

Illustrations by Chris Hodzi

PUBLISHING

Published by ITDG Publishing
103–105 Southampton Row, London WC1B 4HL, UK

First published in 1999
Reprinted 2000

ISBN 1 85339 461 0

A catalogue record for this book is available from the British Library

ITDG Publishing is the publishing arm of the Intermediate Technology Development Group.
Our mission is to build the skills and capacity of people in developing countries through the
dissemination of information in all forms, enabling them to improve the quality of their lives and
that of future generations.

Typeset by J&L Composition Ltd, Filey
Printed in Great Britain Russell Press Ltd, Nottingham

CONTENTS

ACKNOWLEDGEMENTS

A number of people have been instrumental in the publication of Book IV of *Training for Transformation*. We first would like to thank Intermediate Technology Publications, especially Neal Burton. This book has been in the process for more than four years and we are deeply grateful to Neal for staying with us through our overloaded work schedules, illness, and distractions.

Again we thank Chris Hodzi of Zimbabwe Community Publishing, for his insights into community life which he expresses so fully through his illustrations. We find his contribution not only lightens up the pages, but also lightens up our spirits.

The chapter on the environment has been inspired by the work of Emilia Charbonneau of the South African Grail and Sr. Hanna Remke, OP. Their workshops provided a springboard for our own adaptation of this critical issue. Vero Schoeffel who helped begin the DELTA women's training programme in Cape Town added they needed passion and focus to this work.

The gender chapter was developed over time through the DELTA women's training programme in Cape Town. We are grateful to the trainers and participants who helped to refine the exercises. We are also very inspired by the major work produced by Oxfam. *The Oxfam Gender Training Manual* is a must for any practitioner in any adult education field. Adelina Mwau who worked with us in Kenya has added much to the practice of gender education.

The racism chapter has included our own work alongside of work done over the years by Nancy Richardson and Donna Bivens of the Women's Theological Centre in Boston. Their untiring pursuit of racial justice is an inspiration to many. Nancy's work is found in these chapters. We also have been extremely grateful to Margaret Legum, who worked with Organization and Social Development Consultants (OSDC) in England for many years on anti-racism work. Her return from exile to South Africa after the lifting of apartheid laws is indeed a welcome addition to the creative thinking and necessary hard work to put in place anti-racist organizations and institutions.

We also wish to thank the staff of Fair Share, School of Government UWC, the DELTA staff, Catholic Welfare and Development and the Grail for their patience, words of encouragement and advice over the time it has taken to write these books. Funders which have supported the writing and have helped to subsidize the publishing of this book include Canadian Development and Peace, Misereor, Cafod, Rockefeller Brothers, and Trocaire. Many thanks and much praise goes to them for their continued support of this work, and for their confidence in the participatory process of transformation that is the inspiration and hope of this work.

PREFACE

Since the first three books of *Training for Transformation* were published in 1984, they have been widely used in training programmes all over Africa and in many other countries. The books have been translated into Spanish and French, and parts of the books into several other languages. As we revised them in 1994, and as we initiated new programmes in South Africa and the United States, we were surprised and delighted to realize how totally relevant the books still are. This is in spite of the fact that there has been a radical shift in thinking about development. Of course the training programmes on which these books were based never did reflect the dominant model of development sponsored by the West. This Western model focused primarily on economic growth, increased production of commodities, capital accumulation and growth of GNP. Development education programmes concentrated primarily on enabling communities and individuals to identify their own needs and find ways of satisfying them together.

The process of involving local people actively in the transformation of their own reality described in the first three books is as relevant today as it ever was. The recognition has grown steadily during the last decade that the only change which effectively transforms the lives of the poor is one in which they have been active participants, and so the demand for the *Training for Transformation* books has grown steadily. Throughout the series we stress the importance of helping local people to develop the skills necessary for building 'People's Movements', an approach which has been strongly affirmed by David Korten in his network for a 'People Centered Approach to Development.' We also give many proven and practical ways of getting this process started.

But can we now use the word 'development'? The very concept has come under serious attack. For instance, Vandana Shiva writes in her book, *Staying Alive* (p.2):

> The UN Decade for Women (1975–85) was based on the assumption that the improvement of women's economic position would automatically flow from an expansion and diffusion of the development process. Yet by the end of the decade it was becoming clear that development itself was the problem. Insufficient and inadequate 'participation' in 'development' was not the cause for women's increasing underdevelopment: it was rather their enforced, but asymmetrical participation in it, by which they bore the costs but were excluded from the benefits, that was responsible. Development exclusivity and dispossession aggravated and deepened the colonial processes of ecological degradation and the loss of political control over nature's sustenance base. Economic growth was a new colonialism, draining resources away from those who needed them most. The discontinuity lay in the fact that it was now new national elites, not colonial powers, that master-minded the exploitation on grounds of national interest and growing GNPs, and it was accomplished with more powerful technologies of appropriation and destruction.

Whenever we used the exercises on 'what do we mean by development?' most groups came up fairly quickly with the recognition that 'there is good development, bad development and very bad development.' But the current critique goes much deeper than this. It is not only a critique of the dominant model of development, but a sense of urgency that development must be seen in the perspective of the survival of the planet, with the new environmental awareness gathered together at the Earth Summit in Rio, and in the light of the new understanding of the effects of gender discrimination.

Although we did not consciously view all development work in the context of the environmental crisis as we do today, when we look back on the generative themes which rural people were constantly raising, we realize that among those that emerged most frequently were 'earth, water, fire and air', the basic life support systems of our planet. Communities were constantly struggling to get good land, to store water, build dams, set up pumps and piping systems, and to deal with the energy crisis, which for most was the shortage of firewood. At the time, we encouraged communities to find solutions to these problems on natural, social, economic and political levels, but we did not link them all together in a broad environmental analysis of the threats to the Earth and her life support systems. Nor did we realize clearly that environmental issues are of crucial importance to the poor because they are the ones suffering most intensely from the violation of the Earth.

All plans and programmes must also take into account a feminist gender analysis, which recognizes how central women are in the creation and maintenance of a culture. Chapter 2 deals with gender and development and is not meant to be comprehensive. *The Oxfam Gender Training Manual* is a resource no organization can be without. Chapter 2 in this book, however, is an introduction to gender issues in a simple and easy form.

We were also very concerned about the re-emergence of overt and covert racism in many western countries, and of deep and ancient ethnic hostilities in situations of extreme scarcity in Yugoslavia and Africa and other places. In the context of poverty, one finds that the different systems of oppression (race, class, culture and gender) nearly always overlap. It is necessary to make the connections between them, and identify the areas in which people are 'one-up' and in which they are 'one-down'. For example, one may be privileged as an educated person, but discriminated against as a black, or privileged as a white and discriminated against as a woman. Chapter 3 deals directly with racism. Many of the exercises can be adapted to situations where domination occurs because of tribe, religion, ethnicity or clan.

Unless we develop a much more comprehensive and sensitive understanding of our own and other cultures, we will either impose our own culture on others, or miss the surge of energy that rises as people move into creation of new ways of satisfying their needs based on their own cultural norms and values. The exercises in Chapter 4 have been used extensively. They provide a positive way out of the dilemma of racism and sexism, if used fully.

In most countries of the world, the question about whether democracy really works is a serious challenge. Chapter 5 sets out a series of exercises and theories that have been used in South Africa since 1995 to address this issue.

As authors, we have developed new programmes incorporating these new perspectives into our work. Now we feel it is time for a new book, to share some of the theory and programmes we have developed. It is especially for those who have been using the *Training for Transformation* series for years, but it is also for others with a special concern about the topics in this volume.

This volume, Book IV, is arranged in a series of modules on these five themes. The modules are made up of several sections which can all be covered one after the other in a weekend on a particular theme, such as environment or gender, or they can be spread out as parts of a longer programme.

We are well aware that there are numerous books and manuals on some of the work in this volume. Our intention is to incorporate in one place some of the most relevant, accessible and practical work. Some of the exercises have been passed on through generations of trainers and across borders. We have searched our files to ensure credit is given to appropriate authors. However, if we have left something out or have not given credit where it is due, please forgive the oversight.

CHAPTER 1
The environment

Section One: The life support systems of the Earth

Section Two: Environment and Health

Section Three: The road to Rio

Section Four: Challenges to change

Section Five: The Council of All Beings

Section Six: The ways forward

Introduction

Environmental education should be based upon a sense of wonder and delight in the Earth which has been given us for our home, the 'biosphere' on which we all depend for our very lives, and the cosmos, the galaxies of heaven, which give us a sense of awe as we glimpse the vastness of the universe and our particular place within it.

We can start this module on the environment with a positive experience of nature and creation, looking at some of the specific systems (air, water, land, food and trees), sharing ideas about how to protect these systems from further abuse, or we can begin with Section Two, looking at health problems caused for so many by the abuse of the Earth and all its systems. The process is up to the facilitator in relation to the group. We have found it helpful for groups to experience an 'ideal' so that later it is possible to work for those goals.

SECTION ONE

The life support systems of the Earth

We suggest that this section of the programme should begin with an all-day field trip to the most beautiful and fertile place within reach. In Cape Town we have often taken the group to a magnificent botanical garden on the slopes of Table Mountain. Mountain streams run down through the garden. The beauty itself is a stimulus for discussion, contrasting strongly with the squalid urban conditions nearby in which so many people have to live. Immediately this experience puts participants in touch with the two great themes of the Earth Summit in Rio in 1993, the integrity of the Earth and global poverty.

Exercise 1. Field visit of discovery

If at all possible, arrange an outing for the group. Transport may be a problem, but many cities have beautiful parks or lakes or quiet places by the sea, and in most rural areas there are mountains or rivers, national parks, or beautiful farms, which could be a starting point for these discussions.

Advise everybody to wear their most comfortable shoes and clothes. Many people dress up in their best for outings and can then become too uncomfortable to relate to their surroundings peacefully.

Procedure

1. Find a comfortable meeting place in the shade where participants can leave their things.

2. Ask them to divide into groups, each of which will focus on one of the following topics: Water, Air, Earth and Trees. There should be **two to five people in each group**, and if necessary there can be several groups dealing with each topic.

3. Give them time (half to one hour, depending on the size of the place) to wander about in their group thinking about and discussing the following questions about their topic:

    a. Why is this thing (Earth, Water, Fire or Trees) so important in our lives?
    b. In what ways do we depend on it?
    c. In what ways do we show that we value it?
    d. What have human beings done to destroy or pollute it?
    e. Why have humans been devaluing it in this way?
    f. What will be the consequences if we continue to devalue it?
    g. What could we do to save this crucial element, now and for our grandchildren?

4. When the group re-gathers, ask each group to choose a spokesperson. Anyone in the group can add things they thought about.

5. Give each group a chance to report, but keep the atmosphere conversational. Though the observations of the groups are usually extremely interesting, it is important that the facilitator keeps the process moving. Report-backs can become long and boring, so when necessary interrupt the process with a relevant song or some body movement or a break.

6. Ask participants to share any songs they remember about nature. Each culture will have its own songs and poems.

Time   2 hours

Materials   Transport for the group to a park, poems and songs.

Trees

I think that I shall never see
A poem lovely as a tree.

A tree whose hungry mouth is pressed
Against the earth's sweet flowing breast;

A tree that looks at God all day
And lifts her leafy arms to pray;

A tree that may in summer wear
A nest of robins in her hair;

Upon whose bosom snow has lain;
Who intimately lives with rain.

Poems are made by fools like me,
But only God can make a tree.

Joyce Kilmer
(*The Family Album of Favourite Poems*, Edited by P. Edward Ernest, Grosset &
Dunlap, Inc. 51 Madison Avenue, New York, NY.)

Sea Fever

I must go down to the seas again, to the lonely sea and the sky,
And all I ask is a tall ship and a star to steer her by,
And the wheel's kick and the wind's song and the white sail's shaking,
And a grey mist on the sea's face and a grey dawn breaking.

I must go down to the seas again, for the call of the running tide
Is a wild call and a clear call that may not be denied;
And all I ask is a windy day with the white clouds flying,
And the flung spray and the blown spume, and the sea-gulls crying.

I must go down to the seas again, to the vagrant gypsy life,
To the gull's way and the whale's way where the wind's like a whetted knife;
And all I ask is a merry yarn from a
laughing fellow-rover,
And quiet sleep and a sweet dream
when the long trick's over.

John Masefield
(*A Treasury of Great Poems*,
Simon and Schuster Inc.,
Rockefeller Center, 1230 Sixth
Avenue, NY. NY, no date)

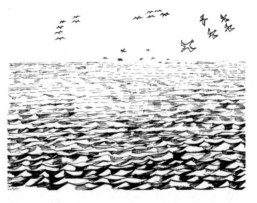

Exercise 2. Chief Seattle's letter

Ask two or three people to prepare to read out this letter from Chief Seattle to the President of the United States in 1855. Explain that Chief Seattle was a native American chief at this time when white people were conquering and making treaties with original habitants of North America.

Today this letter is used very widely in environmental education. Native American culture had a very deep reverence for nature, but, as with many other indigenous peoples, the wisdom within the culture was not appreciated by those preoccupied with economic progress and technological inventions. The very idea of private ownership of the land seemed strange to native Americans, who regarded it as a gift of God for all to share, as did many tribes in Africa.

Procedure

1. Ask the readers to read the letter aloud.

2. Ask people what struck them especially about the letter, **first in pairs and then in the whole group**.

3. Ask participants to choose one phrase from the letter and illustrate it with crayons or watercolour paints. Ask participants to share their drawing and explain why this is important to them.

Time   45 minutes

Materials   Copies of the Letter from Chief Seattle for all participants, crayons and/or paints and paper.

The poor and needy ask for water, and there is none,
their tongue is parched with thirst.
I, Yahweh, will answer them,
I, the God of Israel, will not abandon them.

I will make rivers well up on barren heights,
and fountains in the midst of valleys;
turn the wilderness into a lake,
and dry ground into waterspring.

In the wilderness I will put cedar trees,
acacias, myrtles, olives.
In the desert I will plant juniper,
plane tree and cypress side by side;

so that [people] may see and know,
may all observe and understand
that the hand of Yahweh has done this,
that the Holy One of Israel has created it.

Isaiah 41:17–20

Letter from Chief Seattle

How can you buy or sell the sky, the warmth of the land?
The idea is strange to us.
Yet we do not own the freshness of the air or the sparkle of the water.
How can you buy them from us?
We will decide in our time.
Every part of the earth is sacred to my people.
Every shining pine needle, every sandy shore, every mist of the divine
woods, every clearing and humming insect is holy
in the memory of my people.
We know that the white man does not understand our ways.
One portion of the land is the same to him as the next,
for he is a stranger who comes in the night and takes from the land
whatever he needs.
The earth is not his brother, but his enemy,
and when he has conquered it, he moves on.
He leaves his father's grave behind and he does not care.
He kidnaps the earth from his children. He does not care.
His father's grave and his children's birthright are forgotten.
His appetite will devour the earth, leaving behind only a desert.
The sight of your cities pains the eyes of the redman.
But perhaps it is because the redman is a savage
and does not understand. . . .

One thing we know that the white man may one day discover.
Our God is the same God.
You may think now that you own him as you wish to own our land.
But you cannot.
He is the God of all people.
And his compassion is equal for the redman and the white.
The earth is precious to him, and to harm the earth is to heap contempt on
its creator. The whites too shall pass, perhaps sooner than other tribes.
Continue to contaminate your bed, and you will one night suffocate
in your own waste.
When the buffalo are all slaughtered, the wild horses all tamed . . .
where is the thicket? Gone.
Where is the eagle? Gone.
And what is it to say goodbye to the swift pony and the hunt,
but the end of living and the beginning of survival.
We might understand if we knew what it was that the white man dreams,
what hopes he describes to his children on long winter nights,
what visions he burns into their minds, so that they will wish for tomorrow.
But we are savages.
The white man's dreams are hidden from us. . . .

If we sell you our land, love it as we have loved it.
Care for it as we have cared for it.
Hold in your mind the memory of our land, as it is, when you take it.
And with all your strength, with all your might, and with all your heart,
preserve it for your children, and love it as God loves us all.
One thing we know, our God is the same God.
Even the white man cannot be exempt from the common destiny.

From a letter from Chief Seattle of the Duvamish tribe to the President of the United States, 1855

Exercise 3. **Understanding our Earth and universe**

If possible, continue with this section outdoors after a lunch break during the field trip. If it is not possible to arrange an all-day outing, try to hold this session outdoors at a later stage, perhaps in a nearby garden. Choose three or four of the sections, adapting them to your own circumstances. Do not try to squeeze in too much, but allow the participants time to savour the experiences and share their reactions afterwards.

From dividing everything into parts to a sense of the whole

The great new insight of ecology in the 1950s was that everything is connected. For centuries scientists had been separating up everything into specialized topics of study. We studied plants in botany, animals in zoology, and living things, including the human body, in biology. I got a shock the first time I heard of biochemistry. Could one really combine these two different sciences, biology and chemistry? Ecology recognized that it was pointless to study any of these topics in isolation, because each one depended on all the others, and the connections between them were even more important than the individual thing seen on its own. This insight about the connectedness of all things was new to science, but it was very old to the mystics. Many of them had a deep awareness of the unity of all tribes and of the spiritual dimension in everything that exists. Buddhism is permeated with this awareness. As Thich Nhat Hahn says, 'The rose and the garbage are one. If there were no rose there would be no garbage, but if there were no garbage there would also be no rose.'

Procedure

1. Ask the group to make themselves comfortable. If there is a fine tree growing nearby, around which it is possible for everyone to lie down in a circle on their backs, with their feet pointing towards the trunk, this would be the ideal setting for this meditation. But it can also be done while people sit comfortably in chairs.

2. Ask everybody to close their eyes and pay attention to their breathing. Read the following meditation slowly, pausing where necessary:

   'Slowly breathe in. Feel the air entering your nostrils and travelling slowly down your windpipe to fill your lungs. Slowly breathe out. Breathe in, as deeply as you can, filling your lungs with air. . . . Very slowly breathe out. . . . Breathe in . . . Breathe out. . . . Continue to breathe slowly and attentively noticing what happens to your breath, to the rest of your body.

   'Now use your imagination to follow your breath down your windpipe into your lungs. Notice your chest falling as you breathe out. As you breathe in again, imagine and experience the breath filling your lungs. Imagine all the tiny blood vessels throughout your lungs drawing in the oxygen from the air. Imagine the blood carrying the oxygen moving from the small vessels into larger vessels, passing along the pulmonary artery to your heart; feel the beating of your heart as it pumps out the blood to flow to all the parts of the body, to your head, your arms, your fingers, your legs, your toes; become aware of the blood returning again to your lungs, ready to pass the carbon dioxide it has gathered back into your breath to be exhaled. Think of the oxygen-rich air you are breathing in, and of the carbon dioxide-rich air you are breathing out. Breathe in. . . . Breathe out . . . Breath in . . . Breathe out. . . .

'Now start to imagine where the air you are breathing in has come from. Is it stale air, breathed before by many other people? Does the room smell stuffy? Are there fumes in the air from passing motor cars? Or is the air fresh and sweet full of oxygen as it comes directly from the leaves of trees and plants in a garden or a forest? As you breathe out consider where the air that has passed through your body is going. Imagine it slipping joyously into the green chlorophyll of a leaf on a tree. Imagine the carbon dioxide in the air that was once your breath transformed into oxygen again in the leaves of the tree and coming out again into the atmosphere. As you continue to breathe slowly and attentively, think about all the air around us. Spend a few minutes quietly imagining what has happened to the air, where it has been, how it has been affected in different places, how this might affect your own body . . . your own life. . . .'

[If you are inside, let the group keep their eyes closed and say, 'Imagine there are clouds resting peacefully above you or blowing past in the wind.' Otherwise, say: 'When you are ready, open your eyes and look up through the branches of the tree to the sky above.']

'Think of how the clouds have drawn moisture from the sea, of how they turn the water vapour into rain, how it falls on the earth, soaking the soil, enabling plants to grow, enabling trees to draw up water from the depths of the earth. Think of the sap rising up the trunk, flowing along the branches, bringing life to the leaves (and flowers and fruit). Think of sun bringing light and warmth to the soil, to the plants, and animals, to your own body. Think how the rain and the soil and the sun and the air provide you with fruit and vegetables and grain, provide food for the hens and the animals which give you meat, provide, in fact, all the food you have ever eaten, all the food that has enabled you to grow and given you energy. Can you think of any form of food which does not come originally from the earth, the air and the sun and the rain? The tree like us is connected to, dependent upon, all the life support systems of the Earth.

'Now, keeping your sense of the connection between your own body and the air, the water, the earth and the sun, slowly open your eyes and wriggle your fingers and toes. Start to stretch your arms and your legs, yawn, move, enjoy the life of your body, the life of the Earth. Bring your attention back to this place, to the people around you, to all you have shared, and sit up, smiling.'

3. Ask participants to turn to a partner and share what they have experienced and what has been going through their minds as they did this exercise.

4. Then, in the whole group, ask a few people if they would like to share what they experienced.

Alternative

If it has not been possible to do this meditation in the open air under a tree, you can do a modified version using a beautiful bowl of water, starting with the breathing, and then proceeding as follows:

> We have been thinking about the cycle of the air, and about how we are part of that cycle. Now we are going to think about the cycle of water. We have here a beautiful bowl of clear water. We will pass it around turning the bowl slightly as we pass it to the next person. Everyone will take a good deep drink of it. And as the bowl is passed around the circle let us think about the cycle of the water. Where does this water come from? . . . What happened to it before it came out of the tap? . . . Before it got into the pipes? Before it got into the reservoir? (Name the local reservoir from which the drinking water is drawn.) . . . What role does water play in my body? . . . Where is it going? . . . In what ways are we all involved in the cycle of the water?

Hold up a sheet of clean white paper and ask the participants what they can see in it – then read 'Interbeing' from *The Heart of Understanding* by Thich Nhat Hahn.

Time   45 minutes

Materials   Copies of the 'Interbeing' handout for all participants.

Interbeing

If you are a poet, you will see clearly that there is a cloud floating in this sheet of paper. Without a cloud, there will be no rain; without rain, the trees cannot grow; and without trees, we cannot make paper. The cloud is essential for the paper to exist. If the cloud is not here, the sheet of paper cannot be here either. So we can say that the cloud and the paper inter-are. 'Interbeing' is a word that is not in the dictionary yet, but if we combine the prefix 'inter-' with the verb 'to be,' we have a new verb, inter-be. Without a cloud, we cannot have paper, so we can say that the cloud and the sheet of paper inter-are.

If we look into this sheet of paper even more deeply, we can see the sunshine in it. If the sunshine is not there, the forest cannot grow. In fact, nothing can grow. Even we cannot grow without sunshine. And so, we know that the sunshine is also in this sheet of paper. The paper and the sunshine inter-are. And if we continue to look, we can see the logger who cut the tree and brought it to the mill to be transformed into paper. And we see the wheat. We know that the logger cannot exist without his daily bread, and therefore the wheat that became his bread is also in this sheet of paper. And the logger's father and mother are in it too. When we look in this way, we see that without all of these things, this sheet of paper cannot exist.

Looking even more deeply, we can see we are in it too. This is not difficult to see, because when we look at a sheet of paper, the sheet of paper is part of our perception. Your mind is in here and mine is also. So we can say that everything is in here with this sheet of paper. You cannot point out one thing that is not here – time, space, the earth, the rain, the minerals in the soil, the sunshine, the cloud, the river, the heat. Everything co-exists with this sheet of paper. That is why I think the word inter-be should be in the dictionary. 'To be' is to inter-be. You cannot just be by yourself alone. You have to inter-be with every other thing. This sheet of paper is, because everything else is.

Suppose we try to return one of the elements to its source. Suppose we return the sunshine to the sun. Do you think that this sheet of paper will be possible? No, without sunshine nothing can be. And if we return the logger to his mother, then we have no sheet of paper either. The fact is that this sheet of paper is made up only of 'non-paper elements'. And if we return these non-paper elements to their sources, then there can be no paper at all. Without 'non-paper elements', like mind, logger, sunshine and so on, there will be no paper. As thin as this sheet of paper is, it contains everything in the universe in it.

('Interbeing', pages 3–5, by Thich Nhat Hahn)

Exercise 4. The ecological stretch

This stretch is a wonderful way of celebrating in movement our sense of oneness with the universe.

Procedure

1. Ask the participants to form several concentric semi-circles in front of you and to move around until they all have room to stretch in all directions, but can still see and hear you. Choose a pleasant place outside in the shade if it is hot, or in the sun on a cold day.

2. Ask them to stand erect, planting their feet firmly on the ground several inches apart, and to follow your motions, reflecting peacefully on your words:

   'Raise your hands and hold them one behind the other several inches from your heart. Become aware of your own being, the gift of your own life, of your own history. Realize that you are unique in all the world. There is no other person anywhere who shares the whole of your experience, your history, the web of all your relationships. You are unique, you are precious, give thanks for your being.

   'But though you are unique, you are not alone, you are connected to everything else that exists, that has ever existed. Feel the firmness of the earth beneath your feet. Know your need of it. Slowly lower your hands towards the earth. Stretch your fingers down towards the earth. Become conscious of the solid rock and the life-giving waters beneath the earth.

   'Slowly raise your arms out on either side, growing conscious of all that grows on the Earth,

   the grasses, the grains, the plants, vegetables which nourish our bodies. Become aware of the wealth of wildlife, the insects and lizards, all the small creatures, the larger animals and the birds that find their homes and their food and drink in the earth around us. Continue to raise your arms reaching up towards the sky with the trees. Feel the pull of the sun as you reach up, beyond the trees, beyond the sun, towards the stars, into space, outer space. Know that "you are a child of the universe, no less than the stars and the trees, you have a right to be here." And as you celebrate your connection with all this, draw your arms and your awareness down, into your mind, into your heart, into the core of your being.' [As you say this, lower your hands slowly before your face, your heart, your whole body. Then reach forward, palms up as you say,] 'And offer it all back to the world.'

3. Sometimes it is helpful to do this stretch a second time, as people are less conscious then of trying to do the right thing and can reflect more deeply on the meaning of words and gestures.

Time   15 to 20 minutes

Materials   None

Exercise 5. **The great dance of the universe**

As we consider the movements of the water and the air we begin to see that nothing is static, nothing stands still. The mountains and the rocks may seem to stand still but scientists now tell us that these too are made up of atoms and molecules which are constantly in motion. This is harder to understand, but let us think about the biosphere, that living 'skin' which surrounds the core of rock which is at the centre of the Earth.

The biosphere or ball of life (bio means life) includes the air, the water, the minerals, the plants, the trees the rivers and the oceans, let alone the fish, the birds and the animals. It is easy to see that everything is in motion within and without. All are involved in a great dance, and we too are part of that dance. We do not simply live on the Earth. We are part of the Earth, and just as each part of a body is dependent for health on all the others, so our own health and well-being is linked up with the health and well-being of the Earth.

Our dance with all the creatures of Earth is part of a greater dance, the dance of the Earth with the other planets around the sun. And our solar system, which at first seems so vast to us, is in fact just a tiny part of the universe, the cosmos, with its innumerable galaxies, collections of stars, most of them suns far greater than our own, reaching out beyond our sight and beyond our imagining.

It's the song of the universe,
while aeons roll away.
It's the song that the stars sing
and all the planets play
It's a song to the power
neither you nor I can see
It's a song to the One
who is Mystery.
Sr Miriam Therese Winter

Procedure

1. Read or summarize the introduction above.

2. Ask participants to decide on a song most people will know.

3. Ask them all to join hands and dance, weaving in and out among each other. Alternatively, at an appropriate moment in this programme, which could be at an earlier point if the group needs energizing, invite the group to get up and do a circle dance. This could be a traditional African or folk dance, preferably one that involves different groups moving into the centre of the circle to dance together for a while, and then moving back to the outer circle.

Time   20 to 30 minutes

Materials None

Exercise 6. Collages of the cycles of interaction

We have begun to think about our own connections with the cycle of air and the cycle of water. What about the larger cycles of air and water, in our region and globally? And what about the other movements in the dance? What about the soil, the living things (trees, animals and plants) and what about energy (heat, light, movement)?

Procedure

1. Put up sheets of paper with the following headings on the walls around the room, as far apart from each other as possible:

   AIR
   WATER
   LIVING THINGS (Trees, animals, birds, fish and plants)
   EARTH (Soil)
   ENERGY (Heat, light, movement)

2. Ask people to form **five groups**. Each group will think about the patterns of movement in one of the above cycles, try to understand it as deeply as possible and then make a collage, using coloured pens, drawings and magazine cuttings, illustrating the cycle, the movement of the dance in their particular system. They can use arrows to link the different phases of the process.

   If groups have difficulty at first making connections, spend some time with them asking questions such as: Where does it come from? . . . Where does it go? . . . How does it change in the process? . . . How does it affect our lives?

3. When the collages are complete, place the globe in the centre of the room, and put all the collages in a circle around it. Let the group move slowly around the circle in a clockwise direction, looking at the collages of the other groups, encouraging them to make connections between the different systems (e.g. our blood consists mainly of water, which carries the oxygen from the air to give energy to our bodies). They can show these connections using additional arrows or additional words and pictures on slips of paper.

Time   1 hour

Materials A globe showing natural geographical features of Earth rather than political boundaries, newsprint, felt pens, magazines with pictures, scissors, crayons.

Alternative: Meditation on a tree

If there is a fine tree growing nearby, around which it is possible for everyone to lie down in a circle on their backs with their feet almost touching the trunk as in the breathing exercise at the beginning of this section, one can develop a marvellous meditation on the life of the tree and the way our own lives are connected to that of the tree. The cycle of air, of the oxygen and carbon dioxide, of our own need for oxygen, and the planet's need of the ability of the leaves to transform carbon dioxide into oxygen. The cycle of water can also be woven into the meditation. A tree is a wonderful source for meditation on the environment because it is connected to all the other sources.

SECTION TWO
Environment and health

It is becoming more and more clear that many illnesses are caused by an unhealthy environment. Many of the factors making an environment unhealthy have been introduced by man, especially the waste produced by industrial development. Many forms of cancer, allergies, various types of poisoning by lead, mercury and other chemicals, as well as numerous respiratory problems, such as asthma, pneumonia, bronchitis, sinusitis, and gastric problems such as diarrhoea, cholera and dysentery are caused by pollution of the air and water. Most malnutrition results not from ignorance, but from poverty arising from unjust distribution of land and access to resources.

As all people everywhere are concerned about health, especially where it is breaking down and people are dying for mysterious reasons, it may be best in some communities to start a programme on the environment with this section.

Exercise 7. Survey of your local environment

The aim of this session is to help participants look critically at their own environment and to become aware of any threats that it might present to the health of local residents.

Procedure

This survey should be done by participants in their own areas, preferably in teams, either before a workshop on the environment or in between the phases of an ongoing programme.

1. Hand out the sheet of questions, read it aloud and give participants an opportunity to ask questions of clarification.

2. Give them an opportunity to form survey teams. These must be from the same area and must really be able to work together: if they live too far apart nothing will get done. If participants in the programme come as isolated individuals from very scattered areas, it is better to let them make lists of other people from their home areas who would be interested in working with them on a survey than to settle for teams which have no real chance of getting together.

3. Brainstorm a list of the places they should visit to find the answers to each section of the questionnaire. Each team should define clearly the area they aim to survey, setting reasonable limits so that they do not bite off more than they can chew. It can be a rural village or an urban neighbourhood with definite boundaries.

4. Suggest that they use the questionnaire to summarize their findings.

5. Set the date, at least two weeks ahead, for sharing the findings and debriefing the experience.

Time 20 minutes to introduce the exercise and 30 minutes to plan the survey. Allow at least two weeks to do the survey. This will take several hours of teamwork each week, depending on how large and complex the area is and how ambitious the group is, as well as one to two hours to discuss and combine information in the whole group.

Materials Environment questionnaire for each team.

Questionnaire: Survey of local environment

1. Land
   a. Does the land-use lead to any hazards to health?
      e.g. dangerous roads or railways, holes etc. or growth of potentially dangerous drugs such as coca, from which cocaine can be derived. Are chemical fertilizers used?

2. Water
   a. Where do people get their drinking water?
      Is it pure or polluted?
      Is there adequate sanitation?
   b. Is there adequate water available for washing, at least 25 litres per person per day?
   c. Are there pools or swampy areas where mosquitoes or other insects breed?
   d. Is human or animal waste washed into the water?
   e. Are there any factories or industrial plants dumping chemicals and toxic wastes into the water and poisoning fish?
   f. Is oil from tankers and other waste from ships polluting sea water, poisoning fish and shellfish, and making bathing dangerous?

3. Trees
   a. Are there enough trees in the area to provide shade and adequate firewood?
   b. Are there enough trees to restore the oxygen balance in the air and deal with the carbon dioxide produced in breathing and the carbon monoxide produced by cars?
   c. Have too many trees been cut down, causing soil erosion, floods and drought?
   d. Are there dangerous trees which could fall down, or poisonous shrubs such as oleander?

4. Air
   a. Is the air fresh or polluted?
      If so by what? smoke, fumes, smog?
   b. What or who is responsible for air pollution?
      e.g. traffic, factories, fires, paper mills, chemical plants?

5. Food
   a. Is it possible for most people to obtain a good balanced diet?
   b. Are there adequate laws ensuring that all food sold is safe to eat, e.g. butchering of meat, canning food, fresh supplies of dairy products?

6. *Energy*
   a. Is there pollution caused by the type of energy used:
   coal, oil, gas, paraffin, charcoal?

7. *Waste*
   a. How is human and animal excrement dealt with in your area?
   Are there adequate sewage systems, converting sewage into useful compost and recycling liquid wastes through natural systems, e.g. reed beds?
   b. How is domestic waste dealt with? Is there adequate garbage collection in urban areas? Where is it dumped?
   Are there communities living on the garbage dumps and depending on them for the essentials of survival?
   c. How do local factories and industrial plants deal with their waste? Is the polluter made to pay for cleaning up any pollution they cause?
   d. Are workers informed about any hazards to their health caused by particular types of work, e.g. in mines and chemical plants?

8. *Population*
   a. What are the health hazards caused by overcrowding, e.g. in shacks and informal settlements or urban slums?
   b. How much space per person do you think is needed for a healthy life, both physically and psychologically?

Exercise 8. Case studies on environmental illness

In preparation for this exercise write on separate sheets of newsprint the names and three or four sentences about six children suffering from diseases common in your area, which are caused by environmental pollution, e.g.

- a nine year old boy with asthma
- a baby with diarrhoea or cholera
- a five year old with severe malnutrition
- a three year old with severe burns
- a sixteen year old with AIDS
- a thirteen year old with TB

Procedure

1. Brainstorm in the whole group: what are the most common illnesses in your area caused by pollution or an unhealthy environment?

2. Put up sheets of newsprint with the descriptions of each child on the walls as far apart as possible.

3. Read these short summaries aloud and ask the participants to go and stand under the newsprint about the child they would like to work on, making a second choice where necessary so that the groups are more or less equal.

4. Each group then writes the story of the child's life and the circumstances which probably led to the present crisis in its health.

5. Each story is read to the whole group and then in pairs the participants discuss the probable causes of the problem and the steps which could be taken by the community both to lobby for action by those in authority, and to solve the problem themselves in the spirit of self reliance, to reduce the danger of more people becoming ill.

6. In the whole group, discuss:

   a. In what ways do the poor in urban areas suffer most from environmental problems?
   b. In what ways do the poor in rural areas suffer most from environmental problems?

7. Put the following statement up on newsprint:

   When man violates the Earth and threatens the life support systems which have sustained us for thousands of years, it is always the poor who suffer most acutely. But ultimately there is a backlash which affects all members of society, regardless of class.

   Ask participants to discuss 'Do you think both aspects of this statement are true? Give examples to support your opinions.'

Time   1½ hours

Materials   Newsprint prepared with statements about the six children and the final statement. A globe showing geographical features. Newsprint, markers, masking tape. Paper and pens for groups.

SECTION THREE

The road to Rio

A dramatic presentation of the forces threatening the life-support systems of the Earth and the factors which led to the Earth Summit in Rio in 1992. The importance of this summit was that for the first time it made a clear link between both the causes of and the solutions to global poverty and environmental degradation.

Exercise 9. The assault on the Earth: a simulation

This session is designed to stimulate participants to reflect critically on some of the aspects of modernization which they see all around them. Some will be far more familiar to those living in cities, and others to those living in rural areas. It is important that both groups grow in understanding that many of the things we formerly saw as the great achievements of 'progress' or 'development' are the very things that have led to the current environmental crisis. This crisis is forcing us to rethink all our priorities and strategies for development.

Procedure

1. If it is a small group ask one person to study and represent each of the following ways in which the Earth has been assaulted. If the group is bigger, have up to five people working together on each topic.

2. Each person or group is to choose one of the following topics (see handout for Notes).

   - industrialization
   - colonialism and neo-colonialism
   - urbanization
   - the destruction caused by cars
   - paint and steel
   - air pollution
   - 'scientific' agriculture
   - wasting water

   They are asked to prepare either a collage from the magazines provided, or a short drama revealing the destructive forces involved. For example, a poster for industrialization could show smoking factories, pouring wastes into the river, and the drama might show the ruthless members of the board of a company planning to get rid of their waste materials as cheaply as possible by dumping them in the river, using the cheapest and dirtiest form of energy.

3. After each group has completed their task ask all the participants to sit in a circle around the globe. Each group sends up a representative to make a gesture of aggression towards the globe – a punch, a slap, a stab or a kick (without actually touching the globe) – before making their presentation. (They could also draw and place arrows or spears on pieces of paper around the globe.) It is best to see all the presentations and then to discuss their insights one by one.

19

4. After the last presentation ask for a moment of silence to reflect on the damage that has been done to the Earth, the Mother that has sustained us for so long. Then read aloud 'The world awakens'.

Time   1 to 2 hours.

Materials   If possible get a big globe of the Earth. It is best if it shows the Earth without political boundaries. If this is not available any globe will do or the continents could be drawn with soft felt pens on a large blue balloon. You will also need magazines, pens, glue.

The world awakens

The person who started to open the eyes of the world to the damage that we are doing to the Earth was a woman called Rachel Carson, who wrote a book in 1962 called *Silent Spring*, a sombre and powerful warning to humanity of the consequences of its actions. The pollution caused by Western development was killing vast numbers of birds.

Ten years later the United Nations convened the first international conference on the Human Environment in Stockholm, Sweden. This conference revealed the growing threat that human existence posed to the continued health of the planet and proposed strategies to deal with the problems recognized at the time. Since then a great number of non-governmental organizations such as Greenpeace have sprung up in many countries, all contributing to the Green Movement, which is committed to ensuring sustainable development. They recognize the importance of building awareness of the threats to the environment, encouraging people to change the way they live, and passing laws to prevent big industrial companies from continuing to pollute the Earth.

In 1987 the UN World Commission on Environment and Development linked for the first time two crucial issues which had always previously been tackled separately: environmental protection and global economic growth and development. Headed by the Norwegian woman prime minister Gro Brundtland, this commission produced a stunning report which put the issues of sustainable development into the mainstream of world debate.

In 1989 there was an international conference in Nicaragua, called 'The Fate and Hope of the Earth', bringing together grassroots organizations that were working on environmental issues with those that were working on Peace and those working on Human Rights. As we analysed the causes of the problems each movement was addressing we recognized that the fundamental causes of all the problems sprang from the same source. It was the pursuit of wealth through Western industrial development, in which each company and each nation strove for the maximization of profits at the expense of both human well-being and the well being of the whole Earth community. Greed for short-term profits with no concern for the future lay at the heart of all the problems.

In 1992 the Earth Summit met in Rio, the largest face-to-face meeting of national leaders in history. This conference showed how global poverty was directly linked to the degradation of the environment, and produced 'Agenda 21', a very important set of policy guidelines for the 21st century.

NOTES: The world awakens to environmental problems

We all need more information on the major areas of alarm. Groups seriously interested in their environment will need more up-to-date information on the situation regarding each of these areas in their own part of the world and the facilitator should be able to put the group in touch with local resources where they can obtain the information, and organize a participatory research project with the group. The following are some areas of information that will need to be gathered to understand how the environment is being damaged each day, each hour.

a. Industrialization

The demand for energy for production and transport.
Coal, steam, smoke and air pollution. Mining.
Waste chemicals and hot
water discharged into rivers. Fish dying.
Fog and mist combine to make smog.
Child labour and exploitation.

b. Colonialism and neo-colonialism

The search for raw materials.
Monocrop cultures. Destruction of soil through cash crops like peanuts, tea, coffee, cocoa, sugar.
Destruction of the rain forests.
Scientific forestry. No place for people or other living creatures.
Loss of tropical hardwoods such as mahogany and yellowwoods.
The lungs of the earth are needed for breathing and photosynthesis.
Destruction of species as they lose their habitat.

c. Urbanization

Overcrowding with housing shortage and squatter settlements.
Population outgrows the systems of water and waste.
Dumping sewage in the sea or lakes.
Cities so large and polluted, children and the elderly wear masks to breathe.

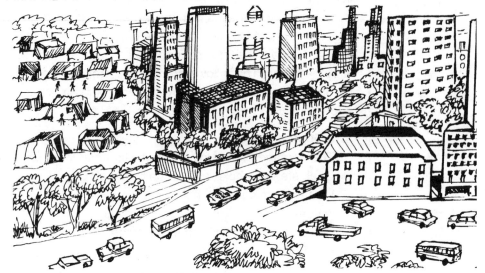

d. The destruction caused by cars

Rapid increase in the numbers on the road
Truck companies win transport business from railways.
The effects of highway systems on nutrition.
Poor public transport.
One by one travel to work.
Fumes and carbon monoxide.
The death of trees along the highway.

e. Paint and steel

Enormous demand for goods from factories that cause
serious air pollution.
The smoke stacks of cities.
The chemical corridors in cities that cause cancer.

f. Air pollution

The dirty brown cloud over most modern cities.
Smog. Respiratory diseases.
Air warnings. 'Smog too thick. Don't go out'.
Destruction of the ozone layer.
Danger of skin cancer.
Global warming and the rising of the seas.
Flooding of low-lying land and islands.

g. 'Scientific' agriculture

From family farms and subsistence to agribusiness.

From intercropping to vast monocrops, as far as the eye can see.

From human and animal energy to tractors, ploughs and combine harvesters.

The creation of dust bowls.

From manure, compost and organic farming to chemical fertilizers and insecticides.

The pollution of rivers and lakes and the death of fish.

The Green Revolution. Why did the poor and hungry get poorer and more hungry?

Land redistribution and small organic farms.

How to grow a lot of food in a small space.

Irrigation and water conservation.

h. Wasting water

Shortage of clean pure water.

Lowering of the water table.

Poisoning of ground water.

Floods due to chopping down the trees above the rivers on the mountains.

In the 21st century people will go to war over water, not oil.

THE ROAD TO THE

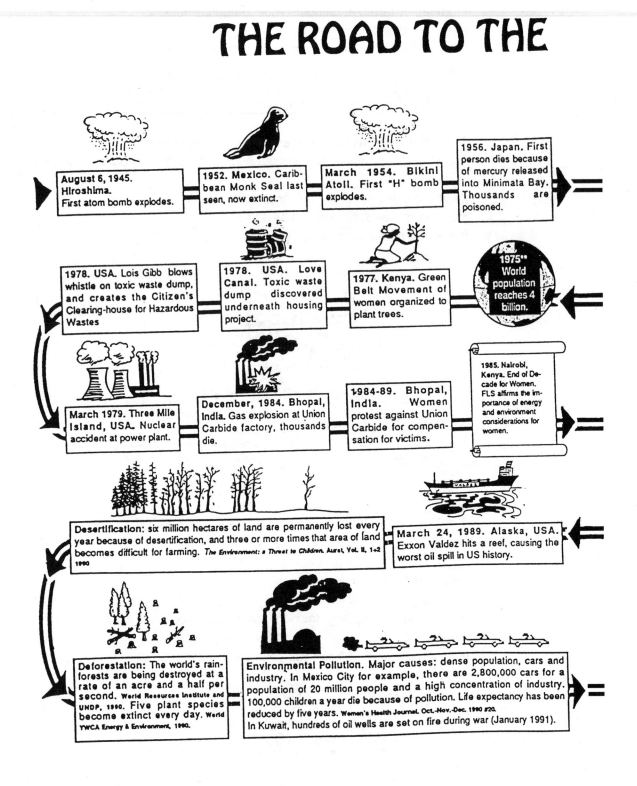

August 6, 1945. Hiroshima. First atom bomb explodes.

1952. Mexico. Caribbean Monk Seal last seen, now extinct.

March 1954. Bikini Atoll. First "H" bomb explodes.

1956. Japan. First person dies because of mercury released into Minimata Bay. Thousands are poisoned.

1978. USA. Lois Gibb blows whistle on toxic waste dump, and creates the Citizen's Clearing-house for Hazardous Wastes

1978. USA. Love Canal. Toxic waste dump discovered underneath housing project.

1977. Kenya. Green Belt Movement of women organized to plant trees.

1975** World population reaches 4 billion.

March 1979. Three Mile Island, USA. Nuclear accident at power plant.

December, 1984. Bhopal, India. Gas explosion at Union Carbide factory, thousands die.

1984-89. Bhopal, India. Women protest against Union Carbide for compensation for victims.

1985. Nairobi, Kenya. End of Decade for Women. FLS affirms the importance of energy and environment considerations for women.

Desertification: six million hectares of land are permanently lost every year because of desertification, and three or more times that area of land becomes difficult for farming. *The Environment: a Threat to Children. Aural, Vol. II, 1+2* 1990

March 24, 1989. Alaska, USA. Exxon Valdez hits a reef, causing the worst oil spill in US history.

Deforestation: The world's rainforests are being destroyed at a rate of an acre and a half per second. World Resources Institute and UNDP, 1990. Five plant species become extinct every day. World YWCA Energy & Environment, 1990.

Environmental Pollution. Major causes: dense population, cars and industry. In Mexico City for example, there are 2,800,000 cars for a population of 20 million people and a high concentration of industry. 100,000 children a year die because of pollution. Life expectancy has been reduced by five years. Women's Health Journal. Oct.-Nov.-Dec. 1990 #20. In Kuwait, hundreds of oil wells are set on fire during war (January 1991).

EARTH SUMMIT, 1992

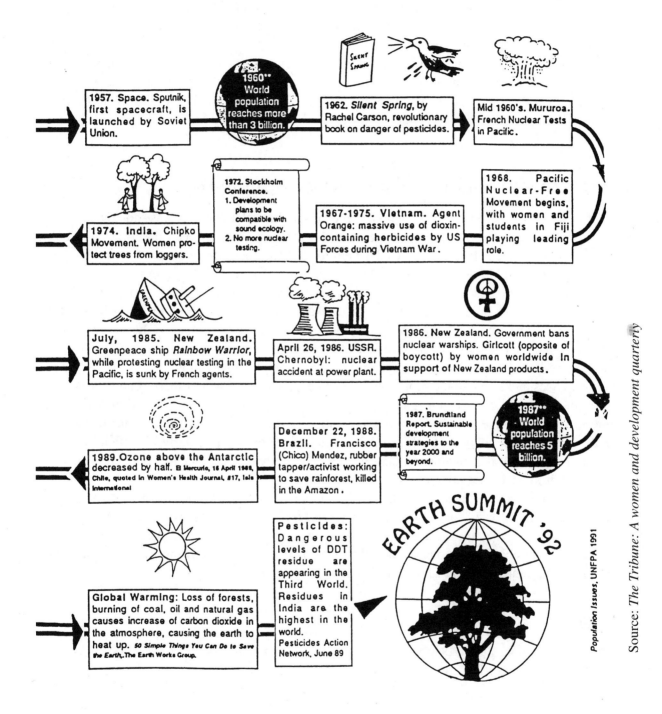

1957. Space. Sputnik, first spacecraft, is launched by Soviet Union.

1960** World population reaches more than 3 billion.

1962. *Silent Spring*, by Rachel Carson, revolutionary book on danger of pesticides.

Mid 1960's. Mururoa. French Nuclear Tests in Pacific.

1972. Stockholm Conference.
1. Development plans to be compatible with sound ecology.
2. No more nuclear testing.

1967-1975. Vietnam. Agent Orange: massive use of dioxin-containing herbicides by US Forces during Vietnam War.

1968. Pacific Nuclear-Free Movement begins, with women and students in Fiji playing leading role.

1974. India. Chipko Movement. Women protect trees from loggers.

July, 1985. New Zealand. Greenpeace ship *Rainbow Warrior*, while protesting nuclear testing in the Pacific, is sunk by French agents.

April 26, 1986. USSR. Chernobyl: nuclear accident at power plant.

1986. New Zealand. Government bans nuclear warships. Girlcott (opposite of boycott) by women worldwide in support of New Zealand products.

1989. Ozone above the Antarctic decreased by half. El Mercurio, 16 April 1989, Chile, quoted in Women's Health Journal, #17, Isis International

December 22, 1988. Brazil. Francisco (Chico) Mendez, rubber tapper/activist working to save rainforest, killed in the Amazon.

1987. Brundtland Report. Sustainable development strategies to the year 2000 and beyond.

1987** World population reaches 5 billion.

Global Warming: Loss of forests, burning of coal, oil and natural gas causes increase of carbon dioxide in the atmosphere, causing the earth to heat up. *50 Simple Things You Can Do to Save the Earth*, The Earth Works Group.

Pesticides: Dangerous levels of DDT residue are appearing in the Third World. Residues in India are the highest in the world. Pesticides Action Network, June 89

EARTH SUMMIT '92

Source: *The Tribune: A women and development quarterly*

Population Issues, UNFPA 1991

SECTION FOUR

Challenges to change

Each of these topics could only be dealt with thoroughly in a long course, but it is important for as many people as possible who are involved in development to get an overview of these environmental problems, in a way that is linked to their own experience. This will help them to see clearly how many of our current practices increase poverty and famine. The people who are most seriously affected are nearly always the dispossessed and the poorest. If these trends continue the life of many poor people will grow harder and harder.

In the past many well-intentioned development programmes have helped to destroy the environment; for example, the over-cultivation of peanuts for salad oil for export and foreign exchange ruined the quality of the soil in Senegal. This is well illustrated in the film *The Business of Hunger* (available through Maryknoll Fathers, New York 10545, USA).

Exercise 10. Developing local problem-posing materials

Each of these areas will be dealt with on both the local and the global level. Teams should be formed to develop pictures, a play or some way to pose the problem that has been described. In Paulo Freire's term, these are called 'codes'. Codes help to start and focus discussions of the problem as people experience it at the local level. Using questions to enable the group to follow the reflection/action cycle described fully in *Training for Transformation* Book I, groups should be encouraged to describe the problem, analyse the causes of the problem, check the ways in which it happens in their own situation and other problems that are related to it, discuss the root causes of the problem and plan actions that are possible and important to them.

Codes have been designed to encourage discussion of the global situation. Teams will be asked to prepare codes and discussion outlines on the local experience of each of these problems.

After this we will try to give participants an understanding of the global dimension and seriousness of the problem by using codes, case studies, simulations and other means of moving from the known to the unknown to stretch their experience. This is particularly important for those planning development programmes so that they can put all their development work into a context of sound environmental development.

After group discussion analysing the root causes of each problem, the group should be encouraged to make plans for action on two levels, the local practical level, and the level of organizing and lobbying to affect policy. Policy suggestions could be compared with those of Agenda 21. If possible discussions should take place on each of the following issues, in the order in which they are most relevant for the participants.

Procedure

1. Divide the participants into **eight teaching–learning teams**, and ask each team to take one of the areas of concern. The areas are:

   ● land and deserts
   ● water
   ● trees and forests
   ● air pollution
   ● food supply
   ● energy

- management of waste
- population and quality of life

2. Ask them to prepare a problem-posing session on the local experience of this problem. Instead of simply talking about the problem they should present a story, case study, newspaper article, picture, play or mime, or collage, which presents the most pressing local aspect of the problem in a way that will be very familiar to the participants. This process is fully described in Chapter 3 of *Training for Transformation* Book I.

3. The teams should also prepare a discussion outline, as explained in *Training for Transformation* Book I (pages 78–81). This should include a set of questions which will lead the group through the process of describing and analysing the problem, considering the consequences and planning action to deal with it. Besides this they should prepare some material on the global dimensions of the problem to present to the group at the end of the discussion on the local experience.

4. You will see that each of Exercises 11 to 18 deals with one of the issues on a global level. The task of the time is to link the local reality to the global analysis.

Time   Team preparation about 1 hour.
Presentations and group discussion 30–45 minutes per group.
Each team can present a session either for the whole group or for three or four other teams.

Materials   Photocopies of the pages from *The Earth Summit's Agenda for Change* for each team.
Newsprint, markers, paper, crayons etc. for preparation of codes.

Facilitator's note

This exercise is meant to give participants an overview of the eight most pressing areas of alarm regarding the environment. Through a process of 'teaching–learning teams' it also gives them an opportunity to practise their skills of group leadership using a problem-posing approach, summing up with some factual information.

If it feels too ambitious or too time consuming to tackle all eight issues, you could just tackle the three or four issues most relevant for your situation.

One of the best resources with good factual information on both the problems and the recommendations of the Rio Summit is *The Earth Summit's Agenda for Change: a plain language version of Agenda 21* by Michael Keating. It is published by the Centre for Our Common Future, 52 rue des Paquis,1201 Geneva, Switzerland.

Rio Declaration on Environment and Development

Recognizing the integral and interdependent nature of the Earth, our home, the nations meeting at the Earth Summit in Rio de Janeiro adopted a set of principles to guide future development. These principles define the rights of people to development, and their responsibilities to safeguard the common environment . . . .

The Rio principles include the following ideas:

- People are entitled to a healthy and productive life in harmony with nature.
- Development today must not undermine the development and environment needs of present and future generations.
- Nations have the sovereign right to exploit their own resources, but without causing environmental damage beyond their borders.
- Nations shall develop international laws to provide compensation for damage that activities under their control cause to areas beyond their borders.
- Nations shall use the precautionary approach to protect the environment . . .
- Eradicating poverty and reducing disparities in living standards in different parts of the world are essential to achieve sustainable development and meet the needs of the majority of people . . .
- Nations should reduce and eliminate unsustainable patterns of production and consumption, and promote appropriate demographic policies.
- Environmental issues are best handled with the participation of all concerned citizens.
- Nations should co-operate to promote an open international economic system that will lead to economic growth and sustainable development in all countries.
- The polluter should, in principle, bear the cost of pollution . . .
- The full participation of women is essential to achieve sustainable development. The creativity, ideals and courage of youth and the knowledge of indigenous people are needed too. Nations should recognize and support the identity, culture and interests of indigenous people.
- Warfare is inherently destructive of sustainable development, and Nations shall respect international laws protecting the environment in times of armed conflict, and shall co-operate in their further establishment.
- Peace, development and environmental protection are interdependent and indivisible.

(Source: *The Earth Summit's Agenda for Change*)

Exercise 11. Energy: the biggest gap between 'the have's and 'have-not's

The aim of this session is to look at the importance of energy in the work of development, and to see how the rapid increase in the use of energy has both enhanced and polluted our lives.

Procedure

1. Give out paper and pens or crayons and ask each participant to draw or write down as fast as they can all the images that come into their minds as they think about the word 'energy'.

2. Then ask participants to form **pairs**, share their drawings or notes and list all the different types of energy they have at their own disposal to help them live their lives as they want to.

3. Ask the pairs to join up with other pairs to **form fours or sixes**. Ask each group to make two lists, the first showing all the types of energy that the average rural farmer in their country is able to draw on, and the other showing the types of energy that a wealthy city businessman uses in his everyday life.

4. Give copies of the Energy handout to all participants and ask a person in each group to read it aloud to their small group. Then ask them to discuss the following questions:

   a. In what ways does an extra supply of energy change our lives?
   b. One of the main driving forces behind industrial development has been the search for greater supplies of energy. How has this contributed to environmental degradation?
   c. How do you see the relationship between energy supply and development?

5. In the **whole group** discuss the questions and insights participants report from their small group discussion. In the whole group, you could also ask:

   a. What other sources of energy are available besides coal and oil?
   b. What are the advantages and disadvantages of using each kind?
   c. What are the possibilities of using water, solar and wind power in your area?

   If they have not been mentioned, add the following points:

   Electricity is clean and efficient. Initially it is expensive to produce, but once the power stations have been set up a great deal can be produced quite inexpensively, using oil, coal, nuclear power, or water, solar or wind power. Does the group know about nuclear power? Do they know of its dangers and the problems of nuclear waste which causes cancer?

6. In the whole group, discuss whether you think there is such a thing as spiritual energy. If so how can you see it affecting the lives of certain people?

Time   About 1½ hours

Materials Paper and pens or crayons for participants, pictures of bicycles, windmills, oxen, etc. (see Facilitator's note overleaf); handout on Energy.

Facilitator's note

Some of the lists from step 2 should include: human physical energy, animal energy, all forms of heat, light, movement; firewood, electricity, steam, coal, charcoal, gas, oil; machines that maximize energy like wheels, bicycles; technology, computers, microchips, etc. If possible collect pictures of dams, windmills, solar heating panels in houses, and old and new types of windmills. Discuss the effects of the power generated at Victoria Falls, Kariba, Cabora Bassa, Oxbow Lesotho dams.

Nature and women

We need to discover our own reality as latecomers to the planet. The world of nature, plants and animals existed billions of years before we came on the scene. Nature does not need us to rule over it, but runs itself very well, even better, without humans. We are the parasites on the foodchain of life, consuming more and more, and putting too little back to restore and maintain the life system that supports us.

We need to recognize our utter dependence on the great life-producing matrix of the planet in order to learn to reintegrate our human systems of production, consumption and waste into the ecological patterns by which nature sustains life.

This might begin by revisualizing the relationship of mind, or human intelligence, to nature. Mind or consciousness is not something that originates in some transcendent world outside of nature, but is the place where nature itself becomes conscious. We need to think of human consciousness not as separating us as a higher species from the rest of nature, but rather as a gift to help us to learn how to harmonize our needs with the natural system around us, of which we are a dependent part.

Such a reintegration of human consciousness and nature must reshape the concept of God, instead of modelling God after alienated male consciousness, outside of and ruling over nature. God in ecofeminist spirituality is the immanent source of life that sustains the whole planetary community. . . . God is the font from which the variety of plants and animals well up in each new generation, the matrix that sustains their life-giving interdependency with one another.

In ecofeminist culture and ethic, mutual interdependency replaces the hierarchy of domination as the model of relationship between men and women, between human groups and between humans and other beings. All racist, classist, sexist, cultural and anthropocentric assumptions of superiority of whites over blacks, males over females, managers over workers, humans over animals and plants must be discarded. . . . The patterns must be reconstructed socially, creating more equitable sharing in work and the fruits of work. . . .

In terms of male–female relations, this means not simply allowing women more access to public culture, but converting males to an equal share in the tasks of child nurture and household maintenance. A revolution of female roles into the male work world, without a corresponding revolution in male roles, leaves the basic pattern of patriarchal exploitation of women untouched. Women are simply overworked in a new way, expected to do both a male workday at low pay, and also the unpaid work of women that sustains family life.

These conversions from alienated, hierarchical dualisms to life-sustaining mutuality will radically change the patterns of patriarchal culture. Basic concepts, such as God, soul-body and salvation will be reconceived in ways that may bring us much closer to the ethical values of love, justice and care for the earth.

Ecofeminism by Rosemary Radford Reuther (p.21).

ENERGY

A person who is full of energy has life and enthusiasm; they accomplish a lot and can move around fast. They don't let the grass grow under their feet. All human beings have energy, some more than others. We all need energy for heat and light and movement. Most of us feel that we would like to have more energy in order to do all the things we long to do.

So, from the beginning of history, human beings have tried to find ways of doing things that took less energy, or ways of increasing the energy at their disposal. We invented wheels because it is easier to pull a heavy load in a cart with wheels than to carry the load. We tamed oxen so that we could use their energy to pull our ploughs and carry our loads. We rode horses because they could move much further and faster than a person. We invented mechanical things like sewing machines and bicycles to help us do our work and move about faster.

Each new invention helped us to accomplish more with the energy we had available in our own bodies. A woman who had to fetch her own water could bring back four times as much water if she owned a donkey. This left her free for other things: to go to literacy classes, or to improve her garden, or to spend more time with children and friends. People used the power of the wind to sail ships. The amount of energy that is available for us to use has a great effect on the quality of our lives. For this reason one important aspect of development has been trying to get more and more energy for people to use.

Three hundred years ago people found that one could make engines move by using the steam from boiling water. With steam engines people could develop trains and machinery to spin and weave cloth. People could move about and make goods much more quickly than ever before. Of course in order to make the steam one needed heat, so coal and oil and electricity were used. Many forms of energy depended on fuel. Coal, oil, electricity and later nuclear energy all became exceedingly precious. The nations that had coal to sell, like Britain or South Africa, and the nations that had oil to sell, like the Middle East countries and Nigeria, all became extremely wealthy. Much research has been put into finding new sources of energy and new technology for using this energy.

One of the biggest differences between rich and poor people is that rich people have far more energy at their disposal than poor people, because of the availability of fuel and technology. It has been calculated that each modern American has the equivalent of the energy of 250 people at their disposal, to help them do their work each day. In practical terms, this means that the average American has 250 times the amount of energy at his disposal that the average rural African has. It is important to see why this could lead to such a high level of efficiency. This is one way of measuring the gap between the 'have's and the 'have-not's. No wonder they are considered so efficient. Many African women have to depend only on the energy of their own bodies.

As people tried to 'raise their standard of living' the search for energy became more and more urgent. Huge quantities of coal and oil are burnt each day and, as they burn, smoke is released into the atmosphere. It pollutes the air. Coal and oil are called non-renewable fossil fuels. They create a great deal of smoke, and the amount of each stored beneath the Earth's surface is limited. If everyone used as much coal and oil as the people in Europe or the USA do then the supply would soon be used up, and the air would be so filled with pollution we could hardly breathe. We have seen this happening in Indonesia and Malaysia when people had to wear masks to protect their lungs. It is always poor people who live in the areas closest to the factories. They begin to get many respiratory diseases such as tuberculosis (TB), cancer of the lungs and bronchitis from the smog that they breathe in.

Exercise 12. **The land**

The aim of this session is to clarify the key issues around land that people in the local community feel most strongly about and then focus the discussion initially on that aspect of this issue.

Procedure

1. Do a listening survey to find out what are the issues of land which most deeply affect the people in your community. (The process of conducting a listening survey is described in the handout for Chapter 2, Exercise 3, and in *Training for Transformation* Book I, pages 54–7.) It might be any of the following or you may find something else that is their deepest concern:

   - longing for a piece of land
   - a small farm in the country
   - a plot of land for a home and a garden in a city
   - overcrowding
   - farms too small to subdivide among all the children
   - poor quality land, stony and dry
   - overused land
   - need for tools and technology to work it effectively.
   - drought
   - soil erosion

2. When the team has clarified what is the main theme around land, they will develop a code (a problem-posing poster or play) that will stimulate discussion with groups. The following are two examples:

A peaceful homestead

Overgrazed land

33

3. Each team needs to also develop questions to fit the code. **Discuss in threes** the following questions or others relevant to your situation.

   a. How would it change your life if you had a piece of land?
   b. Is it possible to get some land? If not why not? Laws? Expense? Land shortage?
   c. Is there anything we could do about this? What are the possibilities?
   d. Can women get land or a house?
   e. Are any political parties working for redistribution of land? Can we work with them? Can we organize? Can we lobby for land distribution?
   f. Do you have any land that you could use? How could you use it most effectively?
   g. Do you understand the principles of permaculture?

   [See Bibliography at back of this book for ideas on food production.]
   [See the Case Study about homeless people in Chapter 5, Exercise 19.]
   [See *The People's Workbook*, 'How to produce a lot of food on a small plot'.]

4. To close this session, you can use a play reading. Ask two people to prepare and then to read the Prologue from *Cry, the Beloved Country: a verse drama*.

Time   1½ hours

Materials   Copy of the play reading for each participant.

"The Earth is the Lord's and the fullness thereof."

"Land ownership is . . . to safeguard the mutuality of belonging, without which there can be no lasting and conserving settlement of human communities . . . it quickly becomes abusive when used to justify large accumulations of 'real estate' . . . In biblical terms the landowner is the guest and steward of God: 'The land is mine for you are strangers and sojourners with me'."

"Creation is nothing less than the manifestation of God's hidden being."

"We are holy creatures, living among other holy creatures, in a world that is holy."

"Economy. The sense of the holiness of life is not compatible with an exploitative economy. If we are to maintain any sense of coherence in our lives we cannot tolerate the present utter disconnection between religion and the economy – the ways by which the human household is situated and maintained within the household of nature".

"What, for Christians, would be the economy, the practices and the restraints of sort of 'right livelihood'? I think the idea of organized Christianity of a Christian economy is no more or less than the industrial economy – an economy firmly founded on the seven deadly sins, and the breaking of all ten of the commandments."

"If Christianity is going to survive as more than a respecter and comforter of profitable iniquities, then Christians are going to have to interest themselves in economy – which is to say in nature and in work".

Wendell Berry, *Cross Currents*, pp 151–3. Summer 1993.

Cry, the Beloved Country: a verse drama

ACT 1
PROLOGUE

The Prologue opens with the stage in darkness except for the two Narrators, the BLACK MAN and the WHITE MAN, to the extreme left and right front of the stage respectively.

There is a lovely road that runs from Ixopo
Into the hills . . .
The hills
Are grass-covered and rolling, and they are lovely
Beyond any singing of it.
The roads climbs seven miles into them,
To Carisbrooke; and from there – if there is no mist –
You look down
On one of the fairest scenes in Africa . . .
Below you is the valley of Umzimkulu,
On its journey from the Drakensberg to the sea;
And beyond and behind the river,
Great hill after great hill;
Then, the mountains of Ingeli and East Griqualand . . .
The grass is rich and matted, you cannot see the soil.
It holds the rain and the mist, and they seep
Into the ground, feeding the streams in every kloof.
It is well tended, and not too many cattle feed upon it;
Not too many fires burn it, laying bare the soil.
Stand unshod upon it: for the ground is holy,
Being even as it came
From the Creator.
Keep it – guard it – care for it –
For it keeps men, guards men, cares for men.
Destroy it – and man is destroyed.

The grass is rich and matted, you cannot see the soil.
But the rich hills break down;
They fall
To the valley below,
And falling,
Change their nature;
For they grow red and bare; they cannot hold
The rain and the mist, and the streams
Are dry in the kloofs.
Too many cattle feed upon the grass.
And too many fires have burned it.
Stand shod upon it, for it is coarse and sharp,

And the stones
Cut under the feet.
It is not kept, or guarded, or cared for;
It no longer keeps men, guards men, cares for men.
The great red hills stand desolate, and the earth
Has torn away like flesh.
Down in the valleys women scratch the soil that is left,
and the maize hardly reaches the height of a man.
They are valleys of old men and old women,
Of mothers and children.
The men are away,
The young men and the girls are away.
The soil cannot keep them any more . . .(*pause*)
All roads lead to Big city.
If the crops fails, there is work in Big city.
If the farm is too small to be divided further,
Some must go to Big city . . .

(Adapted by Felicia Komai, with permission from
Alan Paton, author of the novel, *Cry, the Beloved Country*)

Exercise 13. Drought

It is often helpful to prepare and use a problem-posing play or poster at the beginning of a session, to challenge the participants to think about the problem and raise questions in their minds, before offering them an input with wider facts or possible solutions.

Procedure

1. Ask a group of participants to prepare and then stage a play as described here.

> The play is about women, including a mother and her eldest daughter, returning home after walking 15 km to fetch water during a drought in Machakos district, Kenya. At first they are too tired to say anything. It is clear the mother and daughter walked to the well the previous day and back this day. The water will only last one day and they will have to walk again after one day at home. They must go twice a week to get the bare minimum for the family. The children come in and drink water eagerly. The mother sets aside some in a jar for drinking and cooking, and gives each child a cup to wash with. The second daughter has been trying to look after the younger children. She says there are no greens anywhere. They have all dried up. There is only a little maize. The parents discuss how the land has grown more barren since they were children.
>
> The father has chopped down one of the few remaining trees and burned it to make charcoal to sell to passing cars on the main road to get money to buy some more food. The mother worries that there are so few trees left. They will have to walk very far for firewood. The father says that it is no use planting trees now because they will only die in the drought. The cattle have all died in the drought. There is no milk for the children. There are only a few goats and chickens left. Wearily the mother gets up to go and find a scrawny chicken to kill for supper. [End play]

2. After the participants have watched the play, ask

   a. What happened in this play?
   b. Have you ever known a situation like this?
   c. Are there any signs of soil erosion or degradation in your area?
   d. What has caused it?
   e. What are the effects?
   f. What could the local community do about it?

Input on drought

All over the world dry lands that were used for raising cattle, sheep and goats are becoming drier and turning into deserts. Droughts seem to be more frequent and the land is becoming less fertile. The deserts are growing, very fast in some places – e.g. the Kalahari Desert is marching towards Pretoria at the rate of 2.5 km per year. The Sahara desert is spreading south. The deserts in northern Kenya are growing, and also in numerous other places, dry land, rangeland, that has been good for grazing animals has become more and more barren. The problem is very serious. 70 per cent of all the world's dry lands are already seriously degraded. This is an area the size of the whole continent of Europe. Africa and Asia both have 32 per cent of the world's arid land.

The people in these areas are living on the edge of survival at the best of times and when there is a serious drought many of them die, especially the most vulnerable, the very young and the very old.

---

3. Ask, what are the main results of drought and desertification? (If these have not been mentioned add them and discuss.)

- Increasing poverty and starvation for rural farmers.
- Shortage of food and higher food prices for all.
- Countries become dependent on importing food for scarce foreign exchange.

4. Ask why the deserts are spreading particularly in Africa. Let the group give as many answers as they can and then sum up their answers, adding any of the following points that have been omitted:

- Overcrowding of people due to unfair land distribution.
- Overgrazing by too many animals.
- Use of chemical fertilizers and insecticides.
- Irrigated land that is not properly drained becomes salty.
- Poor farming methods. Planting the same crop all the time.
- Colonial interference with traditional farming patterns. Pressure to plant cash crops, e.g. peanuts in Senegal for export which ruined the soil.
- Drought resistant millet and sorghum have been replaced by maize, which cannot survive droughts.
- No mixed farming. No manure, or else manure used for fuel.
- Loss of topsoil through soil erosion after rain.
- Dongas (deep gullies) formed by soil erosion.
- Chopping down of trees for firewood. Trees hold water in the soil and prevent it from being washed away.

5. Ask what needs to be done about land degradation by governments. If the following points are not mentioned, add and discuss them:

- Fairer distribution of land, to avoid overcrowding and overgrazing and to keep people off fragile land, means finding some other source of income besides cattle, sheep and goats for pastoral people in crowded areas, and for peasant farmers in dry areas.
- Government policies should give priority to many smallholdings rather than huge agri-business ranches and plantations. They should:

  - Discourage use of harmful chemical fertilizers and pesticides.
  - Encourage organic farming methods, composting and use of drought-resistant crops such as millet and sorghum rather than maize.
  - With NGOs, speed up planting programmes using fast growing drought-resistant local trees and other suitable plants.
  - Reduce the demand for firewood by providing other forms of fuel such as electricity, paraffin and oil.

6. What can be done by local people and by NGOs? Where possible the group should try to start a practical project such as one of the following:

- Planting trees
- Starting a tree nursery
- Starting a vegetable garden and a compost pit
- Starting a food for waste project
- Water projects, storage jars, gutters and rain tanks
- Dams, pumps, piped water
- Cleaning up rivers and wells
- Cleaning up the environment. Involving youth.
- Tidying up a cemetery
- Setting up a water filter
- Learning how to produce a lot of food in a small space
- Visit to an agricultural project
- Visit to water recycling plant
- Visit to a paper plant

> In South Africa some squatter communities have organized themselves to ask for title deeds for the land on which their shacks are built and have been successful.

Time   1 to 1½ hours

Materials   Copies of handout for participants.

The God of wildness and wilderness

"God is not to be fenced in, under human control, like some domestic creature; he is the wildest being in existence. The presence of his spirit in us is our wildness, our oneness with the wilderness of Creation."

"The great visionary encounters (in the Bible) did not take place in temples, but in sheep pastures, in the desert, in the wilderness, on mountains, by rivers, on beaches and in the middle of the sea: when there was no choice they happened in prison."

"The Bible is a book . . . open to the sky. That is because outdoors we are confronted everywhere with wonders; we see that the miraculous is not extraordinary, but the common mode of existence. It is our daily bread. Whoever really has considered the lilies of the field or the birds of the air, and pondered the improbability of their existence in this warm world within the cold and empty stellar distances, will hardly balk at the turning of water into wine – which was after all a very small miracle. We forget the greater and still continuing miracle by which water (with soil and sunlight) is turned into grapes."

"Holiness is everywhere in Creation, it is as common as raindrops and leaves and blades of grass."

Wendell Berry, *Cross Currents*. Summer 1993.

Exercise 14. Shortage of fresh water

The aim of this session is to help participants see fresh water as a very precious resource, to think about conservation and fair distribution.

Procedure

1. From your survey determine the way in which local people experience the problem of water most acutely. The problem may include:

   - Queuing for water in overcrowded urban areas and informal settlements where water systems have not been properly installed.
   - Sharing of taps.
   - Slow trickle from taps.
   - Depending on a neighbour for use of their tap.
   - Impure sources of water.
   - Dirty water lying around causing sickness for children.
   - Shortage of water for drinking, cooking, washing and house cleaning.

   In rural areas the most common experience is long and tiring walks to fetch water, taking up much of the time and energy of the women and girls.
   Impure water sources, e.g. rivers where the cattle drink, cause many diseases.
   Inadequate water leads to many diseases, such as scabies for children.

2. Show a five gallon jar filled with water. If this water represented all the water in the world, how much of this water would be fresh? Take one teaspoon of the water, and show that only this amount of water would be fresh. What is wrong with the rest of the water? By far the most of it is in the oceans and it is very salty. One cannot drink it. Sailors who have tried to do so have died from too much salt. One poem about a sailor stuck on a boat which cannot move in the middle of the ocean described it like this:

   > Water, water everywhere,
   > And all the boards did shrink.
   > Water, water everywhere,
   > And not a drop to drink.

   S. T. Coleridge, *The Ancient Mariner*

   Many people have been trying to find a way of turning salt water into fresh water, but so far all the means tried have been extremely expensive.

   So fresh water is very precious because there is very little of it on Earth, and there is none on any of the other planets we have discovered so far. Some people have very little to use and get it only with a lot of hard work, so they use every drop carefully. Others waste a great deal of water.

3. Where do we find the fresh water?

Summarize the answers of the group and include any of the following points which have not been mentioned.

Summary on water

Sources of water include lakes, rivers, dams, reservoirs and huge water tanks in cities, usually built very high so that the water can run down, in pipes in the city water system, and water tanks and storage jars near homes.

Is there always the same amount of water in the world?
Do the proportions of fresh water and sea water remain constant?

There is always the same amount of water in the sea, the land and the clouds, but it is constantly moving in the water cycle. If fresh water comes down as rain and the soil cannot hold it because there is no grass and no trees it rushes down to the sea, usually carrying a lot of precious topsoil with it, and as it enters the sea it becomes salty. So we need to keep as much of the fresh water as possible available for the use of human beings, plants and animals. If there is much global warming many of the places that are now fertile might dry up, and the seas will expand. There will be less fresh water available and many of the low-lying areas near the coast, including many cities and low islands, could be covered by the sea.

Time   1 hour

Materials   None.

> **In the 21st century it will not be oil**
> **over which nations are prepared to go to war,**
> **but fresh water.**

Exercise 15. Down the water line

The aim of this session is to reflect on the need for just laws about water distribution.

Get a local artist to draw a big poster, cartoon style, showing a fine river flowing from the mountains. Near the source several rich farmers have made dams and have fine fields with irrigation. The river passes through a city, near which it is diverted into an enormous reservoir and into several high water tanks. Lower down there are a couple of small towns and water is drawn off for their lawns and vegetable gardens; then a big factory is piping its waste materials into the river.

Some people are fishing in the river, but they are having no luck. One says to the other, 'There used to be so many fish in this river, but now there are none. Occasionally one sees a dead fish floating by.' In the distance one sees a few women walking towards the river with water pots on their heads.

As the river moves downstream there are a few more dams until it has become a mere trickle. There a couple of peasant farmers looking at their dried-up crops. 'This used to be a fine river in our father's time. Now there is hardly any water left in it. I wonder why?'

Procedure

1. Ask participants to go into **groups of three** and discuss:

   a. What do you see in this picture?

   b. We all need water, so we are all situated somewhere on this map. Where are you situated in the map?

   c. Are you getting more than your share or less than your share of water? Is it clean or polluted?

   d. How is water polluted as the river runs towards the sea?

   e. In what ways do modern farmers contribute to this pollution? (Insecticides and fertilizers also pollute the water in the ground.)

   f. Is it possible for everyone to use the same amount of water as the city dwellers with piped water? What would happen if they did?

   g. How do we waste water?

   h. If water has been used and become dirty and polluted can it be reused? (Yes water can be recycled and purified.)

   If there is a water purification plant nearby, it would be interesting for the group to visit it.

2. Ask participants to **come back into one big group** and discuss their responses to the questions. The following short input can be helpful.

   > In what ways are mountains, trees, floods and droughts all connected together? The seas are also extremely important ecologically. They help control the temperature of the planet, and clouds draw water vapour from the seas. This eventually becomes rain which fills the rivers. The seas provide a rich harvest of fish and seafood. Governments need to ensure that certain places are not over-fished, or there will be none left to breed.

3. The group may want to continue the discussion, but keep it focused by asking participants to discuss:

   a. What should governments do to ensure that all people have enough pure fresh water for their needs?

   b. What laws are needed to ensure that factories, farmers and sewage systems do not contaminate the water?

Time   1 hour

Materials   Big poster as described and questions on newsprint.

Mukiri

Mukiri was the nickname of a quiet but very practical Italian lay brother of the Consolata religious Roman Catholic community. It means 'the silent one'. He involved the local people of Meru diocese, Kenya, in a beautiful self-reliant project bringing water down from the hills to the dry Isiola Plains.

For seven years
he has walked
in the Nyambeni Hills,
making his way
through the rainforest.
Quietly he watched the water
filtering through the murram
stopping at the clay.

For seven years
he has walked
through the hot dry places
of Isiola,
through the dusty moonscape lands
with volcanic humps of hills.
Quietly he looked down at the dust
fertile, volcanic dust,
wanting only water
to bring forth life.

For seven years
he has watched
a parched and thirsty people
walking for water;
miles and miles for water
children, dirty,
for want of water
cows, bony,
for want of water.

Men from the dry places
went with him to the hills,
Quietly they gazed
at the cool cascades
of whispering white water,
tumbling from tall ledges
down to deep swirling pools.
They listened to water music
as the drops of life danced down
as the torrents of life surged down.
The forest was alive with water
trees, trunks and leaves

birds, butterflies and flowers,
all alive and throbbing
with this wonderful wealth of water.

The people of the dry places
dreamed of water in the wilderness.
The dream led to the labour
and quietly they went to work,
Mukiri and the people of Meru.
They cut roads in the rainforest
dug dark deep trenches
scooped out damp dark tunnels
through the murram filter
down to the clay floor.

They did not bring machines
to shatter the forest silence;
they did not send overseas for
vast sums for monster machines;
but quietly they worked with their hands
laying pipes, making catchments
to bring the cool clear water,
translucent, life-giving water,
down from the Nyambeni Hills
into the northern plains.

And today
there are pipes in the wilderness,
today
there are taps in the wilderness,
women and children
laughing and talking
as they wait their turn at the tap.
Cows drinking at water troughs
blowing soft satisfied sighs.

Mukiri looks again
at the deep circular valley
of forest beneath the falls.
He dreams of a dam
deep and clear
that will send each year
millions more gallons of water
into the dusty plains,
making the dry land blossom
making the fruit trees grow
making the desert flourish
with living waves of wheat.

by Anne Hope, Easter 1977

[45] TRAINING FOR TRANSFORMATION

Exercise 16. Destroying forests

This session uses one of two stories which will stimulate discussion on the human and the Earth's need for forests. One is the short book called *The Story of the Lorax* and the other is an excerpt from *Circles in the Forest*, by Darlene Mathee which you will find on pages 48–51.

Procedure A. The Lorax

1. If you can obtain *The Story of the Lorax*, by Dr Seuss, from a library or bookshop it can be used as a starting point for discussion on many environmental issues, particularly the importance of trees and commercial logging. This is a delightful story, written originally for children, but much appreciated by adults. If possible make transparencies of the pictures and show them on an overhead projector. Otherwise, if it is a small group, hold up the pictures. Explain beforehand that Dr Seuss was a poet and loved the sounds of words so he sometimes made up his own new words that sounded suitable to him for the thing he was describing. Tell them it does not matter if they do not understand every single word, but explain those that are essential for the story. If possible ask several participants to read the words of different characters in the story. Give them a chance to read over their words and be sure to have a practice beforehand.

2. Ask the group to describe what happened in the story to make sure that it is clear to all the participants.

3. Ask why the relatives of the Onceler started to chop down the beautiful truffula trees.

4. Why did so many people buy the 'thneeds'?

5. Ask if they know of anything like this happening in real life.

6. Discuss any local industry that is using up valuable resources and ruining the environment, such as paper mills for thick newspapers.

7. In an urban group decide which are the main industries. Are they making something that people really need?

8. Is there a difference between good and bad work? What is meant by 'right livelihood'? Review the main points about why trees are so important for human beings, as well as for other living creatures and for the Earth itself.

9. Who is mainly responsible for chopping down trees?

Facilitator's note

This discussion can move to the role of advertising in modern life, and the difference between real needs and true and false satisfiers. (See the Wheel of Fundamental Human Needs, page 248 of this book, and also the passage from E. F. Schumacher about tree planting, page 53.)

Procedure B. The Death of the Kalander Tree

This reading is from the book entitled *Circles in the Forest* by Darlene Mathee and has become a South African classic. This section is a vivid account of the experience of a family of woodcutters, working in the Knysna forest in the early 19th century. Saul, the younger son, is committed to halting the wanton destruction by the timber merchants and the ruthless plundering by the ivory hunters. He experiences a strange mystical kinship with Old Foot, an indomitable and majestic elephant, and is overcome with anger and despair as his father, Joram Barnard, forces him to help chop down a giant kalander tree. The Knysna lourie birds, the bigfeet (elephants) and the wild pigs all seem to share in resisting and then mourning the destruction of the great tree.

1. Ask four different people to read the words of the father, Joram Barnard, the sons, Saul and Jozef, and Uncle Anro, and take time for a practice. Either have one good reader prepare to read the whole narration, or else pass the text around letting each person read a paragraph.

2. Ask participants to get comfortable in order to hear the reading of this story. Read the text aloud.

3. Ask the participants to reflect **with one or two people** next to them on what struck them particularly about this story.

4. In the **whole group** give people an opportunity to share their insights. Other questions:

   a. What other examples can you think of where the environment has been ruthlessly destroyed by a few people making great profits?
   b. How can one balance authentic human needs with reverence for the integrity of creation?

5. Give participants copies of the story, and the input on 'Deforestation'.

Time   1½ hours

Materials   A copy of one of the stories, handout on deforestation and excerpt from *Small is Beautiful*.

47

A Story: The Death of a Kalander Tree

At daybreak they found the kalander hardly a hundred paces from where they had slept. Like a mighty king it stood towering above the white alder and mountain saffron, stinkwood, assegai and hard pear. As if God had planted it there long before the others. Its giant roots anchored it to the ground like giant arms; higher up, where its body caught more of the sun, the grey bark hung like dry strips of skin.

The old man's beard moss in its branches hung like thin green hair, waving eerily in the wind. It was an enormous tree. Where it rose from the forest floor its body was as thick as five oxen together.
"Where is he going to fall, Pa?"
Saul made his own calculations: if they let if fall to the south, it could land straddling an old stinkwood tree; if it fell to the east, it would make a path of destruction through other good wood, and to the north it was just as bad.

"We'll lie him down a little to the south-east," his father announced.

There was a feeling of panic in Saul when they walked towards the tree with axes. Jozef and he watched their father finally weigh up, with an old woodcutter's knowledge, where he wanted the giant to fall. Then he marked a point low down on the grey-green, moss-covered trunk and got his foothold between the roots. When he swung back the axe and brought it forward to hit the first blow on the drop side, it tore right through Saul.
"I think he feels it," he said out loud.
"What?" Jozef asked beside him.
"I think the tree feels it."
"Have you gone daft?"
Behind the kalander, in line with the notch on the drop side and a little higher up the trunk, old Anro's axe fell in; slowly and in rhythm with the front one.

It took them seven days to fell that tree. Seven strange days.

Swarms of louries gathers in the trees around them and at times even the sound of the axes was drowned by their continuous kok-kok-kokking.
"What's the matter with the louries?" Saul asked Jozef.
"I suppose there are bigfeet elephants near – I'm telling you now that white alder over there is mine if we have to run."
The next morning the tracks were right round the shelter.
"Joram!" a worried old Anro called from outside. "You'd better come and have a look here. I think I'm seeing things."
When they got outside, Joram Barnard took one look at the tracks, straightened up and look anxiously into the dark underbush around them. "It's Old Foot!" he said.
"I thought so," old Anro agreed, throwing a huge piece of wood on the fire. "And just see how softly the devil did it! Not even a tin or anything kicked over."
"The dung is still warm!" a terrified Jozef shouted from behind the shelter.
"The bugger! Stood watching us while we slept of course, making up his mind whether to walk us into the ground or not!" his father said, sounding uneasy.

"Why are you standing there like a rock, Saul?"

"He ate all the sweet potato skins, Pa!"

"They do that. But I don't like this one doing it. Once a bigfoot starts walking alone and softly on top of that, you must be wary of him."

At sunrise the louries came back to kok-kok-kok and gurgle and hiss incessantly, gliding red-winged from branch to branch in the streaks of sunlight as if there were unrest amongst them.

On the third day Saul left the sweet potatoes too long under the ash and all the oil baked out.

"Why the heck did you let it happen?" his father raged.

"How can you expect a tired man to sit and choke on a thing like this?"

His father was in a bad mood. "The food must last till we're finished, we cannot waste a single sweet potato! You can see for yourself the kalander is tougher than we thought. He is trying to put us to bed! Our axes stay blunt!"

"Perhaps he just does not want to go dead, Pa." Afterwards he could not think what made him say such a thing.

"What did you say?"

"Uncle Anro says he must be close to a thousand years old. Perhaps he does not want to go dead yet."

"Since when is he alive?"

"He has grown, then . . ." He knew he was vexing his father but he could not stop himself. Since they had started cutting down the tree, a feeling of anger had grown in him that would not lie down any longer. "He had to live in order to grow that big."

"What's going on in your head?"

"Nothing, Pa. It's just that something tells me that kalander is alive! If he was dead he could not have grown and if you live, you can feel and if you feel you'll be afraid to go dead!" . . .

His father turned to old Anro. "What's the child talking about, Anro?"

It was halfday. The louries were quiet. The whole day long not a shot was heard in the forest. Something else was worrying Saul. Was it Old Foot Marais had shot the day before?

His father got up suddenly. "Very well then," he said, "Saul must surely be tough enough now to swing a man's axe?"

Saul's body went limp with fright. He knew at once what his father was going to say next and uncontrollable stubbornness welled up in him. "I'm not lifting an axe at that tree, Pa!"

His father's eyes became cold and stayed on his when he said to old Anro, "Give him an axe!"

"Pa . . ."

"My axe!"

"I'll do it, Pa," Jozef offered eagerly. "Uncle Anro said himself yesterday I cut well."

"Saul will do it!" His father's eyes did not blink. "He will cut at the top side and Anro at the back."

Saul realized that he had started something ugly. "Pa said Jozef and I must go cut the rollers this afternoon," he said, trying to get out of it.

"You can do that after you've felt the axe of a man in your hands! Come on!" His father's face was pale with anger.

"I'm not touching that tree with an axe, Pa." He could not tame his anger and fear. He could not understand what had got into him, all he knew was that he would not lift an axe to the kalander. Never.

But his father spun round in his tracks, grabbed a piece of assegai from the stack of firewood and shouted. "When I say you take up the axe, you'll take it up!" his father shouted and struck him across the hip with the assegai. "Now will you go and take up that axe?"

"Yes, Pa."

He did not look up as he walked towards the tree. He kept his eyes on the ground. "Let Jozef do it, Pa!" He pleaded for a last chance to get off.

"Lift that axe! Swing it high and don't tickle that tree when you bring him down!" Despair swept through Saul's tough, thin body; his hands clamped white round the handle of the axe as the blood pressed from the veins. At the end of the first upswing he hesitated for a second before he brought down the razor-sharp blade and lashed it into the back of the gash. Old Anro's second blow followed almost immediately. Then Saul again. Old Anro. Saul. Old Anro.

"That's it!" he heard his father shout. "Now he suddenly knows how to do it! That's it, show him! Does it feel as if the tree can feel anything?"

The smell of green, bruised kalander wood hung in the air, the chippings flew from the gash like white sparks from a fire and a single lourie cried out in distress over the Forest. With every blow Saul gave, anger and despair knotted tighter within him. . .

The morning of the fourth day they found the tracks of a herd of elephants that had passed between the kalander and the shelter the night before. Old Foot's spoor was not amongst them.

Saul took the knapsack and went looking for the honey. Late that afternoon he found it high up in an upright where a baboon would have trouble getting to it . . .

He hooked the knapsack round his neck, climbed the stinkwood tree next to the upright and clambered along a branch that reached the bees' nest.

He was already getting back again when a branch cracked somewhere below him in the Forest, like the crack of a gun; he knew it was the noise of a bigfoot. As his body touched the main fork of the stinkwood, the second branch cracked below him. It was very close. Above him a lourie started gurgling and hissing; when he looked down he saw the movement in the underbrush and Old Foot coming through the thicket. Like a huge, grey rock moving slowly through the foliage with the two massive tusks curving gracefully upwards. As thick as a man's body where they bulged from their sockets. Relief went through Saul: Marais had not shot Old Foot. What was more, for once he was already up a tree. He saw the elephant stop close by the stinkwood, his trunk coming up and searching the air before he disappeared into the underbush again.

Back at the shelter he did not tell them that Old Foot was in the vicinity.

"Seems to me our Saul was lucky, too," his father said as he opened the sticky knapsack. "A nice bit of luck, I see! And Jozef got us a blue buck!"

The atmosphere between him and his father cleared then.

The next day, at midday, the kalander started creaking. Not where the two huge gashes were cut into the trunk, but as if its whole body was creaking from inside.

"That is the toughest tree I've had under my axe in all my life!" old Anro said, collapsing by the fire shortly before dark. It was Saturday evening and a long, dry Sunday lay ahead for him.

You could hear the creaking of the tree at the shelter.

By midnight Saul felt he was suffocating; old Anro and Jozef snored more or less in unison, then the kalander creaked, then his father snored. He wanted to run outside to shut his ears but he was afraid the bigfeet would come again and trample him. Sunday, the whole day long, the tree creaked like one in pain; the harder he tried to keep his imagination at bay, the more it felt as if every creak went right through his own body.

"You think he'll fall tomorrow, Pa?"

"Yes."

But the sixth day also went by. The tree kept holding on with what was left between the gashes.

"He wants to get us in bed!" old Anro complained as they laid down the axes that night.

"Perhaps Saul was right," his father mocked with a tired laugh. "Perhaps the old tree does not want to give up its hold on life."

The creaking of that tree was something unearthly. Dear Lord, Saul prayed under the shelter that night, let the kalander fall tomorrow. Please. If it is a sin to pay for a tree, forgive me. Amen. Please Lord. Let him fall.

Shortly before quarterday, the kalander slowly started heeling over.

"He's going!" his father shouted, threw down his axe and ran. Old Anro did the same and fled to the north of the tree.

It swayed slowly at first. Then faster, as the last of the wood between the gashes tore loose and the forest giant fell down, bringing everything in its path crashing to the ground. Birds flew in confusion from the underbrush, a bush-buck fled past Jozef and Saul and a pack of wild pigs passed between their father and the stump.

Then all was quiet.

Thank God, Saul said to himself, feeling sick.

The kalander was dead. You could see it.

Above their heads, where moments ago the kalander had spread its branches against the sky, was a huge blue hole in the forest roof.

To the west of them the first shot of the day rang out and shortly afterwards the rain started pouring down.

From: *Circles in The Forest*, Darlene Mathee, pp. 74–85.

Summary input on deforestation

Forests have been called the lungs of the world. At one time Europe was covered in forests, but gradually as agriculture developed these were cut down. Now the whole world depends on the tropical and equatorial forests to maintain the balance of oxygen in the atmosphere. Yet these forests are now also being chopped down by 'developers' who only see value in the trees if they are chopped down and sold for money.

In Brazil ranchers are pushing their way into the forests of the Amazon, chopping and burning the forests to provide more ranching land on which to raise cattle to satisfy the insatiable desire of the wealthy for beef. It takes 21 times as much grain if it is fed to cattle to provide enough calories for human energy as it takes if the humans eat the grain themselves. But it is much more profitable for the ranchers to raise cattle and sell beef than it is for them to grow and sell maize.

The destruction of the forests is destroying the life of many native American tribes, but the ranchers are so determined to take over the land that they have persecuted ruthlessly those who have tried to resist. Chico Mendes, one of the leaders of the resistance movement, was murdered by the ranchers, a hero in the struggle to get justice for the poor, but also one of the first known martyrs in the struggle to save the environment.

In India, when developers started to chop down the forests, the local women, realizing that their whole livelihood depended on the forest, encircled the trees with their bodies, so that the machines could not get at the trees without killing the women. Eventually the trucks went away. Chipko has grown into a major grassroots movement described in Vandana Shiva's book, *Staying Alive*.

The destruction of forests high on the mountains has meant that the soil can no longer hold the rainfall, and has been a major cause of floods. The whole pattern of rainfall has been affected and this has caused serious drought in other places.

Another serious consequence of the destruction of forests is that it destroys the habitat of many species of plants and animals, some of which are rapidly becoming extinct. These things have a right to exist for their own sake, but they also provide human beings with invaluable food, medicine and other benefits.

It is true that poor people are chopping down a lot of trees and this has meant that in many areas where there used to be good woodlots there are now no trees at all. But poor women searching for firewood, or families making charcoal to sell for the necessities of life, really cannot be blamed. They are struggling for survival. It is those who have much good land which they are unwilling to share that have forced too many poor people on to dry and infertile land. It is extremely important to encourage local people to plant and see to the maintenance of at least one tree for every tree they chop down.

However, the worst damage to the trees is not being done by poor peasants searching for firewood. Even more serious than this is the destruction of the tropical rainforests. These dense forests with huge numbers of enormous trees grow in the hot and humid lands all around the equator. [Find it on the globe.] They are in countries like Brazil, Nigeria and Zaire, Burma and Malaysia. Even temperate lands like Europe and North America were once covered in trees. Knysna in the Southern Cape in South Africa had wonderful forests of huge old trees, some of them several hundred years old. For years loggers have been going into these forests to cut down the largest and most useful trees, for building, shipbuilding and furniture, and destroying the trees they did not want. But recently something much more serious has been happening in countries like Brazil. Rich industrialists and landowners have gone in, driving out the indigenous forest people who have lived peacefully with nature for many centuries. The newcomers have cleared the forest using the 'Slash and Burn' method ruthlessly on a vast scale, so that they can use the land for other export crops and for ranches to grow beef to export to America. The forests are being destroyed very rapidly, and the new crops do not do well for very long because the soil and the weather are not suitable for them.

These forests have been called the lungs of the earth. By the wonderful process of photosynthesis their leaves turn the poisonous gases, like the carbon dioxide which we breathe out and the carbon monoxide from cars, into fresh oxygen which we need for our survival. Destroying the rainforests is like destroying the lungs of a living body, and without these lungs human life will not be able to survive on Earth.

Suggested questions to go with this reading:

- What do you think is the root cause of this destruction of the rainforests?
- Is it human greed, the desire of some to make money as quickly as possible with no respect for nature, taking it for granted that everything on Earth comes free?

Tree planting

"Now at the risk of being misunderstood, I will give you the simplest of all possible examples of self-help. The Good Lord has not disinherited any of the children, and as far as India is concerned, God has given her a variety of trees unsurpassed anywhere in the world. There are trees for almost all human needs. One of the greatest teachers of India was the Buddha, who included in his teaching the obligation of every good Buddhist that s/he should plant and see to the establishment of one tree at least every five years. As long as this was observed the whole large area of India was covered with trees, free of dust, with plenty of water, plenty of shade, plenty of food and materials.

"Just imagine if you could establish an ideology which would make it obligatory for every able-bodied person in India, man woman and child, to do that little thing – to plant and see to the establishment of one tree a year, five years running. This, in a five-year period, would give you 2,000 million established trees. Anyone can work it out on the back of an envelope that the economic value of such an enterprise, intelligently conducted, would be greater than anything that has ever been promised by any of India's five-year plans. It could be done without a penny of foreign aid; there is no problem of savings and investment. It would produce foodstuffs, fibres, building materials, shade, water, almost anything that the people really need."

E.F. Schumacher, *Small is beautiful*

Exercise 17. Air pollution

The aim of this session is to enable the participants to think about the problem of air pollution in the urban areas.

Procedure

1. Put up a picture of a city with smoking factory stacks, buses and lorries churning out smoke, people cooking over coal fires outdoors. A heavy brown cloud hangs over the city. The houses are all small, many shacks huddled closely together. On the green hills beyond the clouds are a few big comfortable houses in clear blue sky surrounded by trees. There are no trees in the central city.

2. Ask the participants to turn to the person beside them and **in pairs** discuss:

   a. What do you see happening in this picture?
   b. What causes the smog?
   c. Have you ever experienced this type of air pollution?
   d. Who suffers most from air pollution?
   e. What effects does it have on people's health?
   f. What is the hole in the ozone layer?
   g. Why are ultra-violet rays dangerous?
   h. What is meant by acid rain? Why is it important?

   Discuss how to find out if we do not know the answers.

3. Ask the participants to come together in the **whole group** and share their answers to the questions, each pair giving one point at a time.

4. In **groups of six** ask them to make recommendations about what can be done by individual people and by NGOs in terms of:

   a. planting trees
   b. lobbying the local authorities on the issue of air pollution.

5. What do we expect of the government in terms of:

   a. Laws controlling factory and car emissions, coal burning.
   b. Making the polluter pay.

Time   1 hour

Materials   Poster, newsprint, markers, tape, paper.

Exercise 18. Food: from feast to famine

The purpose of this session is to raise awareness of:

● the causes of famine in Africa
● the effects of agribusiness and global food companies on the lives of the poor

and to discuss the importance of some measure of self-sufficiency in local, regional and national food production.

'Nature Pleads "Not Guilty!" ' This was the title of an issue of *New Internationalist* magazine in September 1984, at the height of one of the worst famines in Africa. After going through the historical analysis of the food situation in Africa, see if the participants agree that famines are not caused by nature.

> **For centuries Africa produced all its own food.**
> **Only occasionally in times of drought was there famine.**
> **For decades during the time of colonialism**
> **Africa exported tons of food each year.**
> **Yet during the last 20 years terrible famines have caused**
> **enormous suffering and death. Why has this happened?**

Procedure

1. Ask the participants to divide into **groups of three or four**, putting those with the widest background knowledge into different groups.

2. Give each group a slip of paper with a short introductory input related to one of the questions below (see handouts: these should be cut along the horizontal lines).

3. Put a large-scale map of the world on the floor. [If it is possible to get the participants to cut out and arrange really large outlines of the continents and major islands in green felt or light cardboard, this is even better than using a large commercially printed map.]

4. Ask the participants to sit next to the other members of their group, in an oval around the map so that all can see it. Have supplies of 'provisions' on a low table at one end.

5. Ask the following questions, giving participants an opportunity to share any information they have on the topic. When there is a gap in the discussion, ask the group with an appropriate input to read it out. They should then illustrate what is occurring by showing it on the map or moving some of the tokens provided; for example, when cash crops are discussed they can add coffee beans, tea, sugar, etc. to the appropriate place on the map. The topic could then be opened for further discussion. Keep enough time for discussion of the final question, i.e. what can be done to ensure sustainable development and adequate food production in Africa?

Questions

1. What did the diet of Africans consist of before the coming of white settlers?
2. How did slavery affect the West and the East coasts? What was meant by the triangular trade?
3. How did colonialism affect the food situation in different parts of Africa?
4. Which cash crops were produced in which countries, and what effect did this have?

---

5. Why did the situation fail to improve after independence during the 1960s?
6. What has been the effect of agribusiness, and the Green Revolution?
7. In what way did OPEC and the oil crisis of the 1970s affect the food situation in Africa?
8. How has militarism and war affected the food situation?
9. What factors made the situation even more serious during the 1980s?
10. What do you think needs to be done in order to ensure sustainable development and adequate food production and distribution in Africa?

Time   1 to 2 hours

Materials   Photocopy the handouts, which provide answers to the questions, on sheets of paper, and cut them into separate slips for each group. Map of the World; provisions, e.g. coffee, tea, sugar (empty containers would do).

'It takes 21 kg of grain protein to make 1 kg of beef protein.'

Diet for a Small Planet

"No artist – no maker – can work except by reworking the works of Creation. By our work, by the way we practice our arts we reveal what we think of the works of God. How we take our lives from this world, how we work, what work we do, how well we use the materials we use, and what we do with them after we have used them – all these are questions of the highest and gravest religious significance."

"The plowman and the potter have cosmic function."

Walter Shewring

"Christianity has for the most part stood silently by, while a predatory economy has ravaged the world, destroyed its natural beauty and health, divided and plundered its human communities and households. It has flown the flag and chanted the slogans of empire. It has assumed with economists that economic forces automatically work for good, and has assumed with the industrialists and militarists that technology determines history. It has assumed with almost everyone that 'progress' is good, and that it is good to be up with the times. It has admired Caesar, and comforted him in his depredations and defaults. But in its de facto alliance with Caesar, Christianity connives directly in the murder of Creation. For in these days Caesar is no longer merely a destroyer of armies, cities and nations. He is a contradictor of the fundamental miracle of life."

"Our destruction of nature is not just bad stewardship. . . . It is the most horrid blasphemy. It is flinging God's gifts into His face, as of no value beyond that assigned to them by our destruction of them."

Wendell Berry, *Cross Currents*. Summer 1993.

Summary of history of food and famine in Africa
[Cut into separate slips and give one to each group]

Before the arrival of white settlers the staple foods of most people were millet and sorghum. In drier places many people grew cassava. Yams grew in West Africa, and bananas in fertile mountain places in Central and East Africa. Hunting and fishing provided meat and fish in many places. Cattle and goats were present from very early times and stocks gradually increased. Sheep were introduced from the Middle East.

During the 18th and 19th centuries one hundred million slaves were taken out of Africa. Most of those from the West coast were taken to Brazil, the West Indies and the southern part of North America, where they worked in sugar plantations, tin mines and cotton plantations. Thousands died during the journey on board ship under horrifying conditions. Those from the East coast were mostly taken by Arab slave traders. The loss of all these able-bodied young adults, besides causing enormous human suffering, had a devastating effect on the local economies and the food production of the places from which they were taken.

The slave traders set up the triangular trade between Europe, North America and West Africa. Weapons and cloth from Europe were taken in ships to Africa where they were sold in exchange for slaves. The slaves were taken to North and South America where they were put to work in the tin mines and on the cotton plantations. Metals and raw cotton were sent to Europe, where they were made into weapons, and woven into cloth. Then the whole triangle started again. Because rival chiefs in some parts of Africa wanted guns, they were prepared to co-operate with the slave traders in rounding up some of their own young men and women to sell them into slavery. There were however some chiefs that pleaded with the European rulers to stop the slave trade.

Before colonialism many parts of Africa were extremely fertile and provided more than enough food for the people. As the European powers established their authority in most African countries they set up patterns of trade based on what they called 'comparative advantage'. This meant that each country would concentrate on producing the things it could grow and produce most effectively. This led to monocrop agriculture. The use of the soil over and over again for the same crop exhausted it and left it far less fertile. The colonies provided the raw materials, like coffee, tea, rice, sugar, cotton. These were sent to Europe for processing and either used there or re-exported to Africa. For example, peanuts were grown in Senegal and exported to France, where they were processed into salad oil and sold at a far higher price than the original peanuts. Meanwhile many parts of Senegal became a desert.

This pattern of trade was greatly to the advantage of the industrialized countries, and still has profound effects on trade patterns today. The prices of raw materials have continued to go down while the prices for manufactured goods go up. As Nyerere once said, 'Today we have to sell twice as much coffee as we did five years ago to buy the same tractor.'

African farmers were persuaded to change from subsistence farming, in which they grew all the food needed by their own families, but did not make much money, to growing cash crops for sale. In the West African tropical forests they started to grow cocoa and rubber. In East Africa they grew coffee, tea, sisal, and later rice and pineapples for export. In Zimbabwe they concentrated on tobacco.

Even though at the time the introduction of cash crops was seen as development, in fact it was a poor exchange. Instead of providing food for local people, the land was used to grow export crops. Malnutrition increased and by the 1980s many African countries were dependent on imported food.

Muranga, one of the richest parts of Kenya, where earlier the people had a very healthy diet of maize and beans, by the 1970s had one of the highest rates of malnutrition in the country. All the most fertile land had been used to grow coffee and tea. The men tended to regard the money they earned for these cash crops as their own and much of it was spent, not on the family, but on liquor. The women no longer had large enough farms to produce sufficient food for their families. This pattern of increasing hunger side by side with prosperous cash crops could be seen in many parts of Africa.

People had very high hopes that after independence, which many African countries obtained during the 1960s, the economies of their countries would improve rapidly and development would put an end to poverty. This did not happen. Colonialism was replaced by Neo-colonialism, the new economic form of colonialism. The European powers and the white settlers no longer had political power but they still controlled the economy. Transnational corporations (TNCs) set up factories in African countries where labour was cheaper. People believed the TNCs were bringing investment and jobs, and governments gave them tax holidays and promises of a stable labour force. Often strikes were outlawed, so wages remained low and working conditions poor. Many of the large corporations made, and took home, vast profits.

Agribusiness meant that transnational food corporations such as Del Monte established huge plantations, ranches and processing plants. This and the growth in population contributed to a situation in which many families no longer had land on which to grow their own food. Scientific research, including the introduction of chemical fertilizers, pesticides and hybrid seeds – known as the Green Revolution – meant that though production sometimes increased, there was often more hunger. Increased technology meant that there were fewer and fewer jobs in agriculture. The unemployed cannot buy the food produced on these big plantations because they have no money. In fact, small-scale farming often produces as much as large farms, and also gives jobs and dignity to people.

OPEC (the Organization of Petroleum Exporting Countries) agreed to raise the price of oil very drastically in 1973. This meant that countries such as those in the Middle East, Nigeria and Venezuela became rich very suddenly, and other countries that had become dependent on oil for transport and industry went into serious debt. They borrowed money from the banks at an interest rate of 9% and very rapidly the interest rate went up to 21%. This meant that for many of the poorer nations a huge percentage of their export earnings were used simply to service their debts.

Famines have been made far worse in many places by war and military spending. Often there is sufficient food nearby but people do not have access to it. When the price of oil went up in 1973, the USA, Britain, France and Germany all made up for the extra costs of

their oil imports by increasing their exports of armaments. Many countries in Africa were persuaded that they must spend far more of their national budget on importing weapons and military equipment. Then, because they had sophisticated weapons, conflicts that would have resulted in small local skirmishes escalated into major wars. The suffering was enormous and money that could have been spent on food and human services was diverted to war. This was true of apartheid South Africa, but it has also been true of Angola and Mozambique, Sudan, Somalia, Rwanda and many other countries.

___

By the 1980s the countries of the South were paying such heavy interest on their debts that, from 1983 onwards, the money that was being paid by the poor countries of the South to the rich industrialized countries of the North was more than the so-called Aid given by the North to the South.

When African countries tried to borrow more money from the International Monetary Fund to pay these exorbitant interest rates, the IMF insisted on 'structural adjustments' in their economies. This meant that they would not be given any further loans unless they cut down radically on government spending. It was a fact that the civil service in some countries was bloated and many people were not doing productive work, but structural adjustment meant that governments radically reduced their spending on education, health and social services. Thus the poor became far worse off. They also had to concentrate on increasing their exports to pay off their debts, even at the expense of meeting the needs of local people. Again more land was used for export crops and less was available to meet local food needs. More countries became dependent on importing food at great cost.

___

Exercise 19. Population and quality of life

The aim of this session is to enable participants to grasp the rate of growth in global population and the implications of this for development.

In advance, if possible, prepare three delicious pies or cakes. Each pie represents the goods and services which will be available for a particular age group over their lifetime. The second pie is a little larger than the first to represent the fact that there has been some growth in the GNP of most countries during a 25-year period, but during that same time the population has increased so that the pie must be divided between more people. Each individual's portion therefore grows smaller as each generation passes.

If pies cannot be prepared, follow Procedure B.

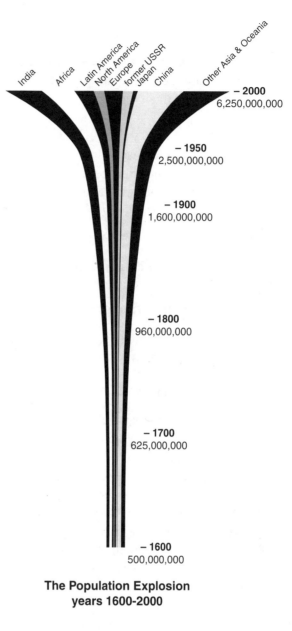

**The Population Explosion
years 1600-2000**

Procedure A. Fair shares?

1. The group is divided into three groups: the '60-year-olds', representing the grand-parents' generation; the '35-year-olds', representing the parents' generation; and the '10-year-olds', representing the children's generation.

    For a group of forty people there should be:
    seven 60-year-olds
    eleven 35-year-olds
    twenty-two 10-year-olds

    For a group of 20 there should be:
    four 60-year-olds
    six 35-year-olds
    ten 10-year-olds

    Explain that this is a fairly accurate division according to the numbers of people in the world today.

2. Each group is asked to choose a song representing their generation or use a song about food, e.g. 'Food, glorious food' from the musical *Oliver*.

3. The first pie is presented to the 60-year-olds. They cut it up. One person is given a very big piece of pie and the rest is divided equally. They eat it while the others watch, singing the song chosen by this group.

4. The second pie is given to the 35-year-olds. Two people are given big pieces and the rest is divided equally. They also eat it up, but their portions are of course smaller than the first ones. The others watch singing the song of this group.

5. The third pie is given to the 10-year-olds. Four people are given big pieces, and they cut up the rest and share it equally, but their portions are much smaller still. The others watch, singing the song chosen by this group.

6. Ask the group to discuss the following questions:
   a. What did you see happening in this play?
   b. Why were the portions getting smaller and smaller ?
   c. In what ways does this reflect what is going on in the world as a whole?

Time   1 hour

Materials   Three different size pies and a knife with which to cut them.

Procedure B. Population growth graph

1. Put up a large poster with the 'wineglass' diagram showing population growth from the 1994 UN Development report, found on the previous page.

2. Ask the participants to study the chart and to discuss in pairs:

   a. What strikes you particularly about the chart?
   b. What are the implications of the present rate of population growth for development and quality of life for all?
   c. How does the increase of population affect: food supply, water, health services, education and jobs, and any other aspects that concern you?
   d. What different factors contribute to the rate of population growth?
   e. What steps are necessary if we are to lower the birthrate?
   f . What do you personally think about family planning and birth control?
      What problems are associated with it for you?
      Has your religion had anything to say about it?
   g. What can we do personally and as organizations to ensure that people will be able to meet the fundamental human needs of all the children alive now and those who will be born in the future?

> **Input**. The graph shows the growth of population from 2 to 8 billion from 1920 to 2020, i.e. population has multiplied by four in 100 years. As the speed of growth has been increasing all the time this means that there are now twice as many people as there were in the world in 1960.

3. Discuss:
   a. Can the Earth meet the needs of everyone, not only of those who are alive today but of those yet to be born?
   b. Can we work out a pattern of sustainable development so that the needs of our children and their children can still be met?

African culture stresses the importance of taking account of the consequences of our actions 'to the seventh generation'. The children yet to be born are as much a part of the community as those of us who are living now. But modern industrial society is so focused on short-term gains that it has forgotten how to 'care for the future'.

We live in a finite world with limitations. There is a limited amount of good land for farming. We might learn to farm some of the other land in a sustainable way, but probably not too much more. There is a limited amount of fresh water. There is a limit to the amount of food which can be grown. We may learn to produce and harvest more, but it is essential that we do so in a way that will not harm the environment. Otherwise in the long run our children, and our children's children, will suffer.

4. a. How do you see the responsibility of governments in terms of limiting population growth?
   b. Are any parties or organizations supporting these policies?
   c. What is our own responsibility?

Time   1 to 2 hours

Materials Graph

Exercise 20. The problem of waste

The aim of this session is to help participants become aware of how waste has become a major environmental problem, and to look at practical ways in which both local communities and local governments can deal with it.

Procedure A. Common waste

1. Bring along an assortment of common waste, including paper, plastic, used cans, glass bottles and jars, and vegetable peelings and garden refuse.

2. Divide the participants into **five groups**.

3. Give each group one of the following:
   - an assortment of tin cans
   - several items of plastic
   - a number of glass bottles and jars.
   - old newspapers, magazines and envelopes
   - old vegetables cuttings, peelings, orange rind etc.

4. Ask each group to discuss:
   a. What are these things made of?
   b. Where were the raw materials obtained?
   c. Where and how were they made?
   d. How much energy was used?
   e. What happens to them when we throw them away?

5. Hand out information on each of these materials.

Notice particularly how much more energy it takes to make new things such as tin cans compared with recycling them. Discuss the possibilities of burning rubbish, putting drinks in reusable bottles and jars instead of tin cans, and using baskets instead of plastic bags for shopping; also of composting vegetable peelings and garden waste.

Time   1 hour

Materials   Enough tins, plastic, glass, newspapers, and food garbage for each group to work with. Information about environmentally acceptable ways to dispose of waste should be available from local councils or from United Nations programmes in your area.

Procedure B. Food for garbage

1. Read Curatiba case study.

2. Questions for discussion:

   - Would it be possible to organize such a scheme in your own city and approach the city council to co-operate by donating money for food?
   - What are the possibilities of **recycling** in your area, if you are in town?
     Or how can we take care of our waste in rural areas?

Input on toxic wastes. Explain that some wastes are extremely dangerous because they poison the water, the soil, the food that is grown in such soil and the air we breathe. These are called **toxic wastes**, and most come from chemicals such as insecticides, fertilizers, paint and oil. The most dangerous of all is nuclear waste. The plutonium which is a by-product of nuclear energy production is highly poisonous and cannot be destroyed for thousands of years.

Industrial societies produce more toxic waste than they can dispose of in their own countries, so now they try to ship it to the poorer countries of the South, which do not have such strict laws for preserving a healthy environment. They are willing to pay other countries to take their waste, and some governments have agreed to this because they are so desperate for foreign exchange. But they are putting the health of future generations at risk.

Homework on toxic waste. Ask the participants to go to their local libraries and ask the librarians to help them do a search of the local newspapers to find out whether there has been any attempt to dump toxic wastes in their country. If so they should consider how they could organize a protest to prevent this happening.

Time   1 to 1½ hours

Materials   Copies of the case study on Curatiba, Brazil

A case study of Curatiba in Brazil

Curatiba is a fairly large city in Brazil. It has had a very enlightened Mayor and city council who were determined to make life in the city as healthy and enjoyable for all the citizens as possible. Development was extremely carefully planned, along a series of major roads radiating out from the centre of the city to the outskirts, like the spokes of a wheel. Along each of these roads ran a good system of public transport. Shops, parks, churches and recreation centres as well as factories and other workplaces were made easily accessible to all the people along these major roads.

As in many other cities, following the invention of plastic and paper packaging and tin cans, people began to drop litter in the streets and parks, polluting this beautiful city. There were also problems of unemployment, poverty and hunger. At a particular point a group of concerned citizens, including members of various churches and non-government organizations, started to organize clean-up projects. The city council agreed to give the equivalent of 3 dollars' worth of food to anyone who collected a shopping bag full of rubbish, and food worth $25 to anyone who collected a big garbage bag full of rubbish, plastic bags, tins etc. The streets and parks became clean, the people had more food available, and the city council found that it was cheaper to donate the food in payment for the garbage than to send their large trucks to collect the refuse.

SECTION FIVE

The Council of All Beings

Exercise 21. A trial of the humans

This role play is based on an exercise in *Thinking like a Mountain*, by Jonathan Seed and Joanna Rogers Macy.

Procedure

1. All the participants are invited to take part in a court case in which the Western model of industrialized development is accused of destroying the environment and threatening the well-being of the Earth, the indigenous people, and numerous other creatures, in a spirit of greed, callousness and domination.

   The Judge is Gaia, the ancient Greek Goddess of Earth. There are two lawyers for the prosecution and two for the defence. Each side calls a variety of witnesses.

2. The judge and the four lawyers are chosen by the group and also a police officer to keep order in the court and ensure the proper procedure is followed.

3. The two lawyers for the prosecution get together to plan their line of argument for the prosecution, and the two lawyers for the defence plan the points they wish to stress to defend modern civilization.

   The rest of the participants are asked to choose which side they wish to be on. The sides should be fairly equal. Each person decides whose voice they wish to present. If the group is very large, ask people to work in pairs.

The witnesses for the prosecution can include: indigenous men, women, children, animals threatened with extinction such as elephants, whales and dolphins, eagles, rabbits and others whose homes have been destroyed as cities spread, penguins after oil spills, fish, Khoisan (Bushmen) and Native American people and any others that those present are deeply concerned about. They can also be joined by scientists, artists, poets, etc.

The witnesses for the defence can include scientists, doctors, astronauts, secretaries using computers, filmstars, businessmen who are making big profits, estate agents etc.: anyone who is gaining a lot from modern civilization.

4. The trial should take place outside, either in a beautiful place, or perhaps in one spoilt by modern developments such as pylons, an oil refinery, a dump, a littered railway yard, etc.

5. The policeman calls the court to order; Gaia, the judge enters; and from this point the judge takes charge of the proceedings. After the witnesses have been heard each of the counsel has an opportunity to sum up and then the judge pronounces sentence and suitable punishments for reparation.

6. Take time to debrief the group, asking what were the most important things they learnt.

Time   2 to 4 hours

Materials   A table, gavel (or hammer for the judge) and any other materials for a court.

'If all the creatures of the Earth had a parliament, they would vote the humans out.'

Thomas Berry

'We humans cannot live without the Earth, but the Earth can live very well, even better, without us.'

Thomas Berry

The ways forward

Exercise 22. Alternatives with our local communities

Various actions have already been suggested in different sections, but it is important, before the sessions on environment close, to make some practical plans for local action.

Procedure

1. Begin by dividing into **neighbourhood groups of participants** who live reasonably close together.

2. Hand out the 'Practical action' chart. Explain that on the left there are two spaces for personal reflection, on the right two for group reflection.

3. Ask participants to work individually in silence for about ten minutes, deciding which of these suggestions, or any other suggestions they have, are most important, and which they could most easily start in their area. Ask them to fill in the left hand columns of the chart.

4. Then ask them to discuss in their neighbourhood groups and try to come to a common decision about which of the suggestions are most needed and most possible. They should then fill in the right hand columns of the chart.

5. Then see if they can make a practical plan to start a project. If appropriate the planning kit from *Training for Transformation* Book III could be used.

Time   2+ hours

Materials   Newsprint, markers, tape and copies of the Practical action handout.

Practical action for taking care of the environment in our neighbourhood

1. Tick two or three items in each column (add your own suggestions if appropriate)

Individual				Group	
Most Needed	Most Possible	ACTIONS		Most Needed	Most Possible
		Composting			
		Litter collection and control			
		Tree planting			
		Tree nursery garden			
		Vegetable gardening			
		Producing a lot of food in a small space			
		Water conservation			
		Flowers and shrubs			
		Recycling projects: paper, glass and cans			
		Food for garbage			
		Other ideas:			

2. Choose an appropriate day to celebrate the environment, e.g. Earth Day or Arbor Day.

3. Organize a competition for the best home and garden, the best street, the best school compound or Community Centre garden.

CHAPTER 2
Gender and development

71

Introduction

In 1975, the first UN conference on women was held in Mexico. There most women believed that if more money and effort were put into the development of women, the economic situation of women would automatically improve. However, they realized that too little research had been done on the situation of women in most countries and they committed themselves to a thorough programme of research. A 'Decade for Women' was declared by the United Nations as an official commitment to improving the situation of women worldwide.

Women and Development

Even before the decade, questions started arising about whether the process called 'development' was really helping women. A very significant book raising new questions was published in 1970: *Women's Role in Economic Development*, by Ester Boserup.

> Boserup has documented how women's impoverishment increased during colonial rule; those rulers who had spent a few centuries subjugating and crippling their own women into de-skilled, de-intellectualized appendages, disfavoured the women of the colonies on matters of access to land, technology and employment. The economic and political processes of colonial underdevelopment bore the clear mark of modern Western patriarchy. While large numbers of both women and men were impoverished by the processes of colonialism, women tended to lose more. The privatization of land for revenue generation displaced women more critically, eroding their traditional land-use rights. The expansion of cash crops (such as tea, coffee, cocoa for export) undermined food production and women were often left with meagre resources to feed and care for children, the aged and the infirm, especially when men migrated or were conscripted into forced labour by the colonizers. A collective document prepared by DAWN (Development Alternatives for Women in a New era) stated at the end of the Decade for women, 'The almost uniform conclusion of the decade's research is that, with few exceptions, women's relative access to economic resources, incomes and employment has worsened. Their burden of work has increased and their health, nutrition and educational status has declined.
>
> (Vandana Shiva, *Staying Alive*, page 2)

The figures which emerged from the decade of research were presented at the Nairobi UN Conference for Women in 1985, and these left no doubt about the level of the injustice done to women:

Women are 51% of the world's population
They do 66% of the world's working hours
They earn 10% of the world's income and
Own less than 1% of the world's assets.

These figures made it very clear that women are discriminated against and that in all fields it is necessary to make separate studies of the well-being of women and of men. For example, it is not sufficient to study economic situations simply by family or household. Often the economic situation of the men and women in the same family is very different, putting them into different social classes.

This is even more striking if one looks at the differences of political and social power between men and women in the same families, and at choice about how the money available in the family will be used. Women now insist that the figures for males and females should be calculated separately when statistics are prepared, to provide a true comparison of the relative well-being, or deprivation, of men and women. This process is called 'disaggregation' and it has already proved very revealing.

Country	Adult illiteracy rate	Female illiteracy rate
Kenya	21.9%	30%
Uganda	38.1%	50%
Botswana	30.2%	40%
India	48.0%	62%

(Source: *UNDP Human Development Report 1997*)

The reports of UNICEF also helped to focus attention on the fact that the well-being of children is directly linked to the well-being of women. If women were living in wretched conditions, children certainly would be too.

The United Nations Fourth World Conference of Women in Beijing, China, in August and September 1995, made it clear that there is a new strength in women. Maria Riley O.P. (Center of Concern) who participated in several preparatory meetings and the conference said, 'There's a new atmosphere in the women's meetings now. We seem to have crossed a threshold. The women no longer feel that they have to apologize for pushing their own issues or fight aggressively to be heard. They have their agenda quite clear and they are very competent and confident in the way they go about their preparations'.

As people began to realize not only that women had been excluded from the process of Western style development, but that the process itself works against the well-being of women, they saw more clearly that men too were adversely affected, and many of them also impoverished by the dominant model of development, and the role expected of men in this model. So the focus changed from Women in Development [WID] to Gender and Development.[GAD]

> **First they gave us a day for women.**
> **Then they gave us a year.**
> **Then they gave us a decade.**
> **Now we're hoping for a century –**
> **and maybe then they'll let us in for the whole show.**
>
> (Bella Abzug, US feminist)

Gender training: separate or mixed groups

In the early stages of the women's movement women felt a great need to meet together in all-women groups. For so long men had defined what it meant to be womanly and had taken it upon themselves to explain the experience and the feelings of women. In the women's groups, women felt freer to share their own experiences and feelings and they found these were often quite different from those attributed to them by men. As they found that other women felt as they did, they realized that men's experience of life is not the 'norm for all people'. They gained new confidence in the validity of their own experience and the value of what they had to contribute. For many women, especially those who had been most silent in mixed groups, these women's groups were a very important experience of liberation. And, having once experienced the freedom and spontaneity of women's groups, many women treasured the opportunity of continuing to meet in these groups, at least from time to time.

However, as they grew clearer about the transformation goals of the women's movement, and realized that unequal power relationships were at the heart of maintaining the old patterns of behaviour and domination, they realized that it was not enough to work only with the women if they were to bring about real change. They saw that the stereotyped expectations of roles that should be played by the different sexes also deprived men of very important human opportunities, such as close relationships with their children. Men of goodwill, who had sensed the injustices under which many women suffered, and men who were confused by the new assertiveness in the women with whom they lived and worked, also wanted to think through their own gender roles. They realized that to be fully masculine one did not need to have dominating 'macho' attitudes. They wanted more dialogue both with other men about gender roles and with women on creating happier, more balanced patterns of life.

What do we mean when we talk about gender?

If we want to understand the issue of women's oppression better, we need to know what we mean by the term gender. There are two kinds of differences between women and men. They are sex and gender.

Sex is the physical, biological difference between women and men. It refers to whether people are born female or male.

Gender is not something physical, like sex. **Gender refers to the expectations people have of someone** because they are female or male.

To sum up, a woman's sex refers to the fact that she was born female. Her gender refers to what she and others expect of her as a female.

When we look at the differences between women and men it is important to separate sex and gender. The main sex difference between women and men is that men can impregnate (make pregnant) and women can bear children. The main gender difference between women and men is that women as a group have a lower status than men.

Everywhere, women as a group, enjoy fewer advantages and work together longer hours than men. Women's work and opinions are undervalued. In many countries women earn less than men, are prevented from owning land, face numerous obstacles to holding positions of authority and face many threats of violence just because they are women.

(Source: *On Our Feet*, E. Mackenzie for Centre for Adult and Continuing Education (CACE), p 16–17)

We therefore affirm the value of a whole range of different types of groups to discuss gender roles: women's groups, men's groups and mixed groups. Some of the exercises which follow are designed specifically for one type of group, others can be used in all three types of groups. As always the facilitator and the steering committee need to consider the actual needs of a group at a particular time, and choose exercises which meet that need.

Many workshops on gender are now run for men and women together. However, there is still a value in running some sessions separately for women and men, especially in situations where women are hesitant to express their views in mixed groups, or in situations where the women have become so articulate that now the men are hesitant to explore and express their true feelings.

Any group that is silent or marginalized needs the opportunity at times to meet alone with others of their kind so that they can explore their thoughts and feelings freely and work out ways of expressing their experience as strongly and clearly as possible in mixed groups afterwards.

The Black Consciousness Movement in South Africa chose to work separately for a time during the late 1960s and 70s, and through this gained a new sense of their own strengths and of solidarity. The same happened in the women's movement in many countries, and this is still definitely needed in many countries where race and gender issues are not yet resolved.

Even though, in the long run, the establishment of a just and caring society requires open and trusting communication between women and men, black and white people, we believe that such communication is helped by some time spent in separate groups.

> Washerwoman God, we know you in the waters,
> Washerwoman God, splashing, laughing free.
> If you didn't clean the mess, where would we be?
> Scrubbing, working sweating God,
> Cleansing you and me;
> Make our hearts as clean as snow
> Wash us through and through
> Washerwomen, let us be like you.
> (Source: *Cry of Ramah*, Colleen Fulmer, p30)

SECTION ONE

The web of women's oppression

Exercise 1. Story telling and sculpture: how women experience oppression

The aim of this exercise it to help women to remember, tell their stories and find common ground about the universal experience of women's oppression.

Procedure

1. Ask the group to divide into **groups of five**, trying to get as much variety of background and experience as possible in each group. If you have a mixed group, ask for separate groups of men and women. If some people resist this division, explain that the purpose of this is to ensure that the insights of each group can be presented more thoroughly in the whole group afterwards. (Use of homogeneous groups is often helpful when one group has been silenced culturally for some time.)

2. The women are asked to 'think of an occasion when you felt undermined as a woman, not respected, exploited, oppressed or discriminated against'. Each woman is asked to share as much of this experience as she feels comfortable doing with her small group. It is important to make it clear that no one needs to share things they do not want to talk about.

   If there are men in the group, ask them to be in their own group. Explain that discussions about gender are often hijacked by people saying how tough it is for men. Ask them to think of a time when they became aware of having more privileges than someone else. Also to think of a time when they had fewer privileges than someone else. Who did they find had more privileges and why? How did that make them feel and why?

3. Each small group is then asked to choose one of the stories. The person who told the story arranges the bodies of all the members of the group to present a 'human sculpture' showing the key moment in their story.

4. Each group presents their sculpture to the whole group. Each presentation is followed by discussion of the different ways in which people experience discrimination, exploitation, alienation or any other form of oppression.

5. Hand out the summary of definitions. Some of these forms of oppression will certainly have been shown in the sculptures, but ask the group to give examples of any of the above not already dealt with and of any other forms of oppression they can think of.

Time   1 to 1½ hours

Materials   Copies of the Summary of definitions.

Summary of definitions

Discrimination is depriving a particular group of fair opportunities (e.g. of education, jobs, promotion, use of resources).

Exploitation is taking unfair advantage of people because they are not in a position to fight for their rights, e.g. paying very low wages to people who are desperate for a job; insisting on sexual favours before offering a person a job or promotion etc.; expecting an unreasonable amount of work.

Alienation is the feeling of being at a disadvantage because you do not know the culture or the 'rules of the game' in the situation in which you find yourself, and so you are unable to offer the best you can do.

Domination is control by those with the greatest power. There can be domination without serious oppression, e.g. a benevolent dictatorship. One person or group makes all the decisions, but they try to make them for the good of the whole. However, domination is always a denial of the others' right to freedom of choice and participation in decision-making.

Oppression is the widest term, covering all the above and any other form of unjust pressure put on a relatively powerless person by someone with more power. This power may be due to physical strength, the use of weapons, rank, class, money, privilege, laws, education, knowledge etc.

Exercise 2. The web of women's oppression

This exercise is best used after the group has been actively involved in a discussion of women's oppression. Then it becomes a useful way of summarizing the points already raised.

Procedure

1. Put up a sheet of newsprint on the wall and write 'The Oppression of Women' in large letters in the centre. Explain that there have been three underlying themes, three areas in which women most frequently experience oppression. Draw three lines radiating out from the title and label them WORK, SEXUALITY and LEGAL RIGHTS.

2. Then explain how problems can be experienced in many different aspects of each of these areas – for example, sexuality can be divided into issues directly relating to biological sex, or issues relating to gender, the cultural expectations of each sex.

3. Work for a while with the **whole group**, asking them to suggest different aspects of each area, drawing on the newsprint the lines branching out from the centre, as in the diagram.

4. As soon as they understand the process ask them to split into **groups of five** (perhaps the same groups as in Exercise 1) and continue drawing the diagram on separate sheets of newsprint.

5. Once they have finished adding different aspects, ask them to think about how these different aspects reinforce one another and to draw lines in a different colour linking the two points together. For example, many women put up with domestic violence because they do not have sufficient income to support the children or the right to ownership of the family home.

6. When all the groups have finished, put the diagrams up on the wall and allow time for a gallery walk, paying particular attention to similarities and differences between the various charts.

Time   1 to 1½ hours

Materials   Newsprint, markers, tape, labels.

Exercise 3. Listening survey in the community

The aim of this exercise is to ensure that the issues and topics discussed by women reflect the reality of the women in our communities.

Procedure

1. Ask the participants to do a survey of the issues on which the women in their programme, neighbourhood or village have really strong feelings.

2. Summarize the points on the handout and then give them a copy of the handout on 'Survey of women's themes' to discuss and decide how they will do the survey. Ask the participants to form teams (of **two to five people**) who live near to each other. Their task is to read the handout and discuss how they will complete the survey over the next 2–4 weeks.

3. After about 30–45 minutes, ask the teams to come back into the whole group to raise any questions as well as to briefly share their plan.

Time   Ideally, the survey is done over a period of 2–4 weeks with listeners meeting once a week to study their results.

Materials   Notebooks, pens, and copies of the 'Survey of women's themes' handout.

Survey of women's themes

This survey is done by listening quietly in informal situations where women can talk freely. It is active listening with a clear idea of what you are listening for. We listen for the issues about which the women have the strongest feelings. Emotion is linked to motivation. Only on issues about which they feel strongly will people be prepared to act.

What are women:
- worried about?
- happy about?
- sad about?
- angry about?
- fearful about?
- hopeful about?

It is not possible to go to a person and ask, 'What are your strongest feelings?' It is instead necessary to be one with the people and to pay attention to the problems and issues of life that bring strong feelings.

The listening survey is done by individuals in a team. Each team member goes to different places and pays attention primarily to unstructured conversations, in which the women feel relaxed and talk about the things that they are most concerned about.

A framework for listening. One of the simplest and most effective frameworks for listening is being aware of the five basic human needs:

Physical needs
Safety and security
Love and belonging
Self-respect
Personal growth

It is interesting to compare the initial insights of the group about which needs are most urgent while other concerns may be on-going. New themes will continue to arise, so the team needs to be open to listening for and including new themes on an on-going basis.

Where to listen? The team will have to find ways in which they can listen to the spontaneous discussion of women, without manipulating or embarrassing them.

Market places	Bars
Buses and trains	Homes
Washing places	Sports events
Hairdressers	Outside church
Clinics	Times before and after public meetings

Team meetings. The team needs to meet once a week to report back to each other about their findings and record, by topics, what they are hearing. The purpose for getting this information is to ensure that women leaders are clear about local women's needs.

Exercise 4. The diamond: a framework for analysis

This exercise helps participants to link the four aspects of oppression. This first step in analysis is preparation for strategic action.

Procedure

1. Put up a sheet of newsprint with a large diamond. In the centre the problem is stated, e.g. 'The Oppression of Women'. The four sides of the diamond represent the causes of the problem: economic, social, political and cultural.

2. Draw and label arrows identifying the factors contributing to the economic, social, cultural and political oppression of women.

3. Start the process in the **whole group**, giving two or three examples from the summary.

4. Then ask the participants to continue in small **groups of four or five** participants.

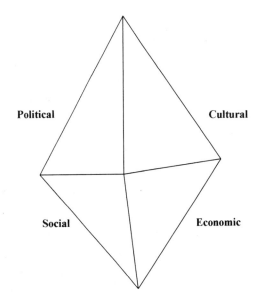

5. Provide an opportunity for them to share their insights afterwards. When the group have contributed all their insights the facilitator could call their attention to any of the points in the summary below which are particularly relevant in the local situation.

6. Then invite a small group to serve as a formulating team to make one composite diagram including all the insights. (If you have an artistic group they can make a border around the arrows illustrating the points mentioned.) Put this diagram on the wall.

Time   1 to 2 hours

Materials The 'diamond' drawn and labelled on newsprint before the session. Newsprint, markers and tape.

Summary: Different angles on the impoverishment of women

Economic   Effects of the development model
             Triple burden of work (see Section 2, Exercise 5)
             Women's work invisible, undervalued and underpaid
             Unequal pay for comparable work
             Job discrimination
             Domestic responsibilities not shared
             Men control the family budget
             From Women In Development (WID) to Gender And Development (GAD)
             Practical needs versus strategic planning for transformation.

Social   Relationships in family and wider community, work
             Role expectations of women in the family

Social conditioning and gender expectations
How gender expectations deprive men
Unequal educational opportunities
Ownership of women's bodies
> Conjugal duties
> Women can't say 'No'
> Rape in marriage

Prostitution: a social economic problem, not a sin
AIDS: Women's health problems less researched
Sexual exploitation for jobs ('Meet me at 4.30')
Control: 'My husband won't let me attend the women's group or literacy class.'
Self-esteem: women have much to be proud of.

Political   Power to make decisions on every level: family, community, city and district councils, national government
Quotas to share power (e.g. in South Africa the African National Congress has a rule that 1 of 3 candidates must be a woman on the ballot lists)
Women and the legal rights.

Norwegian Prime Minister Ms. Gro Brundtland stated that when the cabinet was made up of 50 per cent women, 'it made all the difference in the world. It changed the agenda.'

Cultural   Patriarchy in both traditional and Western forms
Cultural traditions: ownership of bride/Mother-in-law
Lobola (bride price)
Eyes down . . . Kneeling to men
Female circumcision
Success for women chiefly seen in their ability to catch a fine husband
Women's sense of self-worth, dependence on attachment to a man
Feminist theology

SECTION TWO

Women's work

Exercise 5. A fantasy of life without women

This is a warm-up exercise to look at the roles that women play in society.

Procedure

1. Ask the participants to get into **groups of three** of the same sex. Ask them to imagine and describe: 'What would happen in your family, your village or your neighbourhood if all the women went away for a month?'.

2. After about 15 minutes share informally in the whole group for another 10 or 15 minutes. (There will probably be lots of laughter. The atmosphere tends to be much freer in women's groups and much more flippant in mixed groups, so sometimes in mixed workshops it is a good idea to share experiences from the threes in homogeneous (same sex) groups before sharing some points in the whole group. The main point of this introduction is to get everyone involved and to affirm the fact that women play a very central role in life.)

Time   20–30 minutes

Materials   Newsprint, markers, tape.

Variation

A second round can be held in which the groups of three, again of the same sex, imagine what the village or neighbourhood would be like if **all the men** went away for a month. However, in many families this is not a new experience, due to jobs for men which involve a lot of travel and migrant labour, so this is more likely to deal with real experience, and might cause anger, bitterness and stereotyping to surface. It is therefore better, if one wants to keep the atmosphere light in a warm-up, to do just the first round and keep it fairly short. Deeper issues are better dealt with at a later stage.

Summary: The triple burden of work for women

Women carry a triple burden.
They are expected to take care of the needs of the family,
To contribute to family income through a job,
And to bind together the members of the wider community.

Overwork is certainly not confined to rural women. Many women in town were drawn into so-called 'productive' labour (as if their work in the homes was not productive) and got jobs as domestic workers and in factories. Even though they shared with the men the role of breadwinner, they still had to do all the work of maintaining the family and the home. Very few men were willing to share in these domestic responsibilities. And along with the job and family demands, women are still expected to play their traditional role in maintaining the life of the community. If there were weddings and funerals who was expected to cook? These family functions were central in maintaining the bonds within the extended family.

Exercise 6. A 24-hour day*

The aim of this exercise is to examine and compare the work day of women and men coming from different classes and life situations.

Procedure

1. Prepare sheets of paper containing four clock faces for all the participants. The two top clocks are marked a.m. and the two bottom ones are marked p.m. The two on the left are marked 'Woman' and the two on the right 'Man'.

2. Prepare five descriptions on separate pieces of paper, each describing one of the different types of family typical in your country or region. Three of the families should reflect poverty in different situations, one could be a more secure working class family and one a more privileged professional family.

Examples of different types of families

The following descriptions have been prepared for South Africa, but they should be adapted for other countries so that participants are working with situations which are familiar to them. For example, domestic workers know a great deal about the types of families who can afford to employ servants. For some groups it might be better to have all the families from the local area, but showing a range of occupation and class background.

a. *African dockworker and textile factory worker in Cape Town with three very young children. Sick grandmother trying to take care of children.*

b. *Xhosa woman in the Transkei with five children. Husband works on the mines in Johannesburg. She stays with her old parents. They have a very small plot of land.*

c. *Indian family. The husband has small business and the wife is a teacher in Durban. They have four children 16–7 years old.*

d. *White family in Johannesburg. The husband is a bank manager, the wife was formerly a secretary but is not working now. They have two children aged 8 and 5, and two servants.*

e. *Coloured family on a fruit farm in the Western Cape. The husband is a farmworker and the wife is a domestic servant. They have five children.*

---

* Source: *Oxfam Gender Training Manual*

84

3. Divide the participants into **five groups** and give each group a description of one of the different types of families. There should be **three to five people** in each of these groups. If the group is larger, subdivide the groups so that everybody can participate actively.

4. First let each group discuss the life situation of 'their' family, filling out the details to make the family as typical as possible of that group as they know it, but not yet discussing details about timing.

5. Hand out a copy of the clocks to each participant. Then ask the participants to work in silence for ten minutes, individually filling in on the clock faces what the woman and the man will be doing during each hour of one typical working day from midnight to the next midnight.

6. In groups let them discuss their decisions and try to come to realistic consensus. When they reach consensus they should fill in the a.m. and p.m. clocks for the man and the woman on a sheet of newsprint. (20 mins)

7. Ask groups to put the clocks up on the wall, and invite everybody to take part in a gallery walk, with the following questions in mind.

   a. What struck you most as you looked at the amounts of time spent by different people on different activities?
   b. What differences were common between most of the men and most of the women?
   c. In what ways did race and class make a difference to the time different people spent on paid work, unpaid work and recreation?

Time   1½ hours

Materials Newsprint, markers, tape, handouts for all participants on families, and copies of the clocks

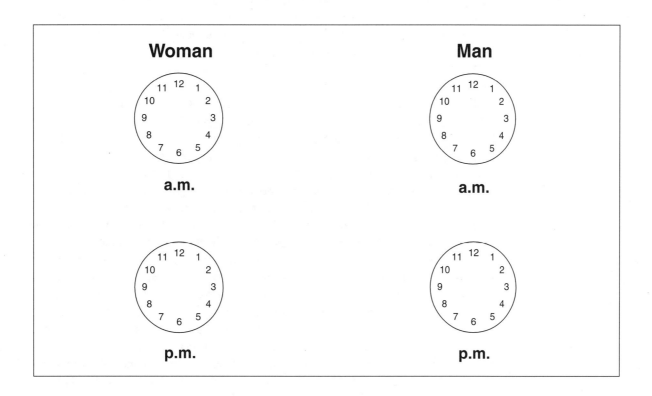

Women's traditional work is invisible, undervalued and underpaid

The industrial revolution put emphasis on 'production' of goods and commodities. Productivity was seen primarily in terms of commodities for sale. Factories ensured that men's work, and later women's work outside the home, was visible. It was part of the Gross National Product (GNP).

Women's work in the home was taken for granted. Those who shaped the economic development of most countries assumed that the work of women and nature came free. Low wages were paid to male workers and miners, taking it for granted that there would be a wife in the background putting food on the table for the worker, and bearing and raising children for the workforce in the future. In a similar way industrialists took for granted that they could use the land, the forests, the trees, the air, the rivers and ocean as if they were in unending supply and their own personal property.

Women's work in the home and in the fields is invisible; it is not even counted in GNP; it is usually totally undervalued.

For centuries women had been spinning invisible threads of love, relationships and communication between different members of the family and weaving webs of trust and co-operation between different groups in the community.

However, as economic need forced women into the 'productive' work of the factories, inevitably, though they tried to respond to all the demands of the triple burden, there was not enough time to pay attention to children, to look after the sick and the elderly, or to sustain the community through celebrations of the great events of human life, births, deaths and marriages. All these functions are sometimes called 'reproductive', because passing on life involves more than giving birth and feeding and nurturing children. It also includes the passing on of the cultural and spiritual values that bind together and give life to the family and the community. The continuity of these intangible things cannot be ignored indefinitely.

The consequences of neglect appear everywhere, ignored children growing into juvenile delinquents and later criminals, the enormous expansion of medical institutions for people who can no longer be taken care of by their families, until the AIDS epidemic made home care the only solution again. Countless needy people turn to psychologists for a listening ear, take meals at cafeterias or from street vendors, if they can afford it, because no one in the family has time to cook.

None of these changes is necessarily bad but it is no wonder that, once the invisible and unpaid labour of women could no longer be taken for granted, the costs of welfare, health care, and childcare rocketed. Governments are shocked and resent paying for these services, but they do not recognize that they were taken care of before by exploiting the work of women. This does not mean that women should go back to providing these services for free, but that **the whole of society should recognize how essential these services are if there is to be any quality in human life**. We must find proper ways of paying for these essential 'non-productive' forms of work.

Poverty adds enormously to the burden of work. There are many things that one can buy to save oneself the use of time and energy, but if one has no money one has to do every step of the work by oneself, e.g. the difference between doing all the laundry oneself, or taking it to a laundrette to be washed in a washing machine. One of the main ways of reducing the unfair load of work on women is ensuring that they earn more money.

Exercise 7. Analysis of women's work

This exercise enables groups to begin to analyse the work women do from the perspective of production, reproduction and community building.

The exercise can be done after the previous exercise, or on its own working from the general life experience of the participants.

Procedure

1. Ask the participants to form mixed groups of about **five people** (with one member from each of the former groups if the previous exercise has just been used). Give each group a piece of newsprint, crayons or markers.

2. Put up a sheet of newsprint headed 'The Work We Do', with two concentric circles divided into three sections. The inner circle is marked 'Paid' along one of the section lines and the outer circle marked 'Unpaid'. Around the outside of the outer circle label the sections 'Production', 'Reproduction' and 'Community Building'.

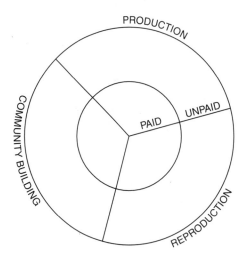

THE WORK WE DO

3. Discuss in the **whole group** what is meant by each of the categories, and fill in a few examples on the newsprint on the wall. The following are some examples.

- **Production**: includes making new goods for people to use, at all levels, from growing vegetables, to mining coal and making tins to can the vegetables, from growing cotton to tailoring smart suits. Some of this is paid and some is not.

- **Reproduction**: includes all kinds of ways of ensuring the life of the new generation; giving birth, but also feeding and caring for children. It includes both unpaid work, in the family and community, and paid work, such as teaching the young, nursing (caring for) the sick and the old. It also includes building up love and trust and co-operation in the extended family.

- **Community building**: includes all the work that is involved in building up the quality of life of the local community, e.g. voluntary community groups, pre-schools, celebrations like baptisms, weddings and funerals, initiation ceremonies, organizing religious services, higher and adult education, campaigns, community organizing, work on the organizations of civil society and participation in political parties, and government all the way up from local and provincial to national level.

  Community groups in South Africa during the struggle were the local authorities created by communities, when people rejected the authority of the Councils set up by the apartheid government. These became very powerful and effective in some places, but are much less so now that we have elected local councils. They are a type of NGO.

4. Then ask each group to fill in what type of work is done by different members of their community. They should consider whether each thing that is mentioned is paid or unpaid, and put it in the appropriate section of the circle. Some things will be written in both paid and unpaid circles, e.g. preparing meals, taking care of the sick.

5. After about 15 minutes, or when the groups are slowing down, show the signs for male and female and ask them to look again at what they have written and make a red male sign beside the work that is done by men and a blue female sign beside the work that is done by women.

Female	Male

6. Ask them to put these posters on the wall, looking for any things that other groups mentioned which they did not discuss.

7. Allow a few minutes for general discussion on the insights which arose during the process.

Time   1 to 1½ hours

Materials   Newsprint with headings and comments prepared before session. Newsprint, markers and tape.

Summary

The facilitator summarizes the findings of the group, adding any points that have not been mentioned from the background sections on 'Overwork and rural women', 'The triple burden of work for women', and 'The traditional work of women has been invisible, underpaid and undervalued'.

Overwork and rural women

In most traditional African societies women have worked extremely hard. The colonists imagined that most farmers were men, as they were in Europe, but in fact in many African countries up to 80 per cent of the food was actually produced by the women. Besides the backbreaking work of hoeing, planting, weeding and harvesting, women also had to fetch the water and the firewood, which often involved walking many miles in times of drought and as firewood grew increasingly scarce. They also had to care for the children, do the washing, clean the house and care for the old people.

Nyerere said, when most Tanzanian villages had been only marginally affected by westernization, that the people who worked harder in Tanzania than anyone else were the rural women. But as 'development' proceeded, two factors contributed enormously to the burden of work on women: the fact that so many men left the rural areas and became migrant workers in towns and

88

the fact that the children, who had traditionally helped a lot with the work, were sent to school and were no longer available to do much work around the home. A major survey done by the *Women's Tribune* in Harare in 1981 showed that a great majority of women said their greatest problem was overwork.

Women work

I've got the children to tend
The clothes to mend
The floor to mop
The food to shop
Then the chicken to fry
Then baby to dry
I got company to feed
The garden to weed
I've got the shirts to press
The tots to dress
The cane to be cut
I gotta clean up this hut
Then see about the sick
And the cotton to pick.

Shine on me, sunshine
Rain on me, rain
Fall softly, dewdrops
And cool my brow again.

Storm, blow me from here
With your fiercest wind
Let me float across the sky
'Til I can rest again.

Fall gently, snowflakes
Cover me with white
Cold icy kisses and
Let me rest tonight.

Sun, rain, curving sky
Mountain, oceans, leaf and stone
Star shine, moon glow
You're all that I can call my own.

Maya Angelou: *Poems*, Bantam Books, 1986, pp 144–5

Exercise 8. Action planning to reduce the overload of work

The aim of this exercise is to get women to start to talk about things that they could do together, rather than individually.

Procedure

1. Ask participants to form **groups of no more than five or six people** who are all from the same geographic area. It is important that the small groups are all of people who have some way in which they can meet after the workshop.

2. Ask the small groups to discuss:

   a. What makes women's lives most difficult?
   b. Of these, what is one thing we could do together to reduce the overload of work on women?
   c. What can we do for ourselves and in what ways could we work together to lighten the load?
   d. What other resources would help us do this?
   e. Where can we find these resources?

   The solutions offered for this problem will be very different according to the local situations of different groups. They might include anything from organizing childcare centres to introducing appropriate technology like donkeys or carts for fetching water; in rural areas, introducing water pumps and piped water projects, making paraffin or gas available for cooking to reduce time spent fetching firewood and chopping of trees, or lobbying for electricity, proper childcare, equal pay for comparable work, etc.

3. In the whole group, share some of the ideas for plans. It is not helpful for groups to share all the details of their plans, as the details can become boring.

Time   1 hour or more

Materials   None

SECTION THREE

Poverty

Exercise 9. Causes of poverty among women

In the last twenty years it has become clear that the majority of those who are very poor are women and children. This exercise is to help participants understand the causes of women's poverty, so that they can plan effective strategies to bring about change.

Procedure

1. Hand out the list of causes of poverty to each participant.

2. Ask the participants first to work on their own, ranking the five most serious and frequent causes as 1, 2, 3, 4, 5. Those which do not apply to their community should be marked with an 'x'.

3. When all the participants have had an opportunity to think for themselves ask them to get into **groups of four or five** coming from similar situations, to share the reasons for the order they chose and see if they can come to a common agreement about rank order.

4. Ask a spokesperson from each group to share which cause they ranked first, then those ranked second, then third, etc. Write each cause on newsprint as it is mentioned and add a tick each time that it is mentioned by another group. Make sure this process is done briskly and does not waste a lot of time, so that the overall picture is presented before the discussion takes place.

5. Allow time for comment and discussion.

Time   2 hours

Materials   Copies of 'Causes of poverty among women' for all participants.
Newsprint, markers and tape.

Summary

Explain the difference between the **practical needs** of women and **strategic goals**. The practical needs are things which ease the immediate experience of poverty, e.g. getting a job even if it is a very low paid one. The strategic goals aim to bring about a long-term change in the situation of women, usually challenging the root causes of discrimination and power relationships, e.g. getting a law passed which ensures equal pay for comparable work, or one that ensures that fathers pay maintenance for children. Another example is ensuring that women have a full share in decision-making on all the issues which affect their lives. Strategic goals usually involve long-term planning and commitment.

Discuss the constant importance of always working on both levels. Helping to relieve the most urgent immediate needs of the daily struggle makes the programme more concrete and makes it possible to celebrate some achievements. However, the obstacles encountered and the failures experienced will depend the understanding of participants that long-term changes in the power relationships between men and women are essential.

Causes of poverty among women

Rank the following in order of importance in the left column

Personal ranking		Group ranking
____	a. Rising school expenses	____
____	b. Pensions too low	____
____	c. Low wages, unequal pay for comparable work	____
____	d. Casual and unreliable work	____
____	e. No maintenance for children from absent fathers	____
____	f. High rent for poor housing	____
____	g. No opportunity for home ownership	____
____	h. Large family of children	____
____	i. Responsibility for members of extended family	____
____	j. Dependent men	____
____	k. Alcoholism of father or mother: wages spent on drink	____
____	l. No plot to grow vegetables	____
____	n. No common land for cattle grazing	____
____	m. No plot to keep chickens and goats	____
____	o. No planning on family budget, husband's wages not shared	____
____	p. Wife's wages taken by husband	____
____	q. No skills for developing home industry	____
____	r. No access to resources: tools, sewing machines etc.	____
____	s. Inflation and rising cost of living	____
____	t. Unemployment	____
____	u. Women last hired, first fired	____
____	v. Low level of education	____
____	w. Responsibility for family prevents taking job	____
____	x. High medical expenses	____

Exercise 10. The gender tree: a framework for gender analysis

The aim of this exercise is to enable participants to analyse the differences between different forms of oppression and the types of needs they have to address.

Procedure

1. Draw the outline of a large tree on a large sheet of newsprint.

2. Prepare small slips of red, light and dark green, beige and brown paper. Explain that you will use the tree as a visual framework for showing the relationship between different aspects of gender oppression from the standpoint of women.

> Light green papers, leaves, represent women's practical needs.
> Dark green leaves represent the long-term strategic needs.
> Beige represents the trunk of beliefs, values and practices.
> Brown represents roots, the underlying systems of oppression which maintain unequal power relationships. This might include race and class as well as gender.
> Red papers represent the fruits, changes in women's situation.

3. Ask the participants to divide into **groups of five** and give each group about 5 red, 5 light green, 5 dark green, 3 beige and 3 brown slips. Give them five or ten minutes to write the practical and strategic needs, the beliefs, values and practices, and the underlying systems of power on the appropriate slips.

4. Then invite each group to bring up their slips of paper and stick them on the tree, explaining when necessary. A different person could come up each time. Start with the practical then the strategic needs, then the beliefs etc. and finally the systems of power. When the tree is complete ask them to give examples of how the leaves, trunk and roots are constantly interacting with each other.

Time   1½ to 2 hours

Materials   Enough coloured paper to cut up for each small group, and on the newsprint the explanations of what each colour means.

93

Exercise 11. A case study: women do pay back their debts

The aim of this exercise is to remind women that they are very responsible members of society and therefore they have every right to insist on loans to increase their capacity to earn incomes.

Procedure

1. Give each participant a copy of the short case study about 'women paying their debts' from the Grameen Bank. Read the case study to the whole group.

2. Ask participants to form **groups of three** and discuss the following questions:

   a. What impresses you most about this story?
   b. Why do you think women are so responsible about paying back loans and with money?
   c. Are there saving and credit schemes in our area or through our church?
   d. What can we learn from this story?
   e. Is there a need for this in our situation and who can we approach for further information?

3. After about 20 minutes, ask participants to come back to the whole group for a general discussion. If there is a need to have another meeting with people in your area who run saving and credit schemes (or community banks), see what arrangements can be made to follow up this discussion.

Time   1 hour with possible follow-up

Materials Case study for each participant.

Women pay back their debts

The Grameen Bank of Bangladesh was founded in 1976 by economics professor Muhammed Yunus specifically to prove the bankability of the poor. By October 1990 Grameen had lent $278 million (about Rs1 billion) and was lending nearly $8 million a month, to its 830 000 members, 90% of whom are women and all of whom are classified as very poor. [There is a] repayment rate of 98%. The benefits that the bank's tiny loans, often only around $50, bring its members in terms of proportional additions to their income and savings are immense. Grameen Bank has doubled in size in the last two years and is still growing fast. It has proved that 'development banking' can work on a large scale and is sponsoring many similar initiatives in other countries.

Source: *Wealth Beyond Measure*, Paul Ekins, Mayer Hillman and Robert Hutchison, Gaia Books Ltd, 1992, p. 37

SECTION FOUR

Sexual oppression

Exercise 12. Violence against women

The aim of this exercise is to help women articulate the pain that they or women close to them have suffered.

Procedure

1. Ask participants to form **groups of three to four people** and show them a picture of a man beating a woman. Ask them to discuss the following questions:

   a. What do you think the man is thinking and why is he beating the woman?
   b. What is the woman thinking?
   c. Does this happen often? Why?
   d. What kinds of programme are there about alcoholism in your area?
   e. How much violence in connected to alcohol?
   f. Why else does this happen?
   g. What do we as women do, that continues this kind of behaviour in the home?
   h. What can women together do about this?

2. Ask participants to discuss these questions in the whole group.

3. Input from local groups about alcoholism (which is a disease), and how it can be treated, could be a useful follow-up to this discussion. Other strategies can be:

   • women forming self-protection groups
   • women forming self-help groups
   • safe havens for women (or women's shelters)
   • battered women courses are offered in most countries
   • women's legal rights against violence (even against their husband's violence)

Source: Violence against women, Eastern and Central Africa Women-in-development Network (Box 49026, Nairobi, Kenya). 1997.

Alternative procedure: women, war and violence

The aim of this exercise is to help men and women, separately and together, to look at violence in society.

1. Ask the participants to form **separate groups of men and women**. These groups should meet in separate rooms to discuss the following statement:

Violence, both inter-ethnic conflict and violent crime, seems to have been at an all time high in our continent in the last twenty years. In what ways are the attitudes of men and women towards war and violence different? What values underlie the attitudes of your own group and what are the values which you think underlie those of the opposite group?

2. When the participants **return to the whole group** ask first the men, and then the women, to sit in a small circle on the floor surrounded by the other group.

3. Ask those in the group in the middle to speak personally, sharing their thoughts and feelings about violence, beginning each time with 'As a man I feel, or think, that. . . . .' Each person should offer only one point at a time and allow pauses for those who have not yet participated to share something before they speak for a second or a third time.

4. When both groups have shared their thoughts and feelings, ask the groups to go back to their **separate sex groups** and answer these questions:

   a. What do we expect our own sex to do to reduce the violence?
   b. What do we expect the opposite sex to do to reduce the violence?

5. Each group should list their main points on two separate sheets of newsprint.

6. They return to the **whole group** to listen to the reports of each group and discuss them and together make plans for further action.

7. The facilitator should gather some resources about assertiveness training, self-defence training, passive resistance and non-violent action for use as handouts.

Time   2 hours

Materials Newsprint, marker, and tape, picture of man beating woman.

Exercise 13. Rape*

The aim of this exercise is to encourage women to articulate either their own or friends' experiences of women who have suffered this crime, and talk about strategies and support needed to protect women in the future.

Procedure

The facilitator needs to collect newspaper articles for three to six months before the session. These can be photocopied for use during the workshop. At least one-third more articles are needed than the number of participants.

1. Ask participants to form **groups of four to five** women and make a circle with their chairs.

2. Then ask participants to walk around a large table where the newspaper clippings have been laid out. Ask each participant to take one of the articles and go to their small group. At this time, have each person read their article in silence to themselves.

3. Ask participants to discuss:

   a. How do these experiences of women make you feel?
   b. What are the usual responses by the different authorities in society?
      (a school principal, police, employer, parents, clergy)
   c. Are the experiences you have read in the newspapers similar to experiences you know about women in your area?

4. Ask participants to remain in their small group, and hand out 'Myths about Rape'. Ask someone from each group to read the handout aloud and then have the participants to discuss this handout. Are there other myths about rape?

5. Ask everyone to come back to the whole group and discuss other myths about rape. Put these up on newsprint.

6. Give an input on some of the rights and protections that women need:

   - police procedures for rape
   - medical check-ups and why go to the hospital
   - legal and court proceedings
   - social and psychological trauma

---

* Source: *Oxfam Gender Training Manual*, p155

7. Ask participants to discuss, in the same small groups:

    a. What kinds of support they can either give to others or that they need themselves:

        - family
        - community
        - doctors
        - police
        - lawyers

    b. What changes in laws are needed to protect women?

8. Discuss these questions in the whole group and put on newsprint those issues that the participants wish to follow up.

Time   3 hours

Materials   Newspaper articles about rape, handout on 'Myths and realities about rape', newsprint, markers and tape.

Myths and realities about rape

Rape is one of those crimes which causes emotional reactions in people. Some even think that rape is impossible, that a woman really wants it to happen. When a rape victim goes to the police station or to a court, she will find that she has to prove that she did not provoke the rapist in some way.

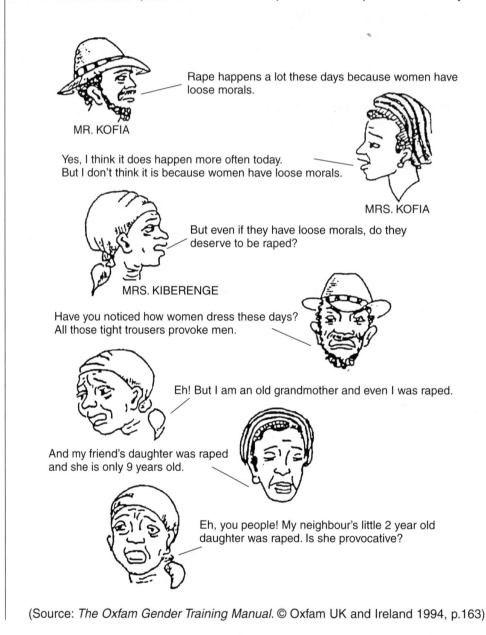

MR. KOFIA — Rape happens a lot these days because women have loose morals.

Yes, I think it does happen more often today. But I don't think it is because women have loose morals. — MRS. KOFIA

MRS. KIBERENGE — But even if they have loose morals, do they deserve to be raped?

Have you noticed how women dress these days? All those tight trousers provoke men.

Eh! But I am an old grandmother and even I was raped.

And my friend's daughter was raped and she is only 9 years old.

Eh, you people! My neighbour's little 2 year old daughter was raped. Is she provocative?

(Source: *The Oxfam Gender Training Manual.* © Oxfam UK and Ireland 1994, p.163)

Exercise 14. **Child abuse**

The aim of this exercise is to encourage breaking the culture of silence about abuse against children.

Procedure

1. Give a copy of the poem 'Atieno' to each participant and read it aloud. Then ask the following questions.

2. Which of the following statements about it do you agree with? [Hold up newsprint with statements on and read them aloud.]

   a. It has always been happening and it just seems more common now because it is reported more often.

   b. Many men in extremely poor areas are deeply frustrated and they have lost their sense of self respect because they cannot get a job and support their families properly. They take out their frustration on the most vulnerable members of society, the children.

   c. Women have become more assertive because of the women's movement, and so some of the sexual violence towards women that was tolerated is now directed towards children because they are more vulnerable and unable to defend themselves.

   d. There is always a moral breakdown in times of rapid cultural change and this is one of the signs of the present change.

3. What can we do in the short term to protect children from all kinds of abuse, but particularly sexual abuse?

4. What can we do to get down to the root causes of the problem and develop deeper self respect in all men, a deeper reverence for all human beings, and a culture which provides special care for those who are most vulnerable?

Summary

There are many different forms of child abuse, ranging from neglect of a child's fundamental human needs to exploitation, cruelty and sexual abuse. Which form of abuse do we see operating in the poem 'Atieno'?. What other forms of child abuse are you aware of in your area?

All over the world there seems to have been a terrible increase of sexual abuse of children in recent years, both in the form of rape of very young girl children and paedophilia, sexual abuse of young boys. Research shows that a very high proportion of this sexual violence towards children is carried out by men.

Time   2 hours

Materials   A copy of the poem for each participant. Newsprint, markers, and tape. Write statements a. to d. on newsprint before the workshop.

101

Atieno

Atieno washes dishes
   Atieno gets up early,
   beds her sacks down in the kitchen,
   Atieno eight years old
   Atieno yo.
Since she is my sister's child
   Atieno needs no pay,
   While she works my wife can sit
   Sewing every sunny day,
   With her earning I support
   Atieno yo.
Atieno's sly and jealous
   Bad example to the kids
   Since she minds them like a school girl
   Wants their dresses, shoes and beads.
   Atieno ten years old
   Atieno yo.
Now my wife has gone to study
   Atieno is less free,
   Don't I feed her, school my own ones
   Pay the party, union fee?
   All for progress? Aren't you grateful
   Atieno yo.
Visitors need much attention
   Especially when I work at night
   That girl stays too long at market
   Who will teach her what is right?
   Atieno rising fourteen,
   Atieno yo.
Atieno's had a baby
   so we know that she is bad
   Fifty-fifty it may live
   To repeat the life she had,
   ending in post-partum bleeding
   Atieno yo.
Atieno's soon replaced
   Meat and sugar, more than all
   She ate in such a narrow life,
   Were lavished at her funeral
   Atieno's gone to glory
   Atieno yo.

        Majorie Mbilinyi, Kenya

SECTION FIVE

Culture

Gender analysis has also thrown light on some of the problems experienced by men in Western cultures because of the rigid gender stereotypes. Many men have been upset at the new roles which women are claiming for themselves, but others have seen this as an opportunity to reconsider some of the expectations which limit their own freedom. For example, even little boys are mocked if they start to cry. It is often suggested that men are weak if they cry or show strong feelings of sorrow or tenderness. But crying is a normal response to intense hurt or sorrow, and men who have shut themselves off from all pain and sorrow do far more damage to the family and community than the slight embarrassment of a few tears.

If men are not supposed to show that they are hurt, women are not supposed to show that they are angry. It is not good for either men or women to repress their feelings, and in the end this blocks interpersonal communication.

Many men feel that they are oppressed by the intensely competitive world in which they have to operate at work. The pressure always to be the breadwinner and earn as much money as possible can be hard on them. Because of this, and also for cultural reasons, many men spend very little time with their children. All the parenting is left to the mother, and the father misses out on the deep family bonds which could develop with his sons and daughters. This is a most serious form of deprivation.

Men sometimes realize that, though they have many acquaintances, very few are true friends with whom they can share their problems and difficulties. Whenever they get together they tend to talk impersonally about superficial interests, like cars and sports, often with a competitive element of one-upmanship, and some men feel that very few deep friendships develop among men.

Women as creators and maintainers of culture

As the evidence grew clearer that the dominant model of development was making women poorer, more powerless, and more overworked, awareness was growing of the central and creative role of women in the life of every community. People began to see that women were the 'backbone of the community'. When men left for the towns to become migrant workers, the women often remained in the rural areas and struggled, against great odds and overwhelming difficulties, to hold the families together.

When men who had been employed were crushed by the devastating experience of unemployment, and turned to despair and alcohol, often abandoning their families, the women continued. Even though women frequently had meagre resources to meet the needs of their families, there was always so much work to be done. Though they suffered in many other ways, women never felt useless, as the unemployed men so often did.

The definition and understanding of culture has expanded from a narrow focus on the fine arts to an understanding of culture as a whole pattern of life, which included all the ways in which a community tries to satisfy its fundamental human needs, and to the values and beliefs on which they base their choices and decisions. People began to recognize women as the primary creators and maintainers of culture.

Women's deeper commitment to the common good of the community

A further factor that began to emerge was that, as men in developing cultures became more caught up in Western values and lifestyles, individualism, personal ambition and greed began to replace the traditional identification with the welfare of the community. Women on the other hand were rooted in the demands of ongoing life. They could not ignore the needs of the children, the old and the sick. To them it was obvious that children and youth had a profound need for a healthy community. Relative economic security in one's own home could not compensate for living in a community riddled with unemployment and crime. Most women therefore have shown again and again that they have a much greater commitment to the common good than do most men. All over the world it is mostly women who do most of the work in community-based organizations and NGOs which are working for social transformation.

In 1992, 45 women were elected into the United States Congress. After one year in office, these women reflected on their experience in a male dominated institution (390 men). They thought that men and women make decisions differently. They agreed that men tend to see 'politics' as a game: who wins and who loses. There is usually much competition between different individuals and between different parties, constant rivalry. Women on the other hand first looked at the problem under discussion (crime, health care, jobs, etc.) and then tried to find common solutions by problem-solving.

(Source: *San Jose Mercury*, Nov. 1993)

Exercise 15. **Cultural conditioning***

The aim of this exercise is to look at the ways in which our own tradition and culture determine beliefs about women and men, to identify the origin of the messages and to find out the effects of these today.

Procedure

1. Ask participants to break up into **small groups** again, and discuss the following questions:

   a. What did you learn about being a girl/boy when you were a child?
   [This should be written on separate lists for girls and boys.]
   b. Where did you learn it?
   c. What are the effects on you today?

2. Ask participants to share their insights in the whole group.

Time   1½ hours

Materials   Newsprint, paper, pens.

Facilitator's notes

1. This activity, when used with both men and women, sets a good climate for discussing how gender roles are constructed, maintained and reinforced. Participants enjoy the songs, stories and proverbs told during the session. It helps participants to see the role of the socialization process in constructing gender roles, and how deep-rooted these roles are. It has been one of the sessions best-received by both men and women.

---

* Source: *Oxfam Gender Training Manual*, p. 176–7

2. Note that modern culture has its own myths. It is important to include these in order to avoid fostering racism or prejudice against traditional societies.

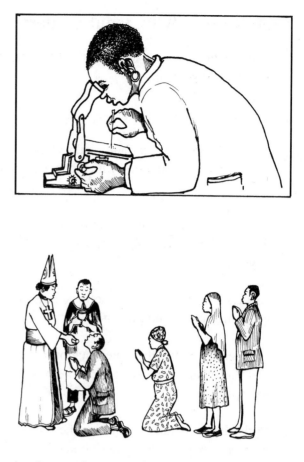

3. Myths address key issues relevant to the particular society, they provide norms of behaviour and reasons for these. They are told as entertainment at an early age, and thus have a great subconscious impact. We do not usually analyse myths for their meaning, and people may be surprised to discover the full implications behind myths.

4. You may find that participants are able to share more deeply if they are in single-sex groups. However, mixed-sex groups may be appropriate where there is tension, hostility or misunderstanding between the men and women in the group.

5. It is important to point out that boys may have as much pressure to conform to their gender role as girls. Note that what is held to be 'proper' behaviour for men and women varies from culture to culture, and over time. The pressure comes from many places, e.g. family friends, school, tradition, the media.

6. There are many effects on us as adults today from the messages we learnt as children. The messages are often internalized and thought of as natural, rather than learned, e.g. it is seen as natural for women to be submissive, and men to be powerful and oppressive. People who do not act according to the stereotype may be criticized or ridiculed.

Exercise 16. **Myths about gender***

The aim of this exercise is to look at the ways in which our tradition and culture express beliefs about men and women.

Procedure

1. Ask each person to list traditional and modern stories, songs, games, sayings, proverbs or rhymes from their own childhood which concern men's and women's roles. Ask them to list as many as possible.

2. Divide participants into 'country or region of origin' **groups of three to six people**, and share the most important songs, games, proverbs and the effect of these on them as girls/women, and boys/men.

3. Ask each group to choose the most striking account, and to prepare a presentation to the whole group in a quick and dramatic way.

4. Each group makes their presentation in turn. Explain that there is no comment or discussion at this stage. As this is going on, write brief descriptions of the stories or songs on one side of the newsprint.

5. In the **large group**, brainstorm the meanings of the presentations and record the ideas on the newsprint opposite the description of each song, story etc.

6. Discuss the implications of the ideas that come up.

7. Summarize the discussion with input on the meaning and use of myths.

Time   1½ to 2 hours

Materials   Newsprint, markers, tape

---

* Source: *Oxfam Gender Training Manual*, p. 175

Exercise 17. Stereotyping[*]

The aims of this exercise are to increase awareness of male/female stereotypes and to initiate discussion about some of the consequences of stereotyping.

Procedure

1. Divide the group into **small single-sex groups** and give them two sheets of newsprint and pens.

2. Explain that 'We are going to look at what we mean by sex stereotypes'. Ask each group to brainstorm all the characteristics of the opposite sex which they believe or which they have heard commonly expressed, e.g. women are talkative, patient. They should write at the top of the first sheet 'women are . . .' and at the top of the second sheet 'men are . . .'

3. Ask them to repeat the exercise for their own sex. They should head the sheet 'men/women are . . .' e.g. men are aggressive, do not show their feelings.

4. The small groups take five minutes to share initial reactions to these lists.

5. Put up sheets and ask each group to present their ideas for five minutes.

6. Ask, 'If these are some of the images of men and women that are commonly believed in our society, what are the consequences for men and women? e.g. if the male image is aggressive and the femal image passive, what can happen?' Each small group lists the consequences they can see.

7. Put up sheets, and allow people time to read them.

8. With the **whole group**, lead a discussion on stereotypes and their consequences. Include points from the summary.

Time   1 to 1½ hours

Materials   Newsprint, pens and tape

Summary

This exercise is a useful introduction to the notion of stereotypes, but be aware that it may cause some tension between women's and men's groups. If it does, follow with a game or activity to bring the group together again. In the final discussion, bring out the following points:

a. We are looking at what is generally believed in society, and some of the results.
b. If these consequences are not as we would like them to be, what can we do to help change them?
c. We are not trying to prescribe – no 'oughts' or 'shoulds'.
d. Why be defensive?
e. There are 'personal' consequences.

An alternative exercise on stereotyping could be the following quiz (see handout).

---

[*] Source: *Oxfam Gender Training Manual*, p. 121 and 122. This activity comes from a course for teachers and careers officers in a training project by Counselling and Career Development Unit, University of Leeds and Careers and Occupational Information Centre.

Quiz on roles and activities for men and women

This is not a test of gender awareness. It is not a test at all. It is just a way of looking at our first thoughts about people's roles and activities. Your answers will be confidential – we will be looking at group rather than individual answers. Please tick whether you think each role or activity is done mostly by men or mostly by women. Do not ponder your answer for a long time – your first thoughts are what we want. If you don't know or can't decide, leave that one and go on to the next one, in order to finish. You have two minutes. There will be a chance to discuss this fully after you have completed the exercise.

Roles	*Men*	*Women*
1. Chef		
2. Housewife		
3. Farmer		
4. Nurse		
5. Tailor		
6. Community leader		
7. Accountant		
8. Mother		
9. Union organizer		
10. Refugee		
11. Politician		
12. Head of the family		
13. Breadwinner		

Activities		
1. Sewing		
2. Carrying heavy things		
3. Operating machinery		
4. Cooking		
5. Selling		
6. Basket weaving		
7. Talking		
8. Planting vegetables		
9. Lighting a fire		
10. Budgeting		
11. Planning		
12. Making decisions		
13. Fetching water		

Source: *Oxfam Gender Training Manual*, p173.

Exercise 18. 'Becoming a man'*

Women can work on their consciousness, but men also have work to do to understand their role in society. Just as whites need to come to terms with their attitudes regarding race, men can be unaware of their dominant roles.

The aims of this exercise are to help men to see the pressures on them to adopt certain attitudes, and to enable men to become aware of some of the origins of their attitudes and feelings towards women.

Procedure

1. Explain the objectives of the activity to the group.

2. Hand out a copy of the list of questions to each participant, and ask them to write completions of the sentences on the chart without consulting each other.

3. Then ask the participants to **form pairs** and to discuss with each other their answers, and their responses and feelings.

4. In the **large group**, draw out similarities in the responses and completions of the sentences, and discuss the following questions:

   a. Do you feel your behaviour is limited by your peers?
      How and when does this happen, and why?
   b. Are there some 'macho' attitudes towards women you would like to reject?
      How can you do this?

Time   45 minutes

Materials   Handout and pens.

---

* Source: *Oxfam Gender Training Manual*, p143. This activity was adapted from one described by D. Thompson: 'As boys become men: learning new male roles' which was published in *Update on Anti-sexist Work with Boys and Young Men*, edited by Janie Whyld, Dave Pickersgill and David Jackson (Whyld Publishing Group, 1990). The trainer described it as providing a good starting point for discussion of the way boys are socialized. Although used in a mixed group, with a similar chart for girls, the trainer felt it would be most useful with a men-only group. We suggest it could be a good introduction to other more challenging activities about male gender roles and attitudes.

Sentence completions

The best things about being a man is . . .

A man would never let a woman see . . .

Men would reject another man if . . .

A man would be praised by his parents if he. . .

Boys can't . . .

The parents of a boy let him . . .

Teachers expect boys to treat girls like . . .

Men get embarrassed when . . .

Parents expect boys to . . .

Men/boys are allowed to . . .

A boy would get teased if . . .

Women really want men to . . .

Men don't like . . .

Source: Thompson D. 'As Boys Become Men: Learning New Male Roles.' *Oxfam Gender Training Manual*, p.145

Exercise 19. **The world upside down**

The aim of the exercise is to help both men and women to imagine a world with different role expectations.

Procedure

1. Ask participants to get comfortable. Tell them you are going to read a story about an imaginary world, and that they may like to close their eyes and focus on the story. You might wish to have two readers alternating sections of the story.

2. After the story ask people to number off into **five groups** to talk about the feelings they had as they listened.

   a. Were they angry, amused or confused? Did any part of the story make them laugh?

   b. Ask them how the imaginary world compares to the world in which we live. Is it a complete role reversal? If you put the word 'man' in each place that 'woman' was mentioned, would you have an accurate description of the world in which we live? Why or why not?

   c. Would people like to live in the world described in the story? What would be wrong with this world? What would be right with it? Would we, as women, want to have the type of power that men currently have? If we did, would we use it in similar ways?

3. In the **whole group** share insights from each question. End the discussion by talking about what an ideal world would be like.

Time   1½ hours

Materials   Copies of the 'A woman's world' handout.

A woman's world

Have you ever been bothered by the way the word 'man' is used to include all people? Does it bother you, for instance, that when people refer to 'the rights of all men', they really mean the rights of men and women, or the rights of all people?

Imagine a world that is similar to our own, but slightly different. In this imaginary world, 'women' is the term that refers to all people. That is, when we use the word 'women', we mean everyone.

Close your eyes and imagine that when you read the daily newspaper or listen to the radio, what you see or hear about are women politicians, women trade union leaders, women directors of large companies. Imagine a world in which most books, plays, films, poems and songs have women as their heroes. Imagine that women are the people you learn about when you study the great scientists, historians, journalists, revolutionaries. Imagine that it is we women who will be making major decisions about the future in this different world.

Recall that everything you have ever read in your life uses only female pronouns – 'she', 'her' – meaning both boys and girls, both women and men. Recall that you have no men representing you in government. All decisions are made by women.

Men, whose natural roles are as husband and father, find fulfilment in nurturing children and making the home a refuge for the family. This is only natural to balance the role of the woman, who devotes her entire body to the human race during pregnancy, and who devotes her emotional and intellectual powers to ensuring the progress and survival of the planet throughout her life.

Imagine further now, the biological explanations for woman as the leader and power-centre. A woman's body, after all, represents perfection in design. Even femal genitals, for instance, are compact and internal, protected by our bodies. Male genitals are exposed, so that he must be protected from outside attack to assure the perpetuation of the race. His vulnerability clearly requires sheltering. Thus, by nature, males are more passive and timid, and have a desire to be protectively engulfed by the compact, powerful bodies of women.

In the world that we are imagining, girls are raised as free and self-confident beings. They play, run, climb trees, take risks with the encouragement of all adults around them. The family puts a priority on the physical and intellectual development of girls since they are the ones who will ultimately be responsible for the future of our society.

Boys, on the other hand, are raised to be timid and obedient. They are encouraged to play quiet games in the home which will prepare them for their life as caretakers of the family. From an early age, they are expected to help their fathers. They learn to look up to women, to try to please and care for them. They are taught to become the mirror in which the strength of women can be reflected.

Now remember back to giving birth to your first child. During your pregnancy, your husband waited with anxiety, wondering what the sex of the child would be. Your first child was a boy. Your husband sat by your side holding this newborn, already instinctively caring for and protecting it. There were tears in your husband's eyes and you knew that at the same time as he was filled with joy at your son's birth, he was also looking forward to having another, hoping for the birth of the girl that would carry on the family name.*

----

* *On our feet: Taking steps to challenge women's oppression*, by Liz Mackenzie, CACE, University of the Western Cape, 1993.

Exercise 20. An alternative to male domination

For thousands of years men have dominated women and some people assume that Patriarchy (the domination of society by 'the fathers', i.e. older men) has always existed. However, recent findings in archaeology have shown that there was a long period when women and men lived and worked in peace and partnership. The text on the handout from *The Chalice and the Blade* by Riane Eisler has been shortened and slightly simplified. It is based on the work of the Californian archaeologist Marija Gimbutas.

Procedure

1. Gives copies of the handout to all the participants.

2. Either read it aloud in the whole group or ask participants to choose a partner and read alternate paragraphs to one another.

3. Suggest that they put a tick in the margin for any thought they agree with, a cross for anything that they do not agree with, and a question mark for anything that they do not understand.

4. Give people an opportunity to ask questions of clarification.

5. Ask the participants to form **groups of four or five** to discuss the following questions:

    a. In what ways do we recognize the influence of 'the blade' in our own societies?
    b. In what ways do we experience the influence of 'the chalice'?

6. In the **whole group**, ask participants to share their insights.

7. Ask the participants to divide into **two groups**. Ask one group to prepare a short mime depicting a society in which the blade is honoured, and the other to prepare a similar mime showing a society honouring the values represented by the chalice. These should be very spontaneous, taking about 10 minutes to prepare and one minute to present.

8. Have each group present their mime.

9. Ask participants to form **groups of three** to discuss:

    a. What did we see happening in each of the mimes and why was it happening?
    b. Do you think violence, greed and cruelty are inevitable?
    c. How do the prevailing values in the community in which we live bring out either the best or the worst in us?
    d. What can we do to bring out the best in those around us?
    e. What changes would we see in our society if the symbol of the chalice grew more powerful again than that of the blade?

10. Share insights in the whole group from each question.

Time   1½ to 2 hours

Materials   Copies of 'The Chalice and the Blade' handout.

The Chalice and the Blade
Human possibilities: two alternatives

The Chalice and the Blade tells a new story of our cultural origins. It shows that war and the 'war of the sexes' are neither the will of God, nor built into our minds and bodies. It provides proof that a better future is possible.

We are all familiar with legends about an earlier, more harmonious and peaceful age. The Bible tells of a garden where woman and man lived in harmony with each other and with nature. . . . The Chinese Tao Te Ching describes a time when the yin, the feminine principle, was not yet ruled by the male principle, yang: a time when the wisdom of the mother was still honoured and followed above all. The ancient Greek poet, Hesiod, wrote of a 'golden race' who tilled the soil in 'peaceful ease' before a 'lesser race' brought in their god of war.

The cultural evolution of societies that worshipped the life-generating and nurturing powers of the universe – still symbolized in our time by the ancient chalice or grail – was interrupted by invaders who worshipped the 'lethal power of the blade': the power to take rather than give life, the ultimate power to establish and enforce domination.

Just as in Columbus's time, when the discovery that the Earth is not flat made it possible to find an amazing new world that had been there all the time, so the new archeological discoveries have opened up the amazing world of our hidden past. They reveal a long period of peace and prosperity when our social, technological and cultural evolution moved upward: many thousands of years in which all the basic technologies on which civilization is built were developed in societies which were not male dominant, violent and hierarchic.

The idea of the universe as an all-giving Mother has survived into our time. . . . It makes eminent sense that the earliest depiction of divine power should have been female rather than male. When our ancestors began to ask the eternal questions [Where do we come from before we are born? Where do we go after we die?] they must have noted that life emerges from the body of a woman. It would have been natural for them to imagine the universe as an all-giving Mother from whose womb all life emerges and to which, like the cycles of vegetation, it returns after death to be reborn again. It also makes sense that societies with this image of the powers that govern the universe would have a very different social structure from societies that worship a divine father that wields a thunderbolt or a sword. It further seems logical that women would not be seen as subservient in societies that conceptualized the powers governing the universe in female form – and that feminine qualities such as caring, compassion and non-violence would be highly valued in such societies. What does not make sense is to conclude that societies in which men did not dominate women were societies in which women dominated men. There can be societies in which difference is not necessarily equated with superiority or inferiority.

Cultural transformation theory proposes that underlying all the surface differences between cultures there are two basic models of society. The first – the **dominator model** – is popularly called either patriarchy or matriarchy, the ranking of one half of humanity over the other. The second, in which social relations are primarily based on linking rather than ranking, may best be described as the **partnership model**. All the modern social movements for social justice, including the recent feminist, peace and ecology movements, are part of an underlying thrust for transformation from a dominator to a partnership system.

(Adapted from *The Chalice and the Blade*, pages xiii–xxiii)

Cry of Ramah

A voice is heard in Ramah,
Hiroshima, Salvador,
Women refusing comfort
For their children are no more;
No garland of lovely flowers
Can dispel the ancient grief
Or silence the anguished voices
That abhor the war machine.

1. If the Herod in us could be faced and then tamed
        with compassion
    all the dark clouds we've cast, we'd bind
        in a murmur of peace.

2. If our leaders could look in the eyes
        of children we carry
    They could forget the bombs they drop
        and their budgets for war.

3. If nations so distant and separate
        could break bread together
    coming to know that they are family
        with warm hearts to share.

4. If the beauty of God's creation could draw
        us to wonder
    humbly we'd drop our fears and pride
        and give birth to new life.

Source: *Cry of Ramah*, Colleen Fulmer, p.9

The 'Cry of Ramah' recalls Rachel, the mother of the twelve tribes of Israel, mourning the death by violence of children and of all the innocent. Ramah was the place of a concentration camp to which all the survivors of the destruction of Jerusalem were taken, and it is linked with other scenes of ruthless destruction in this century, Hiroshima where the first atom bomb was dropped and Salvador in Central America. Herod, the cruel king who massacred all the boys under two years old in his determination to get rid of the child Jesus, symbolizes all cruel tyrants. The grief of women mourning for their innocent children continues all through the centuries.

SECTION SIX

The influence of religion

Exercise 21. Is God male?

The Bible uses many feminine images to describe God, such as Sophia in the Books of Wisdom. Isaiah compares the love of God to the love of a mother for her baby, and speaks of the 'breasts of God's consolation'. Jesus compares his own desire to gather together the children of Israel as 'a mother hen gathers her chicks under her protective wing'. Genesis 2 makes it very clear that both men and women are made in the image and likeness of God. Yet for centuries the Church has only used masculine images and pronouns to speak of God. Feminist theology has shown that this has given a one-sided and distorted picture of God and has undermined the dignity of women.

God is beyond gender, neither male nor female, yet God is no less than a 'person', and 'personhood' is one of the greatest reflections of the mystery of God. It is therefore quite appropriate to use both male and female pronouns and images of God, knowing always that no words can ever express fully the mystery of God. All our insights are but small glimpses of the great reality of the Love behind and within the universe, but every true glimpse is precious, so we should not ignore the light that feminine images can bring to us. One of the most inspiring works of feminist theology is *She Who Is*. We include an extract here for reflection and discussion.

1. Ask the participants to read through the 'She Who Is' handout and underline those phrases and sentences with which they strongly agree, write a cross beside sections with which they disagree and put a question mark beside those they do not understand. Participants could work either alone or with a partner.

2. Then ask them to write down three ways in which their religion has contributed to their own sense of well-being as a woman and three ways in which they have felt their self-confidence undermined by religion.

3. Share these in small groups if the group is large, or in the whole group if the group is not more than about twelve.

Time   1 to 2 hours

Materials   'She Who Is' handout.

She Who Is

By Christian feminist theology I mean a reflection on God, and on all things in the light of God, that stands consciously in the company of all the world's women, prizing their genuine humanity, while uncovering and criticizing the persistent violation of this humanity in sexism. Sexism is itself a paradigm of unjust human relationships, present everywhere. Feminist theology claims the full Christian heritage for women in their own right precisely because they are human. Women are equally created in the image and likeness of God, equally redeemed by Christ, equally sanctified by the Holy Spirit. Women are equally involved in the ongoing tragedy of sin, and the mystery of grace; equally called to mission in this world, equally destined for life with God in glory.

Feminist theology recognizes the glaring contradiction between this theology and the actual, historical condition of women. . . . Sexism is sinful; it is contrary to God's intention and a breaking of the basic commandment, 'Thou shalt love thy neighbour as thyself'. It offends God by defacing this beloved creature created in God's own image. Faced with this sinfulness both church and society are called upon to repent, to turn around, to sin no more, to be converted. Feminist theology calls for the reform of patriarchal civil and church structures . . . to release all human beings for more just designs of living, with each other and with the earth. It is not a theology for women alone. It calls to strengths in women and men alike who care for justice and truth, seeking a transformation of the whole community.

The feminist perspective finds church tradition very mixed in what it has meant for female well-being. It has contributed to the exclusion and subordination of women, but it has also sustained generations of our foremothers in the faith. Along with the need for criticism of church theory and practice, I feel we women should give theology a hearing, listening for wisdom that may still prove useful . . . reflecting a ray of divine light.

It was especially for me the months of teaching in South Africa under the state of emergency in 1986, giving lectures that turned into sessions of mutual grappling with the meaning of faith in situations of massive suffering due to injustice, poverty and violence, that shaped my feminist theology into liberation contours with a global dimension.

For me the goal of feminist religious discourse pivots around the flourishing of poor women of colour in violent situations. Securing the well-being of these, socially the least of women, would lead to a new configuration of theory and praxis and the genuine transformation of all societies, including the churches, to open up more humane ways of living for all people with each other and the earth. The rising of the women is the rising of the race – precisely because women, with their network of relationships, are at the lowest ebb, marginalized, and yet sustaining every society. The incoming tide lifts all the boats in the harbour. Only when the poorest, black, raped and brutalized women in a South African township – the epitome of victims of racism, sexism and classism, and, at the same time, startling examples of resilience, courage, love and dignity – when such women, with their dependent children and their sisters around the world, may live peacefully in the enjoyment of their human dignity, only then will feminist theology arrive at its goal.

Adapted from *She Who Is*, by Elizabeth Johnson, pages 3–16

Exercise 22. 'If God is male, then the male is seen as God.'

The aim of this exercise is to stimulate thinking about how we name God, and how language shapes consciousness.

Procedure

1. Ask participants to form **groups of five people**. Give each person a sheet of plain paper and ask them to respond to the following statement. They will have a few minutes in silence to write their response.

   If God is male, then the male is seen as God

   a. Do you agree or disagree with the statement?
   b. Does it matter how we name God? If yes why? If not, why not?
   c. Does language shape our consciousness, our attitudes? Give examples of how this happens and how change in language changes consciousness.

2. Ask participants to first discuss these questions in their small group and then in the whole group.

3. An interest biblical text to close with, or to share, is Exodus 3: 7–15.

Time   1 to 1½ hours

Materials   Newsprint, markers, tape.

The naming of God has been a problem for humans, even before the days of the great Flood. In the Bible, we have the story of Moses directly asking God about [his] name.

> 'Then Moses said to God, "I am to go, then, to the sons of Israel and say to them, 'The God of your fathers has sent me to you'. But if they ask me what [his] name is, what am I to tell them?"' And God said to Moses 'I Am who I Am.' 'This' he added 'is what you must say to the sons of Israel: "I Am has sent me to you"' Exodus 3: 13–14.

The understanding of God has presented difficulties for centuries. Some consider the root of the name 'yahweh' to come from the verb 'to be'. This would imply that it is impossible to give an adequate definition of God. Others believe that humans can never find a worthy or sacred enough name for God. The absolute nature of God is understood because no human name can describe God. The conclusion of these arguments is that God then cannot be male or female – he or she – but has all the good qualities of both women and men and is infinitely beyond both.

119

Exercise 23. What does your God look like?

The aim of this exercise is to give time for participants to reflect on their own meaning of God and Great Spirit in their lives.

Procedure

1. In preparation, find two women who are good readers to prepare the play reading. They should have enough time to read the parts to themselves and then have a practice session or two before actually reading it to the group.

2. Prepare the participants for listening to the play reading by ensuring that they are comfortable to sit for a while.

3. After the play reading, give out copies of this dialogue and ask the group to reread it in pairs with a person from a somewhat different experience of faith from their own. Ask them to put a tick beside any points they agree with, a cross beside any they disagree with, and a question mark beside anything they do not understand. Ask participants to discuss:

    a. What do you think about Shug's understanding of God?
    b. Why has Celie lost her faith in God and in the Church?
    c. Has that happened to any of the people you know?
    d. In what way do 'good practising Christians' sometimes contribute to this loss of faith?
    e. Jesus says in the Gospel, 'Not everyone who says Lord, Lord, will enter the Kingdom of God, but those who do the will of my Father in Heaven.'
       What do you think it really means to 'do the will of our Father/Mother in Heaven'?
    f. How should we relate to sincere believers of other Faiths? e.g. Muslims and Jews?
    g. How can we be faithful to our own belief, but at the same time appreciative of the faith and spiritual journey of other people?

4. When participants have finished this task, ask them to share their insights in the whole group.

Time   2+ hours

Material   Copies of the play reading for all participants and copies of the questions for discussion on newsprint.

'Tell me what your God looks like'

Black American women have been producing some of the finest literature written during the last twenty years. Through novels they have been sharing their deep, though often unconventional, faith in God. One of the most striking of these is *The Color Purple* by Alice Walker. The first part of the book is written in the form of letters to God from Celie, a poor but resilient black woman who has suffered every imaginable indignity and heartbreak.

At a particular point she becomes fed up with God, and starts to address her letters instead to her sister Nettie who went off to West Africa as a missionary. In this section Celie describes a conversation she had with her exuberant friend Shug about God. The original was written in the dialect of Black American folk but since many people in Africa have difficulty following this we have adapted it slightly into more familiar English, trying to keep as much of the spirit of the original as possible.

It is most alive when read as a dialogue with one person taking the part of Celie and one that of Shug [short for sugar]. A third person can read the words of the narrator, written here in brackets, who often utters Celie's unspoken thoughts.

From *The Color Purple* by Alice Walker

Celie (writing): Dear Nettie, I don't write to God no more. I write to you.
Shug: What happened to God?
Celie: Who's that? (Shug looked at me, serious) Big devil that you are! You're not worried about no God, surely.
Shug: Wait a minute. Hold on just a minute here. Just because I don't harass it like some people we know, don't mean I ain't got religion.
Celie: What did God do for me?
Shug: Celie! (she said, like she was shocked.) He gave you life, good health and a good woman that loves you to death.
Celie: Yeah . . . and he gave me a lynched daddy, a crazy mama, a low down dog of a step-pa, and a sister I probably won't ever see again. Anyhow the God I've been praying and writing to is a man. And acts just like all the other men I know. Trifling, forgetful, lowdown.
Shug: Ms Celie! You better hush. God might hear you.
Celie: Let 'im hear me. If he ever listened to poor colored women the world would be a different place, I can tell you.
Narrator: (Shug talk and talk, trying to budge me away from blasphemy. But I blaspheme much as I want to.)
Celie: All my life I never care what people thought about nothing I did. But deep in my heart I care 'bout God. What he's goin' to think. And come to find out he don't think. Just sits up there glorying in being deaf, I reckon. But it ain't easy, trying to do without God. Even if you know he ain't there, trying to do without him is a strain.

Shug: I'm a sinner. 'Cause I was born. I don't deny it. But once you find out what's out there waiting for us, what else can you be.

Celie: Sinners have more good times.

Shug: You know why?

Celie: 'Cause you ain't all the time worrying 'bout God.

Shug: No, that ain't it. We worry 'bout God a lot. But once we feel loved by God we do the best we can to please him with what we like.

Celie: You telling me God loves you, and you ain't never done nothing for him? I mean, you not go to Church, not sing in the choir, not feed the preacher and anythings like that?

Shug: But if God loves me Celie I don't have to do all that. Unless I want to. There's lots of other things I can do that I 'spect God likes.

Celie: Like what?

Shug: Oh . . . I can lay back and jus' admire stuff. Be happy. Have a good time.

Celie: Well, this sounds like blasphemy sure enough.

Shug: Celie, tell the truth. Have you ever found God in church? I never did. I just found a bunch of folks hoping for him to show. Any God I ever felt in church I brought in with me. And I think all the other folks did too. They come to church to share God, not to find him.

Celie: Some folks didn't have him to share. They're the ones who didn't speak to me when I was there struggling with my big belly and Mr--------'s children.

Shug: Right. . . . Tell me what your God looks like, Celie.

Celie: Ah no. I'm too 'shamed.

Narrator: (Nobody ever asked me this before, so I'm sort of took by surprise. Besides when I think about it, it don't seem quite right. But it's all I got. I decided to stick up for him, just to see what Shug say.)

Celie: Okay. He's big and old, and tall and greybearded and white. He wears white robes and he goes barefooted.

Shug: Blue eyes?

Celie: Sort of bluish gray. Cool. Big though. White lashes.

(Shug laughed)

Celie: Why d'you laugh? I don't think it's so funny. What do you expect him to look like ? Mr--------?

Shug: That wouldn't be no improvement. (Pause) This old white man is the same God I used to see when I prayed. If you wait to find God in church that's who is bound to show up, 'Cause that's where he lives.

Celie: How come?

Shug: 'Cause that's the one that's in the white folks' white bible.

Celie: Shug! God wrote the bible. White folks had nothing to do with it.

Shug: How come he looks just like them then? Only bigger? And a heap more hair? How come the bible's just like everything else they make, all about white folk doing one thing after another, and all the colored folks are doing is getting cursed?

Celie: I never thought 'bout that. Nettie says somewhere in the bible it says Jesus hair was like lamb's wool.

Shug: Well, if he came to any of these churches we talking 'bout, he'd have to have it straightened before anyone'd pay him any attention. The last thing blacks want to think about their God is that his hair's kinky.

Celie: That's the truth.

Shug: There ain't no way to read the bible and not think God's white. When I found out I thought that God was white, and a man, I lost interest. You're mad 'cause he don't seem to listen to your prayers. Humph . . . Do the mayor listen to anything coloreds say?

Celie: I know white people never listen to colored, period. If they do they only listen long enough to be able to tell you what to do.

Shug: Here's the thing. The thing I believe. God is inside you, and inside everybody else. You come into the world with God but only them that search for It inside find It. And sometimes It just manifest itself even if you're not looking, or don't know what you're looking for. Trouble does it for most folks, I think. Sorrow, lord. Feeling like shit.

Celie: It?

Shug: Yeah. It. God ain't a he or a she, but a 'It'.

Celie: But what do It look like?

Shug: It don't look like nothing. It ain't a picture show. It ain't anything you can look at apart from anything else, including yourself. I believe God is everything. Everything that is or ever was or ever will be. And when you can feel that, and be happy to feel that, you've found It.

Narrator: (Shug's a beautiful something, let me tell you. She frowned a little, looked out across the yard, leaned back in her chair. She looks like a big rose.)

Shug: My first step from the old white man was trees. Then air. Then birds. Then other people. But one day when I was sitting quiet and feeling like a motherless child, which I was, it came to me: that feeling of being part of everything, not separate at all. I knew that if I cut a tree, my arm would bleed. And I laughed, and I cried, and I ran all over the house. I knew just what it was. In fact when it happens, you can't miss it. It's sort of like . . .

Narrator: (she grinned, rubbing high up on my thigh)

Celie: Shug!

Shug: Oh, God loves all them feelings. That's some of the best stuff God did. And when you know God loves 'em, you enjoys 'em a lot more. You can just relax, go with everything that's going, and praise God by liking what you like.

Celie: God don't think it dirty?

Shug: No. God made it. Listen, God loves everything you love – and a mess of stuff you don't. But more than anything else God loves admiration.

Celie: Are you saying God's vain?

Shug: No, not vain. Just wanting to share a good thing. I think it pisses God off if you walk by the color purple in a field and don't notice it.

Celie: What's It do when It's pissed off?

Shug: Oh, It makes something else. People think pleasing God is all God cares about. But any fool living in the world can see It's always trying to please us back.

Celie: Yeah?

Shug: Yeah. It's always making little surprises and springing them on us when we least expect.

Celie: You mean It want to be loved, just like the bible say?

Shug: Yes, Celie. Everything wants to be loved. We sing and dance, make faces and give flower bouquets, trying to be loved. You ever notice that trees do everything we do, trying to get attention, except walk?

Narrator: Well, we talk and talk about God, but I'm still adrift. Trying to chase that old white man out of my head. I've been so busy thinking about him, I never truly notice nothing God made. Not a blade of corn. . . . How It do that? Not the color purple . . . where it comes from. Not the little wildflowers. Nothing.

(Adapted from *The Color Purple*, pages 164–8)

CHAPTER 3
Racism

Introduction

Section One: Privilege and power

Section Two: Perceptions

Section Three: Discrimination

Section Four: Racism

Section Five: Moving forward

Introduction

Racism in the modern world is the result of the notion or set of values claiming that white people are superior to black people. That idea or ideology exists all over the world, in one way or another.

Since European colonialism five hundred years ago, black people and their cultures have been subjected to the cultures of white people throughout Africa and through slavery in the Americas. That means not only economic systems, not only political systems, but also the way people think.

We are all affected by racism in some way, because it has become part of our cultures. We have all been taught racism: that means black, brown, red, yellow and white people. Everything we have seen and experienced in our lives, whatever the local culture that formed us, was influenced by the ideas of racism.

Racism is much more profound than individual prejudice or acts of discrimination, although it creates and feeds on both of these. Racism means that people's relationships, even with themselves, are influenced by colour. So are their access to resources, opportunities to name their own reality, make decisions about their lives and set the standards that affect the behaviour of those in institutions or groups.

What is race? 'Race' is a false concept, because everyone's skin colour is on a continuum. Racism is usually around colour, not ethnicity.

What is racism? Racism is revealed in attitudes, behaviour and systems in which one race maintains supremacy over another race. Human beings create and maintain the systems which, in turn, reinforce racism.

This understanding of racism has four essential and interconnected parts:*

Standards	The standards for appropriate behaviour reflect and privilege the norms and values of the dominant culture.
Decision-making	The capacity to make and enforce decisions is disproportionately or unfairly distributed along racial lines.
Resources	There is unequal access to such resources as money, education and information.
Naming reality	'Reality' is defined by naming 'the problem' through the perspective of the dominant culture. Who gets to name 'the problem' determines the framework for solutions.

These four elements of racism make up a definition of power. Those who have power:

- Set the standards by which they and others are judged; that is, they set the standards for appropriate behaviour;
- Have the capacity to make and enforce decisions that affect the lives of other people;
- Have access to resources and control the distribution of resources;
- Define the parameters of a discussion, determine the ideological framework within which

debate takes place, that is, they define the problem and therefore determine the solutions that will be considered.

* These definitions are adapted from a presentation given by Robert Terry in a conference, 'New White Consciousness: Prerequisite for Change in America', Sponsored by the Detroit Industrial Mission and New Detroit, Inc. May 1971. For more detailed discussion see Robert W. Terry, *For Whites Only*, Grand Rapids, MI, USA: Wm. B. Eerdmans, 1970

This definition of racism will be used through this chapter. As a facilitator, one's own understanding influences how one works with groups. Several key principles are important to bear in mind:

- The ideology of white superiority is a historic lie, which the world is learning to reject and deny. Skin colour is no criterion of value. (Legum)
- No one who is alive today is personally responsible for that lie. We were all, no matter what race, born into a system of false thinking, whether we like it or not. (Legum)
- Equality of all people is our natural state. But we will have to work hard to undermine the system of racism, in our personal lives, organizations, institutions and cultures. (Legum)
- We can begin to do that in our groups, by the way we run them, by naming and taming the assumptions of racism, by challenging racist thinking, policies and practices. (Legum)
- Power is central to our understanding of racism. This means we need to examine not only how individuals are affected, but also how organizations and institutions operate in terms of the use of power. (Richardson)
- No one and no people is utterly powerless. We all have personal and spiritual power. We all have the capacity to join with others to enhance our collective power. (Richardson)

Note This chapter comes from work done in South Africa, the United Kingdom and the United States. The authors developed and used some of the exercises in this chapter while working with Community Change, an anti-racist organization in the USA. Margaret Legum's contribution is heavily indebted to the work of Organisation and Social Development Consultants (OSDC) of Sheffield, England, with whom she has had a long association. OSDC produces a range of training manuals for use in a variety of professional arenas. Nancy Richardson's contribution comes from the Women's Theological Centre, Boston, Massachusetts, USA. The Women's Theological Centre focused much of their work on anti-racist and internalized racism training and, at the same time, worked at developing an anti-racist, multi-cultural organization in practice.

SECTION ONE

Privilege and power

Exercise 1. Privilege

This exercise is a warm-up to help participants get to know each other and begin exploring some of their own experiences in society related to racism.

Procedure

1. Ask people to form **groups of three**, with people they do not know well.

2. Participants are then asked to write their responses to the following question: When did you first realize that some people were more privileged than others? List five of those privileges.

3. After each person has had time to individually write their responses, the groups of three are asked to share what they wish to share in their small group.

4. When the groups have had about 15–20 minutes, the facilitator asks the whole group how many of you gave examples of others who had more privileges than you had. Usually the whole group has given those examples. Then ask: When did you first realize that you had some privileges others did not have? Ask the small groups to share their response to this second question.

5. Ask them all to come back to **the whole group** to discuss their insights. This is not a report-back time, but mainly a chance for people to share insights.

6. Some of the issues that arise can help the group to start developing their own definition of privilege, including that of racism. Key words can be put on newsprint for future reference.

Time   45 minutes

Materials   Paper and pens.

Exercise 2. Sharing power*

This exercise will highlight different sources of power and look at the types of power participants have, and how the group would like to establish its own standards and ways of sharing power within the group.

Procedure

1. Write the word POWER on the top of a piece of newsprint.

2. Ask participants to turn to their neighbour and brainstorm by writing a list of responses to the following question: What gives people power?

3. After a few minutes, **in the whole group**, ask participants to give one response at a time. Put their responses on newsprint. (Some of the responses may include money, title, job, education, intelligence, skill with words, language, religion, beauty, physical strength, race, gender, age, class, accent, rural/urban, facilitator in meetings.)

4. Ask participants still in the large group to brainstorm: Which of these different kinds of power exist in this group?

5. Ask participants to turn back to their neighbour and discuss: What are some guidelines that would help participants share comfortably in this group, despite differences in people's levels of power?

Several questions may help facilitate this process:

    a. Who gets listened to best?
       Who takes up most time talking?
       Who does not get heard?
       If someone says nothing, do people notice?

    b. Are some of the kinds of power 'given' to others in the group appropriate? (For example, someone could assume that since a person is white, that person also has money or a high income so those assumptions must be checked out.)

6. Newsprint those norms that the group have come up with to share more equally in this group.

Note In establishing norms of behaviour in the group, highlight points that the dominant cultural groups need to be aware of, which you will find in the summary input.

Time   1½ to 2 hours

Materials None.

---

* Source: Legum

129

Summary *

In most societies, there is a dominant set of cultural values. For historical reasons, many countries have taken on the 'Western' cultural values. Some helpful definitions:

Oppression is a system of domination of one group over another.

The privileged group has societal power to:

- act and define reality
- determine what is real, normal and correct
- institutionalize and systematize discrimination, harassment and even genocide

The excluded group

- to some degree internalizes their own oppressed condition; and thus
- collaborates with their oppressor in some ways.

Race is a sociological, psychological or mental perception. It is not a biological phenomenon. There is no clear distinction between one racial group and another, rather there is a continuum of skin colour and other physical features. Race is an artificial concept. The only race is the human race.

Attitudes include assumptions, stereotypes, prejudices and value systems.

The following words are often used interchangeably with racism. Because they are experienced on the personal and interpersonal level, however, they create confusion.

We have power to take action. Racist attitudes become increasingly dangerous as they progress through the following stages of intensity. They are all aspects of racism but each has a specific meaning.

PERSONAL ATTITUDES	Prejudice	Prejudgement on insufficient information; can be positive or negative.
	Stereotyping	Attributing characteristics to a group and everyone who belongs to that group, and assuming that those characteristics are rooted in significant differences.
	Bigotry	More intense form of prejudice, carrying the negative side of prejudgement. Often describes people who 'cannot change their attitude'.
BEHAVIOUR	Discrimination	The act or practice of giving different treatment to individuals or groups on the basis of assumptions, stereotypes or prejudices.
	Scapegoating	The act or practice of assigning blame or failure to persons or groups rather than placing the blame or failure where it actually belongs.

Racism is a reality because people believe and act as if there are many different races and that some are intrinsically superior to others.

---

* Source: Richardson

Racism is a system by which one race maintains supremacy over another race through a set of attitudes, behaviours, social structures and ideologies. The dominant racial group has power, which is used as follows:

STRUCTURES AND ORGANIZATIONS	Decision-making	The unfairly distributed capacity to make and enforce decisions.
	Resources	Unequal access to such resources as money, education, information.
CULTURE VALUES	Standards	Standards for appropriate behaviour reflect and give privilege to the norms and values of the dominant race/culture.
IDEOLOGY	Naming reality	Involves defining 'reality' by naming 'the problem', 'the solution', 'the situation' incorrectly or too narrowly. Having a set of beliefs, with a bias.

INTERNALIZED RACISM. The perception by the oppressed group that the racists' ideology is true and/or inevitable. It happens within a racist system when a society as a whole rewards the attitudes and behaviours of the dominant group. This affects everyone.

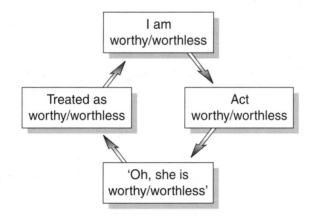

CROSS-RACIAL HOSTILITY A situation that occurs in a racist system when one oppressed race supports the oppression of another oppressed race by maintaining or participating in the set of attitudes, behaviours, social structures, values and ideologies that supports the dominating race's supremacy.

Perceptions

Exercise 3. 'Where is the door?'

Our attitudes describe the spectacles through which we view the world. They help us make sense of the world. Many are based on experience before we could even speak, certainly before we could pass judgement on them; others are more recent. They are based on our own experience. Everyone's attitudes are different, because our experiences are different. Organizations have attitudes as well.

Some of our attitudes are constructive and positive, because they open up choices. Some are less useful, as they are based on false information and fears and so limit our experience. We need to examine our attitudes and where they came from. By comparing them with others' attitudes, we can begin to understand their experience as well as our own.

'Your standpoint is your viewpoint'

This short play is useful to set norms of communication in a workshop, especially if the participants come from very mixed backgrounds. Its purpose is to help those people who consider their way of seeing things as 'the way things are'. It helps them to understand that their view comes from where they themselves 'sit' in society. Our views and priorities are profoundly affected by our personal experiences (e.g. our class background).

The play takes less than one minute to prepare and requires 3 people.

Procedure

1. Ask two people to sit facing each other with one person facing the door (if there is more than one door, choose an object in the room of which there is only one, for example the blackboard or the window or the table). This is important. Ask the second person to sit with his/her back to the door.

2. The third person comes to the two of them, from one side, and asks, 'Where is the door?' They both respond immediately. The one facing the door says 'in front'. The one with his/her back to the door says, 'behind'. The third person looks perplexed and asks again 'where? and the responses are: 'in front', 'behind' – each out-shouting the other. The play then ends.

3. Possible questions for the **whole group** to discuss:

    a. What did you see happening in the play?
    b. Who was 'right'?
    c. Was anyone right for the third person?

4. **In pairs**, discuss:

    d. In what ways have we all been taught to see things from one perspective?

132

e. What makes up our individual 'vision'?

f. What does this mean in terms of how we interact with people from other races?

g. Is there a dominant culture (or group) in our society which shapes our attitudes, expectations of others and our behaviour? If so, name some expectations that the dominant culture has of other cultures.

5. In the whole group, discuss the responses to these questions.

Time   20–30 minutes

Materials   Newsprint, markers.

Exercise 4. **The island***

This exercise is to enable groups to clarify how we inevitably stereotype, have prejudices and make assumption by race, gender, sexual preference and disabilities. You may need to change the categories of people used in the exercise to suit your own situation. It can help participants to look at the relationship between values and attitudes.

Procedure

1. Explain that the participants will receive a list of 20 people from whom they will select 12 who will live in isolation on a recently discovered island for the next fifty years and will have to create a new society. All 20 people on the list have volunteered to go forward.

2. Ask participants to form **groups of five**.

3. After they are in their groups, give them the handout and ask them to select in silence 12 people from the list to go to the island.

4. Ask them to write notes on their paper to explain the criteria for selecting or rejecting people to go to the island. (8–10 minutes)

5. After most people have completed this work, ask the groups of five to come to a consensus of who should go and who should stay behind. They are asked to write their criteria for selection. (20–30 minutes)

6. When the groups have completed their selection, ask them to come back to the whole group, and put up the list of people on the wall with some newsprint.

---

* Source: Legum

7. Ask each group to report on one person they chose to go to the island and put this on newsprint and, in a second column, write the criteria that group used. Do not have one group report all their choices as this will limit participation. Ask other groups to add to the list of criteria as you go along.

8. After completing this list and hearing the criteria, discuss their decisions in the **whole group**.

9. Then ask people to turn to their neighbour and discuss, 'What I have learnt from this exercise?' (about 5 minutes).

10. Ask participants to share their insights in the whole group.

Facilitator's notes

You will find that the choices participants made come from different sets of values that may not necessarily be in conflict in the final choices. However, they could be controversial if a person selects from a very narrow perspective. It might be necessary to remind them of the door exercise. Two obvious criteria are skills and balance in a society.

Participants usually feel they have been logical and have decided on skills, particularly in relation to survival or procreation. However, very little is actually known about people's skills, and even less is known about their reproductive abilities. Little is also known about the twenty people to ensure that those chosen will create a balanced society. What is the standard and who decides what is balanced?

Some participants may leave the nurse behind because of their prejudice against gays. Others leave the doctor behind because their experience of doctors has not been positive. Others might leave the old woman with a walking stick, but is she 55 or 75 years old? Some might explain that they are leaving her behind for 'her own good', but she could be among the most physically and mentally fit of the whole group.

Assumptions, stereotypes, prejudices will surface. Stereotyping can be very powerful and even if our own experience contradicts the stereotype, we often find it hard to let go. Some participants might say 'there is not enough information and therefore I cannot do the exercise'. A helpful response from the facilitator is, 'You are right. But in reality, we do have to make choices with little information. We are using this exercise in order to develop criteria later'.

Depending on the amount of time available, you can move the discussion to a deeper level with the following questions discussed in **groups of three:**

a. Do we have experience of others making assumptions about us or stereotyping or prejudging us? How has that happened?
b. How fixed are our attitudes? Do we really have open minds about others? Do we really treat people 'as we find them' or do we expect certain groups to behave and react in particular ways?
c. Can you identify a stereotype or prejudice you used to have, but have abandoned? How and why did that happen?

Note This exercise is very helpful to an organization before a group has to do any selection process (like job interviews). It helps to clarify how decisions are made and who could lose out (e.g. minority groups).

Time   About 1½ to 2 hours

Materials   'The Island' handout, newsprint, markers and tape.

The Island

It has been decided to send a group of people to a recently discovered island where they will live an isolated life for the next 50 years in order to create a new society.

Choose 12 of the following people to go to the island. Circle the number of each person you choose to go to the island. Then in your small groups, tick the 12 people you agree on as a group.

1. A white middle manager

2. Shop assistant, age 19

3. Zambian doctor

4. Old woman with a walking stick

5. Maize farmer

6. Trade union shop steward

7. Immigrant shop keeper

8. Army sergeant, aged 50

9. Peace campaigner/activist

10. Barman

11. Ex-beauty queen

12. Pregnant school teacher

13. Unemployed black teenager

14. Exile returnee

15. Carpenter from a distant area who speaks a language which is not well known

16. Gay nurse

17. Methodist minister

18. Disabled bank clerk

19. Farm labourer

20. Jazz musician

Exercise 5. Labelling*

The following exercise can enable people to understand how we label ourselves and others, and the results of labelling.

Procedure

1. Give all the participants a large label or a quarter of a piece of paper with a stick pin. Ask participants to write their name at the very top of the paper only. Tell them not to write on this paper until asked to do so.

2. Write the following word on newsprint – SEX or MALE/FEMALE. Ask participants to brainstorm other words related to people's sex which the facilitator writes up on newsprint. Then ask participants to choose one word from the list (or another word that they identify) that they feel comfortable with in describing themselves. Ask them to write that word on their own label.

3. Repeat this process with other themes, such as:
   Location/origin
   Status/class
   Values
   Ethnicity

4. When you have completed this process, ask participants to turn to their neighbour and explain why they chose the labels they did, and why they rejected other labels.

5. When they have finished discussing this, ask participants to put on their label and walk around the room presenting themselves to others in the group.

6. Ask the participants to come back to the whole group and discuss the following questions.

   a. Did you find it easy or difficult to label yourself? Why?
   b. Which people find it easiest? Who might find it most difficult? Why?
   c. Do you expect to be labelled when you go to communities you do not know? How do you feel? Why does this happen?

Facilitator's note

It is difficult to label ourselves because we know people will make assumptions based on these labels and because it means others will only know part of you. If the label indicates your race or ethnicity, this can be stereotyped by others. Discuss why some people can label themselves more easily than others. (Usually those in the dominant group, white males, for instance, see themselves as the norm, therefore failing to recognize the need for a label compared to groups who feel more insecure and need to have a recognized identity.)

---

* Source: Legum

7. Give each participant a clean piece of paper and ask them to write a list: 'where do I come from – what are my origins?' This list could include:

   - location
   - family
   - education
   - class
   - gender
   - religion
   - language
   - diet
   - money
   - political alliances
   - organizations important to them

8. Now ask participants, 'Where are you now?' and to write next to the first list the changes they have made, reasons they changed, and what impact these changes have had on them.

   Their piece of paper will be set out as shown.

Origin	Changes	Reason for change	Impact on me

9. Give each person about 10+ minutes to complete this exercise and then ask them to go into **groups of three** to share what they would like to share with their group.

10. Then ask them to respond to the following questions:

    a. What similarities did you find in the group?
    b. What differences did you find in your group?
    c. What are the factors that influenced change?
    d. How did race or ethnicity bear on these changes or differences?

11. In the **whole group**, ask participants to share any insights they had from this exercise.

Summary

The following may usefully be drawn from the group.

Similarities If we have similar backgrounds, we will have similar choices, access to opportunities and resources, our role models and support for our own identity will also be similar.

Differences Depending on a person's class, race, education, or childhood location, the choices, access, role models will most likely be very different.

Sharing These differences need to be shared and listened to, because the dominant group often believes that their experience is the same as everyone else's experience, or that it is superior.

Changes Our backgrounds are not static, but continually shifting. It is important to recognize where change comes from and to give credit where credit is due. It also can help us to identify how we can change our own behaviour in the future.

Ethnicity White people are just as 'ethnic' as people of colour, but often an aspect of being white is to deny or fail to recognize white 'ethnicity', seeing white as the 'norm' and others as 'ethnic'.

Time 1½ to 2 hours

Materials Paper, stick pins, markers, newsprint, tape.

Exercise 6. Identity

This exercise is to enable participants to focus on their own identity, and to look at areas of race and colour where one might have stereotypes.

Procedure

1. Explain the purpose of this exercise and say that each person will receive a handout with incomplete phrases. Participants will have about 10 minutes individually to fill out the form. Ask participants to form **groups of five** and then hand out the forms.

2. After most people have filled out the form individually, ask them to share each of their responses on the form in their small group. After each response, ask participants to discuss:

   a. Are there issues or things about that 'group' that are not on your own list? Did you think that you or others were stereotyping or ignorant?
   b. What insights did each statement give to you?

3. After the small group discussion, bring the participants back into **the whole group** and ask them for any particular insights they had from this exercise. Find out which question they had most difficulty answering and why.

Time   About 1 hour

Materials   Handout on identity.

Facilitator's note

The identity questionnaire was mainly prepared to help whites to think about their own white identity. However, the questions can be changed to match any type of group you are working with (that is between tribes, clans, multi-racial groups). In this case, we use black and white. More questions can be included to cover multi-racial situations. The words 'black' and 'white' may have to be explained (i.e. 'black is used to characterize all those in South Africa who were part of the struggle and oppressed').

139

Identity

Please complete the following sentences. You can have as many ideas or sentences as you wish; however, be aware of time so you can complete all the questions.

1. To me being black means . . . .

2. To me being white means . . . .

3. White people have been responsible for . . . .

4. Black people have been responsible for . . . .

5. Black is beautiful because . . . .

6. White is beautiful because . . . .

7. The role of white people to bring about change on race issues is . . . .

SECTION THREE

Discrimination

Exercise 7. Discrimination*

If our attitudes towards a certain group of people are negative, then we are likely to behave in a negative way towards them. We may well use any power we have to disadvantage anyone who falls into that group. We may not even be aware of discriminating against them, because it seems natural to exclude them if we think they are unworthy in some way. People can experience discrimination for a whole variety of reasons, so for one reason or another we are all vulnerable to discrimination.

There are physical and psychological mechanisms that we adopt to protect ourselves from the experience of discrimination. It is important to identify these behaviours, for ourselves and with others, in order to limit the damaging effects on our self-esteem and our ability to work with others.

A. WHO IS DISCRIMINATED AGAINST?

Procedure

1. Ask participants to turn to their neighbour and quickly brainstorm: What groups in our society are discriminated against?

2. Ask participants to share one point from their list until you have the full list from everyone on newsprint.

3. Ask participants to turn to their partner and discuss: What strikes you about this list?

4. In the whole group, ask participants to share their responses to the question.

Facilitator's note

The key points from this discussion usually include:

- Discrimination includes everyone;
- Some categories are temporary while others are permanent;
- Some are invisible, some can be hidden; others are obvious;
- Some you can move in and out of; some apply to only a part of your life;
- Many people could find themselves in more than one kind of discriminatory situation.

---

*Source: Legum

Summary   It is helpful to share with the group the 'multiplier effect' of discrimination. If a person is in one category, it can lead to others. For example, if a person has a disability, that person may find it hard to get a job, which can lead to poverty, which could lead to crime, abuse of alcohol or other anti-social behaviour. The same applies the other way round. If you are white, you may have a superior education, a good job, decent surroundings and this will privilege your children as well.

B. BEING DISCRIMINATED AGAINST

This part of the exercise helps participants to get in touch with their own feelings of being discriminated against and the different ways of responding, reacting and coping with discrimination. This also helps to identify the power relationships in discrimination.

Procedure

1. Ask participants to identify one experience of being discriminated against. Give people time to think about that experience and write about it. They should write about:

   a. how did they feel?
   b. how did they react?
   c. who did the discriminating?
   d. what power that person had.
   e. what they now see as an alternative strategy to deal with that discrimination.

2. After about 5 minutes, ask participants to form **groups of four** and share their experiences and responses to the questions. Then ask each group to put on newsprint those things they found they have in common and those they did not have in common under the following headings:

Feelings	Reactions	Power relation	Strategies

3. After each group has completed this task, ask them to share briefly their newsprints. Ask participants to look for similarities and types of discrimination: individual, cultural or institutional discrimination.

Facilitator's note

During this discussion, it is important to discuss the relationship between attitudes and discrimination. Discrimination is an action based on prejudices, stereotypes and assumptions. It is also important to discuss the notion that while we are all free to think what we like and to hold any prejudices we wish, we are not free to discriminate. Most countries have laws which makes it illegal to discriminate, and many organizations have policies and codes of practice which outline the expectations of the organization's staff which back anti-racist behaviour and sometimes punish or stop discriminating behaviour.

C. WAYS IN WHICH I HAVE DISCRIMINATED

This third step of the exercise is to explore how some of us may also be in a role where we discriminate. This exercise helps us look at ways we could counter this behaviour in the future.

Procedure

1. Ask participants to recall a time when they were being discriminatory. These will be times when we had to make judgements and it required us to make a decision, for example the distribution of resources. An easy example is about one's children or brothers or sisters, wife or husband. Ask people to think about how they felt when they discriminated, what were the consequences (reactions of others) after they discriminated, and what alternative strategies they now think they could use in that kind of situation in the future.

2. Similar to the previous part of this exercise, ask participants to go back into their **groups of four** and discuss the experience and develop a chart on newsprint that has the common points on it under three headings:

Feelings	Consequences of action	Alternative strategies

3. In the **whole group**, ask groups to share what they have written on newsprint briefly and then discuss any insights that have come to them.

Facilitator's note

At this point it can be helpful to share with the group the 'Cycle of discrimination'.

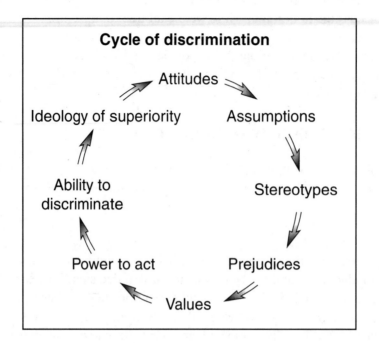

Cycle of discrimination

Attitudes

Ideology of superiority

Assumptions

Ability to discriminate

Stereotypes

Power to act

Prejudices

Values

Time   About 2 hours

Materials   Paper, pens, newsprint, markers, and tape.

Exercise 8. Cushions*

This exercise enables participants to look at how people protect or 'cushion' themselves from discrimination and the effects cushioning can have on everyone involved.

Procedure

1. Ask participants to brainstorm ways in which we protect (or cushion) ourselves from experiences of discrimination. List these on newsprint.

2. Ask participants to discuss with their neighbour the following questions:

   - What are some of the effects and consequences of such behaviour?
   - What are some of the positive and negative outcomes of these personal strategies?
   - What is the worst thing that could happen if you were more direct about feeling discriminated against? Is what you describe based on facts or a fear that is inside yourself?
   - What effects does this behaviour have on the organizations or institutions we work with?

3. When the small groups are ready to share, discuss these questions in the large group.

Note One example of a way a person cushions herself from discrimination is 'withdrawing'. The consequence of withdrawing is the dominant group can use this behaviour against the person: 'You see, they really don't care about this'. The worst thing that can happen if a person is more direct is being fired from a job or physical harm being done. Such fears may not be based on reality. Continued withdrawal means that the organization, and those with power, do not have to change behaviour or policies.

Time   30 minutes

Materials   Newsprint, markers, and tape.

Summary

Most of the strategies that people use to protect themselves include avoiding the situation, joking, rising above it, fighting back, closing off, running away and/or forming support groups with people with similar experiences. These are very common strategies that many people use to avoid conflict. However, these strategies can be understood by others in a different way. For example:

- avoiding   – might be seen as sitting on the fence
- joking   – not taking the discriminatory act seriously
- rising above it – being snobbish
- closing off   – being aloof
- fighting back   – being aggressive
- support group   – ganging up to cause trouble

---

*Source: Adapted from Legum

145

Most of these strategies protect the discriminator from knowing they have damaged the other person. These behaviours 'enable' the discriminator to continue to discriminate.

Our own personal approach to conflict is one we have developed for years. Sometimes we are unaware that we are behaving in this manner as we have done so for such a long time. However, it is helpful to be in touch with what we are feeling, identify what makes us uncomfortable. If we know what kinds of behaviour in others make us feel discriminated against, we can be more direct and more helpful. People who discriminate may not know they are doing it because they also have been doing it for many years. We need to develop strategies to communicate what we are feeling to the discriminator. First, we need to know what we are really feeling.

Other ways that people can cushion themselves against discrimination are more formal. These include:

- money
- education
- class change
- authority
- status.

Although these cushions protect us from the sharp edges of discrimination, they too can have negative consequences. For example, those who change class can lose touch with their roots, become ashamed of their relatives. Those who are educated may feel superior to others without as much formal learning. Those who acquire money may become so involved in 'making money' that they lose their own purpose in life; while those who gain authority may abuse it and alienate those with whom they work.

Institutional practices and policies are often thought of as neutral, and challenging them can be seen as very aggressive behaviour. We live in a society where 'we all know our place' and working in an anti-racist way can upset the status quo.

In dealing with conflict on a personal or institutional level, it is very important to do the hard work of developing several options or alternatives. On the personal level, one can say to the person, 'I really felt offended when you did . . . . . I would appreciate it if in the future you would do . . . .'

On the institutional level, one needs to study the policies or gather information on the practices that you consider discriminatory. With a group of people, develop alternative policies and/or practices that you think would be anti-racist. Then, when you approach those who would have authority to act on the issue, you can describe the problem and offer, in a constructive way, alternative solutions. Be prepared to negotiate other alternatives. In this way, you can help the person discriminating to 'buy into' the new policy or practice.

Exercise 9. Self-assessment of non-discriminating behaviour*

This exercise is to give people time to reflect on their own behaviour in relation to racism. It may be done as an individual exercise with no discussion, or it can first be shared in small groups and then in the whole group, depending on the amount of time one has and the purpose of the training event. If the training is to give feedback to one another, it can be helpful for participants to form small groups of people who know each other well and/or who work together in a unit. This is a way of encouraging people to commit themselves to future behaviour to which they can be held accountable.

If participants do not know one another, a self-assessment tool used only for personal reflection can give them something to take home and think about at a later time.

Procedure

1. Rate yourself on the following checklist using a '5' as highest and a '1' as the lowest mark. Try to be as honest with yourself as possible.

2. When you have completed the checklist, make a list of areas in which you think you need improvement.

3. Create specific goals for becoming more non-discriminating.

Time   30 minutes

Materials   Personal self-assessment handout for each participant.

---

*Source: Adapted from materials from the World of Difference Program, Anti-Defamation League, 1100 Connecticut Ave, NW, Suite 1020, Washington DC 20036, USA.

147

Personal self-assessment of non-discriminatory behaviour

Discriminatory behaviour rating (1 is low and 5 is high)

_____ 1. I educate myself about the culture and experiences of other racial/religious/ethnic/economic groups by attending classes, workshops, cultural events, reading, etc.

_____ 2. I spend time reflecting on my own childhood/upbringing to analyse where and how I received racist, sexist, anti-[a specific religion], heterosexist and other prejudiced messages.

_____ 3. I look at my own attitudes and behaviours as an adult to determine how I am supporting (even unconsciously) or combating racism in our society.

_____ 4. I evaluate my own use of language to see if I use terms or phrases that are degrading or hurtful to another group.

_____ 5. I avoid stereotyping and generalizing about people based on their group identity, gender, etc.

_____ 6. I value cultural differences and avoid statements such as 'I never think of you as a _____,' which discredit differences.

_____ 7. I am aware of, and can explore and discuss with comfort, issues of racism and pluralism.

_____ 8. I am open to having someone of another race point out ways in which my behaviour may be insensitive.

_____ 9. I give equal attention to all staff whom I supervise or work with, regardless of race, religious, socio-economic class, or physical ability.

_____ 10. I am comfortable giving constructive criticism to someone of another race, gender, age, or physical ability.

_____ 11. I include materials about all racial/religious/ethnic/economic groups in my programmes even though other groups may not be represented, because pluralistic programme material is important for all.

_____ 12. I make special efforts in my job to develop practices which are inclusive, such as scheduling meetings, locating meetings, and changing participation costs, when needed.

_____ 13. I consciously monitor TV programmes, newspapers and advertising for biased content due to race, gender, class or other biases.

_____ 14. I monitor the environment in my home, my office, my house of worship and my children's school for multicultural visuals and request such materials if they are lacking.

_____ 15. I feel free to ask people who use discriminatory language and behaviour to refrain, and am comfortable in stating my reasons.

_____ 16. I am willing to be proactive within my organization to achieve the goals set for diversity in hiring and programming.

_____ 17. I am actively anti-racist in my personal life by supporting campaigns and other means of achieving equality.

_____ 18. I am aware of the ways that I and my group benefit from the consequences of my beliefs and value system.

Areas where I need improvement:

My personal goals are

Source: Adapted from materials from the World of Difference Program, Anti-Defamation League, 1100 Connecticut Ave, NW, Suite 1020, Washington DC 20036, USA.

Guidelines for achieving communications free of racial and ethnic bias*

More and more countries are becoming multicultural and multilingual. Groups from various cultural backgrounds are challenging the dominance of Western European influence on daily life.

Discrimination based on race, colour and national origin has been with us for centuries. It remains with us now, despite these trends and claims to being enlightened. Our language – with all its power to reinforce bias and shape thought – is still stubbornly preserving the 'old order' as the standard against which all other groups are judged. Bias is subtle. The more deeply it has been taken into our consciousness, the more difficult it is to uncover.

Teachers, managers, government officials, and communicators are in key positions and need to examine language and select ways of communicating that recognize a broadening racial and ethnic society.

1. Beware of words, images, and situations that suggest that all or most members of a racial or ethnic group are the same. Stereotypes may lead to assumptions that are insupportable and offensive. They cloud the fact that all attributes may be found in all groups and individuals. (Example: 'The Kenyan children were well-dressed . . .' may unconsciously portray that only these Kenyan children are an exception to a mental image of all other Kenyans as 'poor' or 'unkempt'.)

2. Avoid 'qualifiers' that reinforce racial and ethnic stereotypes. A qualifier is added information that suggests an exception to the rule. (Example: 'The intelligent Black student . . . '.)

3. Identify by race or ethnic origin only when relevant. Few situations require such identification.

4. Be aware of language that, to some people, has questionable racial or ethnic connotations. While a word or phrase may not be personally offensive to you, it may be to others. (Example: 'non-White' – this word implies that White is the standard. Similar phrases such as non-Black or non-Yellow do not exist.)

5. Be aware of the possible negative implications of colour symbolic words. Choose language and usage that do not offend people or reinforce bias. (Example. 'It sure was a black day when we lost that money.' This suggests 'black' as negative.)

6. Avoid patronizing and tokenism toward any racial or ethnic group.

7. Substitute information for ethnic clichés.

8. Review media to see if all groups are fairly represented.

9. When confronted with offensive humour or racial slurs, clarify for yourself what you want to get out of the interaction with the person who made the slur. If you want to give vent to your anger, this might be good for you, but it may not be a successful interaction with the other person. Embarrassing a person in public can have the opposite effect.

10. In confronting others, the point is to let the offender know how you feel about what was said. You do have the right to request that this type of humour or language not be used in your presence.

---

*Adapted from *Without Bias: A Guidebook for Nondiscriminatory Communication*, Judy E. Pickens, Editor, NY: John Wiley and Sons, 1982.

Racism

Exercise 10. Understanding cultural racism

The aims of this session includes understanding cultural racism, an analysis of five key issues that make up cultural racism, how cultural domination and alienation is increasing through 'globalization' and mono-cultural imperialism, and raising the question of resistance to, coping with or accommodating the 'new world order'.

Identity and belonging are key fundamental human needs. In an increasing process of globalization, the threat to cultural identity for those who want to move up the economic ladder is real. The definition of becoming successful is often linked to meeting a standard imposed by Western culture. Certain behaviours and styles of work are the measure of success.

This exercise enables participants to analyse some of the key areas of how values and orientation towards life itself affect our daily living together in an multicultural society and world. The following chapter on culture goes into more depth to explore ways to understand one's own culture and what that culture brings to the human race.

Procedure

1. Explain to the group that this session will focus on some of the key areas of cultural differences which we will analyse and discuss. The group will be divided into five smaller groups. Each group will be allocated one of five areas of cultural differences based on the work of James Jones, a psychologist.* These areas are: time, rhythm, improvisation, oral expression and spirituality.

2. The task of each group will be:

    ● Have one person read out loud to the group the description of the areas of cultural orientation.
    ● Discuss in your group your understanding of that topic, how it applies from your own experiences and what could be a way for authentic multicultural respect and mutuality to be developed.
    ● Make a play that would describe your understanding of the topic and one response to the dilemma.

3. Ask participants to **number off** (from 1 to 5) and have all of the number 1s go to one part of the room, 2s to another part, and so on.

4. Hand out copies of one of the topics to each group. (Group 1 receives 'time', group 2 receives 'oral expression', etc.) Give only one topic to each group. Explain to participants that they will receive all five topics at the end of the session.

5. The groups have about 45 minutes to complete their task.

6. When all the groups have prepared their plays, bring them back into the **whole group**. Each group presents their play and describes verbally some of their discussion and response. Begin the presentations with the topic of time and end with the topic of spirituality.

---

* This exercise is based on an article called 'Racism: A Cultural Analysis of the Problem' by James M. Jones.

7. After all the plays have been presented, ask participants to find someone who was not in their small group and discuss, 'What does this mean to me? What have been my insights from all five presentations?'

8. In the **whole group**, discuss insights and the impact this analysis has on our own work and our daily lives. A summary of Jones's points can be given to all participants at the end of the session.

Time   2 to 3 hours

Materials   Copies of the five topics and the 'Some ways forward' handout for all participants.

Summary

Cultural racism is often difficult to detect. Most oppressed groups in the world have lived in two cultures, their own and that of the dominant culture. Those who are part of the dominant culture are often unaware of their attitudes, language, behaviour, and practices. A helpful tool was developed by James M. Jones in 'Racism: A cultural analysis of the problem'.

Jones suggests there are five dimensions of human experience: time, rhythm, improvisation, oral expression, and spirituality.

'These five dimensions reflect basic ways in which individuals and cultures orient themselves to living. They refer to how we experience and organize life, make decisions, arrive at beliefs, and derive meaning.'

These five areas are important because we will find differences between cultural groups in our behaviour and expectations of one another.

Time

Ways of perceiving and experiencing time
Linear or nonlinear
Present or future

Rhythm

Patterns of behaviour within a given time
Individual and cultural
Regular and irregular control

Improvisation

Individual creativity in a time period
Individual style or technical rules
Limited uncertainty or expected possibilities

Oral expression

Social basis of information

Action based results
vs possible abstraction

Social
vs academic knowledge

Spirituality

Belief in non-material

Unknowable forces
act on world

Holistic or undivided
view of world

One of the problems these ideas provoke is the extent to which the dominant culture understands the ways in which it carries out its cultural bias and creates structural barriers to people whose culture differs from that norm. There are strong ethnocentric biases operating in the new global economic and institutional reality. These are seldom questioned and are accepted as the superior values of Euro-American origin. This dominant cultural position further supports itself with power to define the inputs, standards, decision-making and access to resources. Cultures with other values are required to adapt, develop strategies to conform in order to become successful in the 'new order'. Those who have the power to define the standards also decide on who is deficient, whether or not those differences constitute a legitimate basis for judging outcomes towards the goals of institutions.

153

Time

Cultures differ significantly in how they organize, perceive and value time. Western cultures have a 'future time perspective' which is linked to achievement. This strongly affects their attitudes and behaviour. Western cultures think 'into' the future and see the present as a stop along the way.

This way of thinking uses time to shape and influence the present towards that future outcome. Things that happen now are valued for their 'use' toward a future goal or outcomes. The use of time is seen in a frame of urgency to produce. Western cultures also put a high value on individualism. The individual must have an attitude and behave in ways that can demonstrate a high value on using time.

For many other cultures, time is not future oriented. For example, in Swahili there is not a word for 'future'. Time is valued for events that take place in the present. Things that happen in the present are valued for their own worth, not as events leading towards a future outcome. Time is not measured, but valued for what happens during that moment.

Western cultures' future time orientation is a linear view of time. If we are at a point in time, the present moves us to a future point – in a straight line. The present is only a stopping point on the way to the future. For other cultures, time is present-oriented and not in a line. Time is functional.

Cross-cultural conflicts therefore emerge in our perceptions of time. For some, if a party is to begin at 8 p.m., a person who does not come at that time is considered 'late'. A non-linear approach perceives that the party actually begins when people arrive.

Different expectations, assumptions and judgements are made based on these differences about time. There is a continuum, of course. In globalized Western culture, the linear perspective of time is valued, and those who do not use time in this manner are deviant. (Jones, p. 299)

Rhythm

Rhythm is the flow of energy which directs behaviour. A person can feel the energy flow. One's behaviour seems to flow easily without much tension or tiredness. One is in tune with nature or the flow of events. There is a momentum. Different cultures have developed different rhythms and approaches to accomplishing tasks.

Studies have shown how many Western cultures have developed patterns in workplaces that 'fit' their rhythm. Other cultures often do not 'fit' into this pattern and again are put at a disadvantage. Other studies have shown how cultural groups which approach the world more attuned to the present actually succeed more easily when the pattern is not rigid but has variations. Another way to describe the two approaches is a 'fixed' format and a 'variable' format. Which of these is of higher value needs a very serious and long debate.

Institutions that develop from a culture which places a high value on performance in a certain manner with rigid procedures will therefore have difficulty developing high performance outcomes compared with a multicultural staff, who may work with flexible patterns more successfully.

Improvisation

Improvisation is usually defined as composing, reciting or singing on the spur of the moment. Another meaning is making, inventing or arranging offhand (Webster's Dictionary). Put another way, improvisation expresses creativity under pressure of something to be done urgently. Improvisation usually includes problem-solving, and is goal-directed but with the individual's own style.

Inventiveness under time pressure requires:

- 'knowing' the situation,
- a range of relevant skills, and
- the presence of mind to organize and implement

The Western achievement-oriented approach to work relies on a step-by-step and predictable route to reach the goals. For people outside those cultures, these routes have not been generally available because of discrimination or exclusion. There are many examples of how some people have had to be inventive to gain access which those from the dominant culture take for granted. One example that is common is how some black people would pretend to be working for a rich white person in order to get what they needed because they did not expect to get it in their own right. This inventiveness is creative and has style.

Western style achievement-oriented behaviour seeks to control each step of the process. The improvising approach accepts the challenge of a situation without knowing in advance what will be required. These two very different styles produce fertile ground for conflict within a team or organization. But they represent two styles of achievement, both of which are needed for success.

The Western style anticipates and tries to control the future by assuming that a prescribed plan and style of training is what is needed. Future achievement depends on practice, hard work and discipline. Improvisation develops skills through ongoing practice and rehearsals, thus building a range of abilities available on the spot and achievement in unpredictable situations.

Judgements in management and teamwork are often made because of these differences. Present-based behaviour is often seen as an inability to plan or decide direction. Organizations are 'managed' by crisis. Improvisation often comes from a 'context of oppression in which the future was unreliable, unpredictable and not guaranteed to occur at all, much less to occur with certain predictable features. Thus, an improvisational style for Black people [in the USA] is preferred by many and even demanded as a consequence of their struggle for survival. It represents, in other words, both evolutionary and reactionary ingredients of Black culture.' (Jones, p. 303)

Oral expression

'Oral expression is the social basis of information exchange. If important information is communicated orally between people and over time, then interpersonal relationships will be important, as will social knowledge and judgment. The broad implication of this view is that all forms of performance, judgment, and accomplishment will evolve from a basic social foundation.'

In literate cultures where written expression defines merit-revealing intelligence, opinion, ability and accomplishment, oral traditions are put at a disadvantage. This has serious consequences for evaluating work, outcomes and progress. In oral traditions, 'language plays a critical role in information exchange and social relations. Because of its centrality, all features of language are important, including . . . nonverbal communications.' Communication is in the context of social reality. However, formal systems and institutions often lack interpersonal social interaction. Communications are usually 'literal' and mostly written in a memo, a policy or a handbook. They lack social context.

'The oral tradition is more than mere verbal interchange.' In many Bantu languages the word 'word' means life itself. It is the 'life force', the spiritual–physical fluidity that gives life to everything. A newborn child does not have being until she or he is given a name by the father and that name is pronounced! The word embellishes and completes creations. It accompanies acts and gives them meaning.

With this profound significance of the spoken word, an action or a thing becomes important through speaking. It then has meaning. Understanding how the spoken word functions in a culture is an important step in knowing that culture. Our failure to recognize the importance of the link between social relationships and the spoken word will certainly hinder our ability to develop multicultural future. Without this understanding, Western cultures will continue with a racial–cultural bias when looking at performance, belief systems and outcomes. (Jones, pp. 304–5)

Spirituality

According to a number of scholars who have studied African philosophy, it is understood that everything that exists must be seen not as matter but as a force. 'Spirituality is merely the force that resides in all beings, things, places-times, and modalities.' In Western thought, 'force' was traditionally understood to be reserved for the origins of the planet.

But human beings (muntu) are only one force in the world. Muntu includes the dead as well as the living: the ancestors. If the force is in all beings, that force is capable of exerting influence. Then all that is material is only one way of making things happen. The living and the dead, places and time, and processes themselves, all contain force. This spirituality springs from a holistic understanding of the world and universe in which we live. Over recent decades, a number of theologies in Western thought have also been emerging with this same understanding. Co-creation theology, physics, and the blending of Eastern religious thought with Western religions makes these notions more understandable to those schooled in traditional Western spiritual training.

If the traditional Western belief was that force was related to control, then

'one of the clear consequences of this form of spirituality is a lessened sense of personal control. The practical implication is how much direct personal control of events do humans have? Psychologically this has enormous consequences. If one's self-worth is based on accomplishment and control, and this is deep in a culture, then any other type of behaviour is seen as deviant and threatening. In dualistic thinking, a person might be seen as either controlling his/her world or a pawn – being acted on. But if African spirituality brings in a new dimension, a whole value system is being transformed.

'If, by tradition, philosophy, and religious practice, a people believes that causation and control are best shared with other forces in the universe, then a person's worth will be less highly associated with control. Perhaps it is a belief in and value placed on personal control that lies behind the capacity to engage in such controlling activities as the exploitation of slavery, colonialism, and continuing in more subtle forms of racism, discrimination, and prejudice.

'If we add the new global economic pressure to compete and perform in efficient Western ways, a new form of cultural imperialism is rapidly overtaking most societies.

'Thus, to understand the dynamic implications of spirituality is to understand the operation of psychological control and the philosophical context within which it resides. There are positives and negatives in every systematic position, especially as it unfolds in behaviour sanctioned by culture. We have, it seems, accepted and taken for granted the notion that we are, can be, and should be in control of ourselves and the world around us. This belief has obvious positive consequences, but may have negative consequences as well.' (Jones, pp. 305–6)

This can easily be seen in the way Western cultures damage the earth. The dominant Western culture has rapidly extended to most of the world, and without skills to protect one's own identity and to shape one's own destiny within the new context, cultural forms will soon lose their unique contribution to the world.

Some ways forward

There are several ways to move forward on this complex issue of cultural racism.

1. Reduce cultural boundaries which leads to a wider concept of what is normative.

This approach helps groups to see who is in the 'in group' and what are the norms that govern their cultural and individual behaviour. Those who perceive themselves outside of the dominant group also need to articulate and do the hard work on understanding their own cultural boundaries and what is positive that they bring to the wider group.

This leads both groups to develop increased possibilities of using and working with a variety of responses within and across groups.

2. Acknowledge the potential of perceived differences, not as a problem, but as a contribution to the capacities in the total social and cultural fabric of a multicultural society.

'To do this, we clearly need to think differently about human diversity than we do now. We readily accept in principle the notion that diversity is good. Yet when it comes to practicality, the question always becomes what value or instrumentality does such a difference have for important goals in this society?

'When one experiences multiple cultural components in his or her own daily life, tolerance of diversity and respect for difference tend to follow. The result is potentially a society in which diversity is itself a virtue and accepted as commonplace . . . .There are several models in social psychology that suggest that diversity of opinion [and approaches] improve decision-making.' (Jones, p. 309)

There is also research that has shown that a homogeneous cultural approach tends to stagnate groups within their self-contained positions. In organizations which incorporate different cultures and articulates those conscious differences, more creative thinking is stimulated within all individual members.

For the individualistic, 'time-urgent perspective' culture, there is a higher risk of heart disease. Other health studies have shown where there is collective action and a cultural norm of inclusiveness, it becomes an antidote to the negative consequences of individualistic competitiveness. An emphasis on cultural evolution of a group value system that downplays individualism and control can be seen as a healthier work environment.

> 'The emphasis on the written word in the dominant culture permits a certain abstraction of human experience. Shall we send a memo or stop by and chat with an employee or colleague? . . . Increasingly good management is seen as including personal and social skills perhaps associated with an oral approach to interpersonal relationships. The aloof and powerful manager is giving way to the sensitive and accessible colleague.' (p. 309)

Most oppressed people of the world 'know' at least two cultures: their own and the dominant culture. But 'biculturality' should be a two-way street. While oppressed people 'have and must necessarily develop the same skills as those of the dominant culture, those in the dominant culture need to recognize the negative sides of their own approach and norms'. (p. 310)

This raises a number of points for discussion:

- How does a person raised in an oppressed culture convert a disadvantage to an opportunity for growth and development?
- What skills and abilities go into converting different qualities into a wider acceptance and opportunities?
- How can we advance our own appreciation of differences? [Tolerance is not enough.]
- How can individuals and groups evolve to reduce prejudice and its corresponding discriminatory effects?

This handout assumes that it is critical to look at the human experience through differences that are real but changing. The cultural approach, rather than race, emphasizes the content of experience and its historical basis as a means of coming together. By coming to understand culture in a modern society, this can help reduce the expressions of prejudice, discrimination and racism. This approach would reduce the negative understandings with the positive many-sided view of incorporation and inclusion.

Exercise 11. Institutional racism – drawing the web

This exercise is planned for a group in which all participants come from the same institution. There are facilitator's notes to give suggestions for groups that come from different organizations or institutions. This session enables participants to do the following:

- Identify those parts of an institution that support racism;
- Identify specific policies, practices and structures of an institution that support racism;
- Look at the links between different parts of an institution that make a web which reinforces one culture over other cultures.

Procedure

1. In order to understand institutional racism, the facilitator starts by asking the participants in the whole group to brainstorm the institutions that have been created in our society to meet human needs. These institutions are quickly written up on newsprint. Then ask each participant to note on a piece of paper which institutions are meeting the needs of all the people within our country. After a few minutes, ask participants to share which institutions they believe are meeting the needs of all the people, and on an equal basis. If there are differences within the group, have them share those differences, asking if everyone agrees to the suggestions given.

The web of racism in society

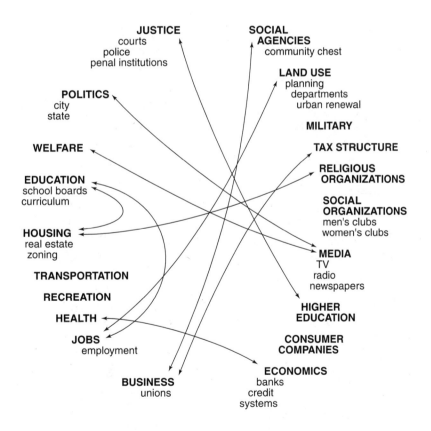

---

* Many more arrows can be drawn to illustrate the interrelationship of all the institutions. Drawing these arrows and giving an example of how the institutions are dependent on each other, and give privileges to whites and subjugate minorities.

The web of racism in society is to help participants understand that each institution reinforces the other institution until, like an insect caught in a spider's web, it is trapped. Show on a diagram how many institutions are linked. If one institution changes, the other institutions are all affected and may change. The real work now begins by understanding the institutional web of racism.

2. Ask participants now to form **groups of six**. The facilitator has the following tasks written on newsprint and explains these tasks to the whole group.

   a. Brainstorm a list of the different units within your organization (or institution).
   b. Take each part of the organization and discuss the policies, practices and structures of that part of the system and how it supports racism or actively works against it.

Facilitator's notes

This task will take 30–45 minutes. If the group comes from different organizations, ask people to go into small groups of those from similar structures. Try to get the same number of people in each group so that they will take about equal time to do the tasks.

If all the participants are from the same organization, the analysis of different sections or parts of the organization might be very detailed. This is fine. It is most useful if the whole *group* brainstorm the different parts of the institution, and then each small group works *only* on one area (or sector) of the institution.

3. Give the small groups about 30+ minutes to do this task. The facilitator should circulate among the groups to restate the tasks and clarify any points that arise.

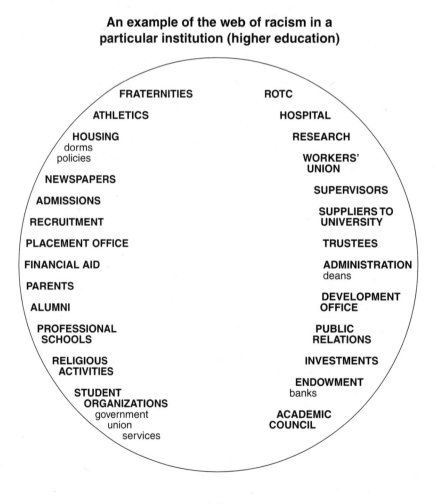

An example of the web of racism in a particular institution (higher education)

FRATERNITIES   ROTC
ATHLETICS   HOSPITAL
HOUSING   RESEARCH
dorms
policies   WORKERS'
        UNION
NEWSPAPERS
        SUPERVISORS
ADMISSIONS
        SUPPLIERS TO
RECRUITMENT   UNIVERSITY
PLACEMENT OFFICE   TRUSTEES
FINANCIAL AID   ADMINISTRATION
        deans
PARENTS
        DEVELOPMENT
ALUMNI   OFFICE
PROFESSIONAL   PUBLIC
SCHOOLS   RELATIONS
RELIGIOUS   INVESTMENTS
ACTIVITIES
        ENDOWMENT
STUDENT   banks
ORGANIZATIONS
government   ACADEMIC
union   COUNCIL
services

162

4. When the groups have completed the tasks, ask the participants to come together in the whole group and ask them to share the points on their newsprint.

5. The facilitator then writes the name of each part of the institution on newsprint, arranging them in a circle rather than making a list.

6. Ask the participants now to discuss with their neighbour how each part of the institution is interrelated (or linked) with other parts. Give them a few minutes to discuss this.

7. Then ask participants to explain one point at a time. The facilitator draws lines linking the various parts.

Summary

The importance of this exercise is to become aware of how each part of an institution reinforces the other parts of the institution through its policies, practices and structures. When looking at each part of the institution, it is important to look at who controls and sets the policies. Some participants might say that the important thing is for people to change their attitudes and then everything will be fine. This is only part of the problem.

Our lives are involved in institutions, but if people change their attitudes and yet the policies remain the same, there is fundamentally no change. Institutional practices can be changed through policies. But policies cannot change attitudes unless the new policies can be enforced.

Practices reflect the types of behaviour within an organization that have been sanctioned either formally or informally.

Policies are guidelines for practices within an institution (length of maternity leave; procedure for promotion; where, who and how to recruit). These are usually developed over time to be consistent to all those in the institution. Obviously, some policies are grossly unfair.

Structures are the formal groups (Board of Directors, Executive Director, committees, departments, regular meetings), formal practices etc. These should be known to the public and all employees in order to be transparent and help employees, clients, or students to know where decisions are made in the institution. It is important to know who is in each part of these structures in order to understand the power of any one group.

Time   About 1 to 1½ hours

Materials   Newsprint, markers and tape.

A supplemental exercise on power structures

The following is a more analytical means of understanding the formal power structure. After looking at how each part of an institution reinforces the other parts, the following questions can be applied to each part:

1. Who are the people who have formal responsibility for making and enforcing decisions that make the policy and/or control the practices within the institution?

2. To whom are they accountable?

3. What capacity do they have to affect the lives of others in the organization through processes such as hiring, evaluation or firing?

4. What is the racial make-up of the administrative and/or supervisory staff? All other departments?

   a. How are they chosen?
   b. Have there been significant changes in the racial make-up in the last five years?
   c. Are there plans for change at this time?

5. What is the racial make-up of the Board of Directors?

   a. How are they chosen?
   b. Have there been significant changes in the racial make-up in the last five years?
   c. What are their primary areas of power and responsibility?
   d. What members of your organization have direct contact or influence with them?

Role play

After the group has discussed the questions above, the participants go into small groups and act out a play on one aspect of an institution which reinforces racism within the institution. These plays are presented to the whole group and are discussed.

Exercise 12. Defining the problem

This exercise is to help participants deal with a controversial issue within the society in order to clarify their thinking and also to help people look at a problem from many different perspectives. Every country may have a different way in which they are dealing with their problems between races or ethnic groups. The facilitator may need to change the statement to fit your own situation. This particular statement has been used in both the United States and South Africa.

Procedure

1. The facilitator first needs to explain that this session is to help deal with an issue in our society that is controversial and complex. Explain that each person will receive a statement to focus the discussion. After each person has time to reflect on the statement, you will discuss it in small groups.

2. Ask participants to form **groups of five**. Give each participant a copy of the Affirmative action handout for them to think about and write their individual responses. Give them about 5–8 minutes. When the groups have finished their discussions (about 20+ minutes), ask all the participants to come back to the whole group.

3. The facilitator asks the whole group what their insights were from this discussion. It may not be necessary to go through all the questions, as this could be too repetitive. It is important, however, to focus on the different options that could be a fair and just policy to redress the inequities of the system based on race. These suggestions can be put on newsprint for further work.

Time   1 to 1½ hour

Materials   Newsprint, pens, Affirmation action handout for each participant.

Affirmative action

Below is a statement on Affirmative Action. Read the statement to yourself, then respond to the questions below in writing. Just putting notes for the responses is fine. When you have completed your responses, discuss the questions in your small group.

Statement

Equal rights, yes, but Affirmative Action, no. Giving preference to people because they have been disadvantaged hurts not only the company (or organization) but the person who gets that preference as well. We all want to be treated equally and get jobs because of our abilities, not special consideration. Standards will fall and then our country will be in a worse situation. We need to make sure people get good education so that they can compete at an equal level. Companies and organizations should not have goals to hire people in order to have a 'politically correct' racial mix on their staff. It is reverse discrimination.

1. What is your first reaction to the statement?

2. Write down the different issues that are contained in the statement. Are any based on fact, prejudice, fear, stereotyping, or historical discriminating patterns? If so what?

3. What are some of the ways (or policies) that could change the pattern of job discrimination?

(When you have completed your responses, share with your small group. Do not feel you must write full sentences. This is for your own use.)

Liberal racism

We often think of the racist as being the active bigot who tells demeaning jokes and engages in violent physical acts. This accounts for a very small minority in most countries. The more subtle and covert acts of the liberal, intentional or unintentional, maintain a system of white superiority. The following are some behaviours which fall into this category.

1. Invisibility	Ignoring. Failing to recognize a person of colour as 'regular' or even a citizen of the country. Noting white people only or predominantly. Ignoring black people's contributions.
2. Colour blindness	'I don't even think of you as black.' Assumption is that this is a compliment, and that it is not good to be perceived as black.
3. Dominance/Paternalism	Ease of whites in taking charge and helping. Difficulty with relating to people of colour in positions of authority.
4. Defining the other	Defining who is a person of colour and what their experiences are. Inability to listen and accept their experience.
5. Denying differences	Comfort of whites in accepting people of colour who talk and act like whites.
6. Stereotyping	Assuming all individual people of colour conform to the cultural patterns (e.g. they are all poor, uneducated, lazy, caring, musical, technical).
7. Assuming things are better	Failure to recognize perceptions of people of colour about current racial inequity. 'Racial oppression existed in the past and it is not productive to continue to compare today with the past.'
8. Fear of assertiveness	Hesitancy of whites to engage in confrontational dialogue. Fear of giving feedback on performance appraisals or assignments.

Source: Richardson

Exercise 13. Who benefits and who loses?

This exercise enables participants to look more deeply at how some groups benefit from institutions and others are caught in them. The assumption that we have freedom within these institutions is not always correct. The exercise also helps people to wrestle with the choices we need to make as we work towards anti-racist institutions.

Procedure

1. The facilitator needs to begin this session with a summary from the previous session where the group has identified the various institutions in our society. The facilitator reviews with the group the interrelated and interdependent nature of all the institutions. It is important to emphasize how one institution can reinforce another institution in society. (Poor housing for blacks can lead to poor health, which can lead to poor performance at school, and poor schools can lead to unemployment, etc.)

2. If your group has people from different racial groups, ask each racial group to form smaller **groups of five or six people.** The groups will now be in homogeneous racial groups, with perhaps more than one group being of the same race.

3. Ask each group to respond on newsprint to the following questions:

   ● How do we personally benefit from these institutions?
   ● What do we think we would lose or gain if the system were changed to give people of all races in our society the same benefits? Are our fears based on real dangers?
   ● If some of the fears are real, what are the consequences if we do not change the situation?
   ● How do we feel caught and unable to change the situation in the institution?

   Remind the groups that they are talking about themselves, not about someone else. Give them at least 30 minutes.

4. When the groups have finished their task, ask them to come back to the whole group and share the insights from their discussion. Their newsprint will be put on the wall after the discussion for everyone to see. In the whole group, these questions might move the discussion along:

   a. What did you discover through this exercise?
   b. What does this tell us about ourselves, this group, this organization?
   c. Can we identify some of the values, standards, and practices of the organization that need to be changed?
   d. Did you find some areas that can be worked on in this organization to work against racism? If so, name them for further work.

Time   1½ to 2 hours

Materials   Newsprint, markers and tape.

Summary on power and privilege*

When we look at how we either benefit or lose through the institutions created in our society, it is interesting to note that we often think there are many many people who are more privileged than

---

* Source: Richardson

168

ourselves. Yet the fact of the matter is that most of us (especially if we are reading this book) are more privileged than hundreds of millions of people on this Earth. It is very difficult to keep the lines clear between the issues of race and class. Racism in most societies has perpetuated an underclass who are usually people of colour (or a group that has little formal power).

Power is about the possibility of deciding.

Privilege is reflected in the fact of getting private education and inherited wealth.

Power is involved in deciding that crime prevention requires more money for law enforcement and drug wars rather than for schools and jobs.

Privilege is about reaping the benefits.

Power is involved in deciding that universal health care is 'too expensive' or that it will 'limit my choices'.

Privilege is reflected in the fact that being born white gives one a far greater chance of survival than most people in the world.

Power involves defining the parameters of the discussion.

Privilege is about not needing to know that parameters have been set.

It is here, at the intersection of power and privilege, that racism is most clearly revealed: the capacity to make and enforce decisions and to have access to resources. When power and privilege combine in an institution uncritically on the issue of racism, the institution makes and enforces decisions in favour of the dominant norms. One group decides whose fear of whom makes sense, is legitimate, and deserves compensation. It is those who have access to resources who have the privilege of living with their stereotypes and prejudices safely affirmed by the judicial system.

In looking at power and privilege, we do not assume either that power is always bad or that privilege is always chosen. A white infant is born to live with white skin privileges without exercising either choice or power.

There are very few people in most societies who experience themselves as having power. Even many people who hold powerful positions experience those positions in relation to others who are more powerful and are thus able to significantly affect their work for good or ill. Because this is true, it is easy, especially for white people, to confuse power and privilege: I do not feel personally powerful; therefore, the notion of 'white privilege' does not apply to me.

Privilege has little to do with individual power, but is integrally connected to access to structural power. Consider again some of the issues raised with the example of white skin privilege of a new-born white infant who, of course, has exercised no individual power. However, the institutional structures which affect the well-being of the infant are numerous: housing, education, job opportunities, health insurance – to name only a few.

It has been well documented that white people have easier access to all of the basic necessities than do people of colour whether or not they personally exercise structural power within the institutions that deliver them. Whether it is banking policies that favour housing loans in white communities or employment practices that keep people of colour in low-paying jobs or no-benefits jobs. The white skin privilege of the infant is integrally connected to that structural reality though neither she, nor her parents, have control of it.

Peggy McIntosh lists over 50 ways that she has experienced white privilege. Her access to privilege does, however, depend, as does that of the infant, on the collective power of the dominant white society. White people who want to combat racism need to understand this link between power and privilege. It is important to recognize the type of power that surrounds our privilege whether we feel powerful or not, even if we do not actually exercise substantial institutional power.

> White privilege is 'an invisible package of unearned assets which I can count on cashing in each day, but about which I was "meant" to remain oblivious.' (Peggy McIntosh, 'White Privilege and Male Privilege')

It is not only white people, however, who need to understand power. Just as very few people in most countries feel powerful, so very few people understand power. Our feelings of powerlessness are connected to our lack of understanding. This is no accident. It is rooted in the radical individualism of the dominant global culture and consequently, of the dominant modes of education. We are not taught to analyse power. As a result, we learn to see systemic problems like racism as problems of interpersonal relationships.

While it is true that there are personal and interpersonal dimensions of any systemic problem, including racism, the problem of racism cannot be solved by improving interpersonal relationships. That is why efforts to increase 'multi-cultural understanding' or 'diversity' workshops are rarely effective in dealing with racial tensions in organizations and institutions. They may, indeed, broaden the perspectives of members of the dominant white group and increase the level of understanding among individuals, but if the power dynamics are not addressed, the underlying tensions will remain.

But how do we do this when so few people experience themselves as powerful? The first step, as we know from the popular education approach of developing critical consciousness, is to learn to analyse the problem and address the power dynamics. Who controls policy decisions? What are institutional priorities as reflected in budgets, staff time, programme emphases? Whose voice counts in making those decisions? Who evaluates staff performance? Whose needs are served by distribution of organizational resources?

In many situations there is both a formal or 'official' power structure, and informal relationships that affect decision-making in an indirect and, often, unacknowledged way. In order to analyse the power in an organization accurately, it is essential to look at both formal and informal power distribution in the institution. Such an analysis can be revealing both to those who hold official positions of power and those who do not. For example, it is often the case that people who think they have power in an organization realize how little they really have when they attempt to make changes and encounter resistance within the informal power relationships. On the other hand, those who have little apparent power are sometimes able to exercise their influence beyond the boundaries of their status within the formal power structures.

Exercise 14. Anti-racist behaviour*

The following exercise was developed for South Africa. The case study should be adapted to fit the racial or ethnic situation that is appropriate to a particular country. It is another approach to help participants deal with controversial and complex issues.

Procedure

1. Introduce this session by explaining that this will be a role-playing session about an organization which has taken clear policy decisions to create equality and end discrimination. However, the Managing Director has received a letter (which all participants will see) resigning on the grounds that, in practice, the new policies are not being implemented.

2. Explain that participants will be divided into **three** groups to discuss how to deal with this situation and ensure it does not happen again. The three groups are:

   - senior managers,
   - a staff group, and
   - the organization's 'Equal Opportunities Committee'.

3. Ask participants to number off (1, 2, and 3) and ask all the 1s to be the managers, the 2s to be the staff and the 3s to be the Committee. Ask the groups to go to different parts of the room so they have space to discuss easily.

4. Give each person the letter written by the employee who resigned. Their task as a group is to prepare a response to the letter. Besides writing their response, ask the group to prepare their strategy for any changes they want to make in this organization.

5. Ask participants to use their own values and not to behave as stereotypes of managers, trade unionists or whatever, but really be themselves.

6. Give the groups 30 to 45 minutes to complete this task.

7. When the groups are finished, ask them to come to the whole group and share the points on their newsprint. During the discussion the facilitator asks the following questions:

   a. What insights did you gain from this exercise?
   b. What strategies did you come up with?
   c. What do you think was the race and gender of the letter writer?
      (In fact, it was a white man, confident that by leaving he was not jeopardizing career. He quickly found another job. The case study is true. One of the solutions that was used by the organization was to call in a black consultant who identified that the drop-out rate of women and black people was very high in the organization.)
   d. What does this mean in terms of who decides policies, standards, and other issues within our own organization?

Time   1½ to 2 hours

Materials   Case study handout for each participant, newsprint, markers.

_____

* Source: Legum

Summary

To understand how integral is good practice on racism to good management, read through the principles again, applying them to any group of people including women, people with disabilities, etc. For that matter, people with different eye colours?

Thus good management will always:

- Systemize the policies it considers important;
- Acknowledge the sources of effective contributions to policy;
- Develop its own image to reflect the way it values its employees, makes them feel welcome
- Ensure that informal business is done in settings to which all relevant employees have comfortable access;
- Develop problem-solving groups to expand communication across potentially difficult areas;
- Encourage networks within the organization which enhance self-confidence and display trust;
- Make public its commitments to good practice.

(Source: Margaret Legum)

Case study on organizational practices

Your organization has an equal opportunities policy. You are an NGO that is committed to justice and becoming multi-cultural. Your organization has a reputation of being on the side of justice. You have just received the following letter. Your task, as a small group, is to:

a. Ask one person from your group to read this letter out loud to the other people in your group.
b. Write a brief response to this letter. (Suggest that the group avoid rescuing the resigned person and stay focused on the future of the organization.)
c. Identify parts of the organization that need to change.
d. Decide on a few strategies to begin implementing these strategies.

Put all of this information on newsprint.

Case study letter

20 November 1999

Dear Manager,

I was glad to be offered a job in your agency and I was looking forward to working with your staff. However, my first weeks at work have raised a lot of questions. I had expected the organization, given recent changes to its staff recruitment and management practice, to be sensitive and aware of other cultures. What I experienced was totally contrary to that. At the morning staff meeting on my first day at work I was depressed at what I heard. Some people made remarks derogatory to women and black people. The person 'in charge' did not challenge these remarks, but in fact smiled, giving an indication that there was support for these comments. It felt obviously that there was little commitment to making the organization multi-cultural. The attitudes that underlie these comments were reinforced by the lack of positive images of black people and women and negative ways they were referred to in other comments and reports which I have read.

I have worked very hard to sensitize myself to the issues of racism and sexism. I had expected the agency to have done the same. Given the collusion between managers and workers which I experienced, I feel I cannot work for such an organization. I have better things to do than constantly challenge, particularly in places where I expect support. Therefore I have decided not to continue with this job.

I am writing this letter to you because I think you are in a position to do something about correcting this kind of behaviour and to create a supportive environment for black and white men and women so that we can all work together to provide the best service to our multi-racial community.

Yours sincerely,
A worker

Principles of good practice: working against racism in the work place*

An organization either contradicts racism or it reinforces it.

1. Good practice in contradicting racism is good management: race is not to be added on.

But developing every employee's potential will not happen automatically. Past racism has delivered affirmative action for whites. It has come to seem 'normal' for whites to be in control. Good management must contradict that norm to create equal access for black people.

Affirmative action programmes will only work inside an organization seen to be contradicting racism at all levels. Tangible procedures will take root only in a culture positively welcoming change right from the top.

2. Making the contribution of black people visible, demonstrating its value, not only to output but to policy-making.

Who do the organization's top white executives consult over future strategy? If black people, is their participation public and acknowledged? If only white people, why?

In your own work, what could a black person contribute as a result of their experience of being black? Can you answer this? If not, how could you find out? What would make it difficult? If you already value the contribution of black people, how are you using it in your own practice? When you use it how do you acknowledge its source or inspiration?

3. Examine the images by which the organization presents itself – to the world and to its employees.

Are white and black people shown in a variety of settings?

What are the images on the walls? What artefacts are displayed? Who staffs the reception area, how are they dressed? Who does the organization honour? How? What food is served and where? What drink? What company perks are offered?

Does the organization's view of itself make assumptions about the superiority of whiteness as a norm? If a black person walked into your organization, spent a day there and kept eyes and ears open, examined your public noticeboards and displays and read your printed literature, would they feel valued as a black person?

How could you find out, rather than speculating?

* Source: Legum

How could you set about working against racism in this area?

4. Examine the norms of informal organization culture to expand two-way communications between black and white employees.

Who meets where informally, in and out of office hours? What 'business' is done in these settings? Are the settings always 'white'? How easy and important is it for black employees to get into those settings? Should senior executives patronize settings which exclude their colleagues, even by implication?

Do black employees ever host informal meetings?

What is the organizational culture around food, drink, clothes, inclusion of families, hobbies and sports in out-of-work socializing?

5. Provide opportunities for employees, in mixed colour groups, to review together how they experience the organizational culture as a means of promoting or hindering communication.

Engage black people in problem-solving over areas of cultural-based difficulties. White people neither can nor should take responsibility for solving all problems arising from racism. Take advice from the experts. Make sure mixed colour groups do not include only a small minority of black people.

Do people congregate along colour lines during breaks? If so, do you know why? Is this segregation voluntary, based on common language, interests, etc.? Does it signify hostility? Get help if you don't know.

6. Review the organization's attitude towards the formation of support networks.

All organizations contain networks. Would a formal black group be supported, discouraged or disallowed?

Where disadvantaged people are in a minority in decision-making levels, they need mutual support. It will enhance their confidence, self-development and effectiveness. Black employees should feel free to form black associations within and outside the organization. This will build their trust in the organization's understanding of racism.

When, after research and consultation across colour lines, you have agreed on your affirmative action as part of equal opportunities policy, publish it widely and prominently.

Affirmative action programmes must be integrated into all personnel policies on recruitment, selection, promotion and appraisal policies. Otherwise, they will be seen as a marginal/option extra.

Ensure everyone knows your policy carries the conviction of management and that its implementation will take a high priority.

7. Provide training on racism and equal opportunities and the details of your own policy for all line management. Even if you think you have goodwill, it will not be enough to contradict the experience of decades, if not centuries.

Publicly allocate resources for staff, for training and for procedural back-up.

Advertise the principles of your equal opportunities policy in all public spaces and in your published material for the public.

Emphasize these policies in recruitment, selection and interviews for all new staff, black and white.

Build affirmative action criteria into appraisal systems for line management – in an orderly and reasonable manner, and after training.

Design internal training and monitoring systems, to overcome past disadvantage, as far as possible with participation from employees of all colours.

8. Be clear why your organization is introducing policies to contradict racism.

Are you suggesting affirmative action is about being kind/fair to black people? If so you are perpetuating racism through white paternalism.

Race privilege which favours or rejects people by skin colour is wasteful and inefficient. So privilege must be shared until it is ended. That is the reason for contradicting racism.

If you find yourself in difficulties with a black employee (or group of black employees) ask yourself if you would have the same difficulty if they were not black. If not, racism is involved. Why are you not using normal principles of good management to solve the problems? Get help if possible from a black confidante, to discover what form racism is taking place between you.

SECTION FIVE

Moving forward

Exercise 15. **Making a personal commitment to anti-racist practice**

'One of the most serious pitfalls of anti-racism work is mistaking new understanding or good intentions for structural change . . . . Racism is imbedded in the cultural values and institutional practices that give shape to social and political reality. Unless we find ways to transform these practices, racism remains in place and white supremacy continues to define our corporate life.'

N.D. Richardson

Racism is having access to systems of power (through privilege), access to resources, setting standards for appropriate behaviour and definitions of reality that perpetuates white supremacy. The following exercise helps participants to explore types of behaviour that is effectively anti-racist.

Procedure

1. Explain that this session is to help a group decide how it will move ahead in changing its way of acting against racism.

2. Ask participants to form **groups of three or four**. Hand out the Grid on behaviour against racism. Have participants discuss this Grid for about 20 minutes.

3. When the small groups have finished their discussion, ask the participants to return to the whole group and share their insights.

4. Some of their main insights can be put on newsprint. Issues that have not been identified can be added by the facilitator from the Summary which is at the end of this exercise.

5. At the end of this session, ask participants to find a quiet spot in the room and ask them to write at least three points they want to change in their own way of working and approaching life. When most participants have completed this task, ask them to find one person with whom they feel close. Ask each to share with their partners whatever points they wish to. The session ends with no group discussion. This ensures that the participants can make their personal commitment as a serious issue without peer pressure.

Time   1 hour

Materials   Grid handouts, newsprint, markers.

GRID on behaviour against racism		
	Racist behaviour	Anti-racist behaviour
ACTIVE	Overtly support policies and practices that maintain White supremacy	Work for change
PASSIVE	Maintain the present situation	???

Questions for discussion

1. Read the Grid to each other in your group. Do you think there is a behaviour that is 'passive anti-racist' behaviour? If so, what? If not, why not?

2. What would you have to DO to be an 'active racist'?

3. What would have to DO to be an active 'anti-racist'?

4. What are the consequences of becoming an active anti-racist? What are the risks and what are the gains for you personally?

(Source: Women's Theological Center, Boston, Massachusetts, USA)

Summary*

'Being passive in a situation that is already racist allows the present situation to continue. It is not possible to work against white supremacy and be passive. This, however, is what many liberal people of goodwill try to do. As a result, they unknowingly and unintentionally get stuck in a pattern of maintaining the present situation by doing nothing to change it.'

It is easy to get stuck in keeping the present situation rather than working for change for several reasons.

- The complexity of the problem can be overwhelming. It is easy to get discouraged when it is not clear where the best places are to begin to act. If one does an analysis of the structures of society, one begins to see that housing, education, poor health, good roads all are linked together. There is no way that one person can change all those situations. It is easier to conclude that people of colour need to work themselves out of poverty rather than considering one's own position that maintains it.

- Our own lives are very complex and busy. Earning a living, taking care of children, the home and other work all take time. Many people complain that they do not have time to do one more thing. However, acting for change may require a change in the way we approach our lives daily. In our work, our neighbourhoods, we can either ensure or stop the possibility of racial justice in our own situations.

- In many societies, we believe that working for change requires strong individuals to confront powerful structures. Working with others, however, is more effective and draws on the strengths and resources of others.

- Another reason is that we often expect quick solutions and think that there is only one correct solution to solve a problem. In fact, the opposite is usually true. Different organizations need to work in different ways and change is a step-by-step process. Some organizations may need to be very clear about becoming multi-cultural, while another organization may consider that their work against racism would be more powerful if it is mono-cultural. A good example of this was the effectiveness of a white women's organization, the Black Sash, during the apartheid era in South Africa.

---

* Source: Richardson

Exercise 16. Power inventory

This exercise will enable participants to identify resources within a group, clarify the power of that group and the range of influence it potentially can have. If participants are from the same organization, the power inventory is shared in the whole group and used for future strategic planning sessions. If participants come from different organizations, ask people to form small groups that have a similar mission (e.g. women's groups, or land use groups, etc.)

Procedure

1. Ask participants to find a quiet place in the room to fill out the Power inventory form they will receive from the facilitator. Hand out the Power inventory form.

2. Give the participants about 20 minutes to fill out the form. Then, or when most of them have completed the form, ask them to form **groups of five** with similar missions to share their insights from answering the form.

3. Ask the group to take a newsprint and make a group power inventory. Their newsprint will have less information than the personal power form, but gives an overview of the power within the group (see Group power chart).

4. Give the small groups at least 20 minutes to make and fill in this chart.

5. Call all the small groups back into **the whole group** and each group puts up their newsprint and shares their Group power chart.

6. The facilitator can then ask the whole group some of the following questions:

   a. Does our group have some forms of power?
   b. Where and in what fields do we have the most power? How can we use this power to cause the kind of change we are looking for:
      ● within the organization
      ● in a specific field
      ● in our communities?
   c. What kind of action can we take to use our power?

Time   1½ to 2 hours

Materials   Power inventory form for all participants and copies of the Group power chart for each small group, newsprint, markers, and tape.

Power inventory form

1. What organizations do you belong to?

2. What job do you have? What jobs do your relatives have?

3. What organizations are your friends and relatives affiliated with?

   Name   Organization

4. What businesses do you use?

   banks

   supermarkets

   clothing

   housing

   medicines

   transport

   property

   insurance

   newspapers

   social organizations

   churches/religious groups

   political parties

   other

5. a. Contacts you have in each of these organizations.

   b. Influence you have in each of those organizations.

   c. Power you have in each of those organizations.

6. a. Contacts your friends have in those institutions.

   b. Influence your friends have in those institutions.

   c. Power your friends have in those institutions.

7. Which of the following powers and how much power do you personally possess? (a lot, some, little)

   a. Formal office in an organization
   b. Elected or appointed office in some level of government
   c. Control over and responsibility for use of:
      - money
      - physical property
      - personnel
      - various skills

   d. Ability to introduce or to control the introduction of new ideas or actions:

   Where?

   How?

8. Which of the above powers (a–d) are possessed by people with whom you have informal and personal relationships? List.

9. Which of the following powers are possessed by organizations with which you are affiliated and by the place you work? Give specific examples and rate the amount of power you think it has in a specific area. Rank '4' as high, '3' as second high and '1' as low.

   a. control over and responsibility for use of:

   money   _____
   property   _____
   personnel   _____
   various skills _____

   b. Representation in other groups _____

   c. Representation in groups established by government _____

   d. Influence with its members _____

   e. Influence with other groups in the community _____

   f. Influence with newspapers, radio, and TV _____

   g. Ability to introduce or control the introduction of new ideas _____

[182] TRAINING FOR TRANSFORMATION

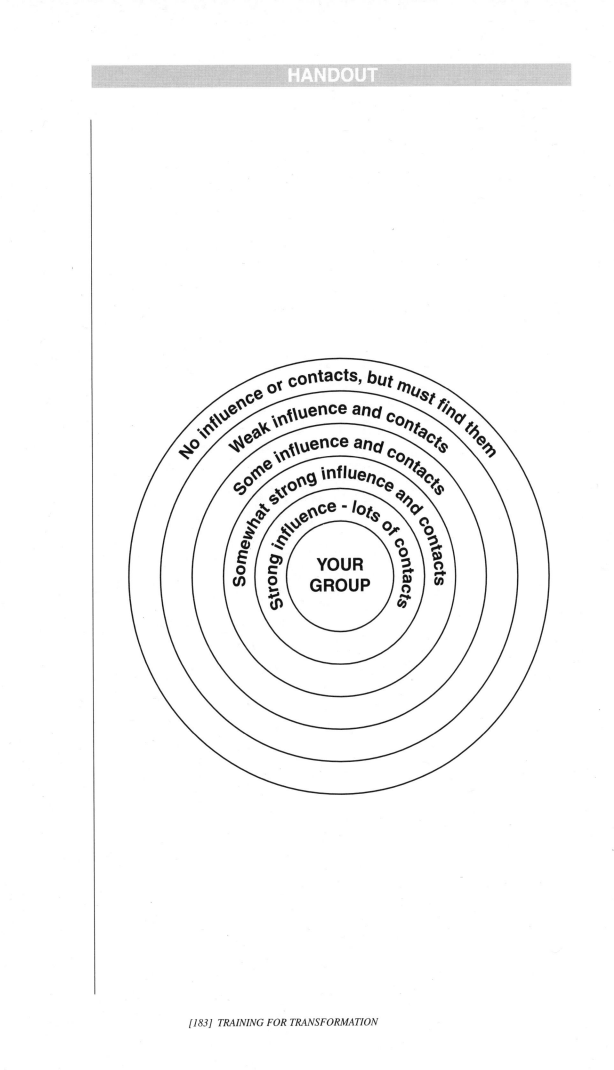

No influence or contacts, but must find them

Weak influence and contacts

Some influence and contacts

Somewhat strong influence and contacts

Strong influence - lots of contacts

YOUR GROUP

CHAPTER 4
Culture

Introduction

Section One: Appreciating our own culture

Section Two: Different experiences of a culture

Section Three: Other cultures

Introduction

There is an increasing awareness, personally and globally, of the importance of culture in every aspect of our lives. There is also a far deeper understanding of what we mean by culture than was current a few years ago. By culture we do not mean only the great artistic achievements of a people, or the peculiar customs of those we do not fully understand. Culture includes all the different ways in which any community strives to satisfy its fundamental human needs, both physical needs for subsistence, and psycho-social needs such as affection, understanding, creativity, and most profoundly its values.

Culture is not static. It changes as the situation of the community changes. It is affected by geography, climate, history, wealth and poverty, urbanization, opportunity, technology, and contact with other cultures. Even within the same culture, people of different age groups, different gender, or different social classes will experience their culture in very different ways. What is life-giving for one section of the population might be experienced as very restrictive, or even destructive, by another section.

Culture reflects values. Our values shape our culture, and our culture shapes our values. Therefore the culture changes as both the values and the circumstances of a community change. The fabric of life is made up of many different strands: economic, social, political, educational and so forth. But the colour, the warmth, the texture and the design of the fabric are formed by culture. Culture is deeply connected with our sense of identity. Only those who live within a culture can fully appreciate both its positive and negative aspects.

Very often in workshops we have found that, as the group wrestled with the economic and political analysis of their situations, they felt overwhelmed by the oppressive forces dominating their lives, and people became quite depressed. However, as we started to deal with culture, a new energy seemed to be unleashed in the group. They participated eagerly both in discussions on the subject, and in practical opportunities to express their creativity.

Human beings are made in the image of God, the great Creator. We are all made to be creative. There is a clear link between violent behaviour and the lack of opportunities for people to be creative. The use of our creativity gives most of us much happiness. It gives us a heightened sense of identity, and purifies our emotions. Any group seeking cultural renewal needs to provide everyone with satisfying opportunities for creativity.

Artists of all kinds can make a special contribution to society by revealing the truth of a people's experience in a way that brings new insight and understanding. But 'an artist is not a special kind of person: every person is a special kind of artist' (Eric Gill). Great works of art such as sculpture, drama, films, music and song, novels and poetry, as well as spontaneous creative expressions, can be used as problem posing codes and have a vital role to play in the process of transformation.

The following exercises on culture help a group to understand more fully the dynamic nature of culture, to look both appreciatively and critically at their own culture, and to become more sensitive to the values in other cultures.

SECTION ONE

Appreciating our own culture

Exercise 1. Introduction to culture

The aim of this brief exercise is to enable participants to focus on the meaning of culture and to begin exploring what culture means to us.

Procedure

1. Ask participants to discuss, with their neighbour, what culture mean to them.

2. After five minutes or so, ask participants to share their ideas and insights. Write the word in big letters on a piece of newsprint, and then write all the words suggested at different angles all around it. Explain that we are going to use our own experience to understand more deeply the meaning of culture and its effects upon our lives.

Time   20 minutes

Materials   Newsprint, tape and markers.

187

Exercise 2. My grandparents, my parents and me

The aim of this exercise is to enable participants to identify the main differences between the lives of their grandparents, their parents and their own generation, and to recognize the ways in which their culture has changed during the last 50 years.

Procedure

1. Give each participant a copy of the diagram of the Wheel of Fundamental Human Needs (see handout).

2. Ask the women and men to form separate groups of no more than **five people**. Both women's and men's groups can include people of different cultures.

3. Ask the **women** to think first about the life of one of their grandmothers (or a woman of her generation if they did not know their grandmother personally), making notes in the first circle:

   ● How was each need experienced and satisfied, more or less satisfactorily, in her life?
   ● What work did she have to do in order to satisfy these needs for other members of her family?

   (They need not work systematically around the circle, but deal with each point as it strikes them, e.g.: 'My grandmother lived in quite a different house from mine. She had to walk 2 km to fetch water, and carry it all on her head, whereas I have a tap in my house. Perhaps the dangers, or the expression of affection and respect etc. were very different in her time.')

   Meanwhile, the **men** in the group do the same, thinking about one of their grandfathers, or if they did not know them, about a man they knew well of his generation, living in similar circumstances. Allow 15 minutes for this step.

4. Ask the participants, in their groups of five, to turn their attention to the life of their mother or their father, using the same questions. Make notes in the second circle (10 minutes).

5. Finally, ask them to think about their own life. What are the main changes that they see both in the ways their own needs are met and in the responsibilities that are expected of them to satisfy the needs of other members of their family? (10 minutes).

6. Ask each person to list the three most striking changes in the culture, either for the women or the men of their family, during the last 50 years. What values, practices and customs have remained constant during these years? (10 minutes).

7. In the same **groups of five** share, 'What did you find most striking as you compared the lives of these three generations of men or women? What new insights did you have about the values and culture of your own family?' (20 minutes).

8. In the **whole group** share your insights on the most striking differences in the lives and values of the men and the women of your culture during the last fifty years. (30 minutes).

Time   About 1¾ hours.

Materials   Newsprint, tape and markers. Copies of The Wheel of Fundamental Human Needs handout.

The Wheel of Fundamental Human Needs

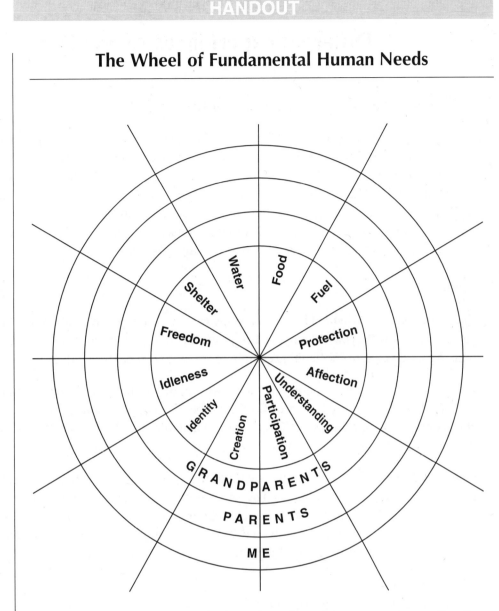

Make a note of the main changes in culture for your sex over the three generations.

SECTION TWO

Different experiences of a culture

Exercise 3. The Pawpaw/Banana game

The aim of the game is to clarify the meaning of culture by enabling participants to learn, and live in, two very different imaginary cultures, and then to examine their reactions when they have to interact with one another. In the debriefing after the game we will discuss how each culture has not only customs and practices, but is built on underlying values. We will look at the importance of understanding the values which underlie any culture, if we are to develop respect for diversity in cultures other than our own. This will lead into discussion of the positive and negative aspects of our own cultures, and the experience of encountering other cultures.

Procedure

1. The participants are divided into two groups with different names, values and customs. The two cultures are the **Pawpaws** and the **Bananas**. In this simulation both groups are working on housing. Each culture meets in a separate room, with a separate facilitator.

2. Each participant is given a copy of their own culture's rules. The group begins by reading the rules of their own culture out loud. They must be given enough time to reread any parts they find confusing and ask questions of the facilitator. Then they start to practise 'living the culture'. They need at least 15 minutes to practise doing this before the next step.

3. Once both groups have got into the swing of their own culture, each group sends an observer to the other culture for five minutes. The rules are not explained to the visiting observer and the rules of each culture must be kept out of sight at all times. Observers are not given an envelope and do not try to participate actively in the life of the culture they are visiting. Their role is simply to watch, observe and listen carefully, and then to report back what they have seen and heard to their own group.

4. Visitors are then sent in **groups of 3–5** from each culture to 'live in the other culture' for five minutes. They are given an envelope with the things they need, and told to try to participate fully in the life of the other culture while they are there.

5. When they return, **another group of 3–5** people from each culture is sent to live in and experience the other culture, again for about five minutes.

6. When all have had an opportunity to participate in the other culture they return to their own group. The facilitator in each group sums up the achievements of the group and the game ends. The facilitator in the Pawpaw group gives the prize to the person who has built the most houses, and the facilitator in the Banana group asks the chief to give the prize to the family which has contributed the most to the well-being of the community.

7. Give the participants an opportunity to discuss, in pairs in their own culture groups, the following three questions:

   a. What did you think of your own culture?
   b. What happened to you when you went to the other culture?
   c. What did you think of the other culture?

8. After a short break bring the whole group together and ask the participants:

    a. What did the Bananas think of the Pawpaw culture?

    b. What did the Pawpaws think of the Banana culture?

    c. Which culture did you like best? Why?

    d. Give each group a chance to explain their culture to the other group.

    e. What were the positive and the negative points of each culture? List the answers on newsprint.

    f. How did it feel to be in a strange culture?

    g. What parallels do you see between what happened in this game and what happens in real life when people of different cultures meet one another?

Time   2 hours to play the game and at least 2 hours for debriefing.

Materials   Materials for each culture put in individual envelopes, with rules for each participant. The numbers given assume 32 participants in all, 16 in each group. It will take a facilitator a few hours to ensure that all materials are properly in the correct envelopes and enough copies of all materials described in the handouts have been photocopied.

Materials needed for the Pawpaw group

16 Copies of the Rules for the Pawpaw Culture
16 Pawpaw Badges with Pins
32 Envelopes marked with Pawpaw symbol, each containing 20 cards of Building Supplies (Half the envelopes marked V for Visitors)
40 cards with Houses
40 Cards with Roadbuilder
40   ''   Plumbers with Water Pipes
40   ''   Foundation Drillers
40   ''   Work Tools
40   ''   Brick Walls
40   ''   Roof Frames
40   ''   Wooden Doors
40   ''   Glass Windows
40   ''   Telephones
40   ''   Light Bulbs.

[Just make 40 photocopies of each of the pages of pictures provided.] Cut them up and sort them into envelopes. Each envelope should have only one or two different kinds of cards. At least 24 of the doors, windows, and telephones should go into the envelopes prepared for the visitors from the other culture.]

Blackboard and chalk or newsprint and markers for scores.

Materials for the Banana group

A large map on newsprint of Bananaland (similar to map provided)
16 copies of the Rules for the Banana Culture
32 Envelopes marked with Banana symbol, containing Banana badges with pins, two slips of gift wrapping paper and one slip of coloured paper (at least 3 of each colour should be given out); half of these are marked V for Visitors

6 copies of page with different houses (2 sheets cut into cards)
6 copies of page of community service (4 sheets cut into cards)
60 copies of page with 'C' and 'F-H' cards (cut up)
Crown or special hat for chief
Caps for guards
Headscarves for women if necessary (if playing in an all-women group, a clear distinction should be made between women and men, e.g. all women should wear headscarves)

[For chief] Newsprint and tape and markers
4 of each of the following Community Service Cards:
Serve on Local Council
Plant Trees
Start a Youth Club
Build the Church
Teach Adult Literacy
Train the Band
Serve Tea at meetings
Create a Park
Organize a Pre-school
Start a Football Club

60 small squares gift wrapping paper used for gifts to the chief.

Rules for the PAWPAW culture

These rules must not be shown or explained to visitors.

The Pawpaws are an extremely efficient, competitive and productive culture. They like to get things done fast and thoroughly. They are impressed by numbers, quantity, speed and achievement. There is much individual 'freedom' and no difference in treatment of men and women. They can be impatient, use people, and take advantage of those who are ignorant or slow, but they are making a heroic effort to deal with the national housing shortage.

They aim to build as many houses as possible, at least one for every member in both cultural groups, but more if possible, in the shortest possible time. The person who builds the most houses will be the winner in this group, and will receive a prize.

They speak an international **language** (like Swahili, Funagalo, Esperanto) designed for business. It involves gestures, sounds and numbers, but no languages known to group members. The facilitator will confiscate two cards (see below) from anyone seen speaking a previously known language.

Envelopes

Each person in the Pawpaw culture is given an envelope with a pawpaw badge which they must wear, and a list of the ten things they need to build each house. They also receive 13 cards with the resources they can supply to others, e.g. one person might get 7 roof frames, and 6 wooden doors; another person 13 light bulbs, etc. Some people supply only one thing but some have a mixture of supplies or equipment.

There is always a slight shortage of some supplies. Envelopes are also provided for the **visitors** from the Banana culture. They may have more of some of the items which are in short supply among the Pawpaws.

The aim of this game

The aim of each person is to build as many houses as possible. Each individual first aims to get one of each of the ten items on the list. As soon as he/she gets all ten items, he/she gives these to the facilitator in exchange for a finished house. The facilitator then gives the person ten more resource cards, about five of one kind and five of another. The person goes back into the group to continue trading and exchanging complete sets for new houses. The facilitator keeps score on the blackboard (or newsprint), showing how many houses each person has built. At the end of the game each participant sticks the houses they have built on the board beside their name, with Blu-tack (prestik) or sticky tape. The prize is given to the one who has built the greatest number of houses.

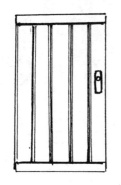

Requirements for building each house

1. Roadbuilder
2. Water Pipes, plumber
3. Foundations, drilling
4. Work Tools
5. Brick Walls
6. Roof Frame
7. Wooden Doors
8. Glass Windows
9. Telephone
10. Light Bulbs

Rules on how to make a trade

Pawpaws begin any transaction by shaking hands with the left hand, gently bumping right feet, and grinning broadly. This means, 'I want to do business with you, and I will be honest.' If people do not do this they cannot be trusted. The person approached responds with the 'yes' or 'no' sign which means they do or do not accept the agreement.

Yes sign: two claps

No sign: hands flat, palms down, moving in and out

I want: hands out, palms up, rapid movement, fingers to palms.

I will give: Tap chest twice and offer hand, palm up.

Repeat sign: Three taps on right ear.

Language

The first letter of each word or syllable of the thing has been combined with a vowel: ro, wapa, fedete, wutu, biwi, rafa, widi, gawa, tuluphu, libi. If you are asking for item 6 you must use six syllables; for item 10, ten syllables. Therefore if you want brick walls (5), you make the gesture for asking and say 'biwi biwi bi'. If you need item 7, a wooden door, you say 'widi widi widi wi'. If you want a telephone, item 9, you make the 'I want' gesture and say 'tuluphu tuluphu tuluphu'. If you need the drill to dig the foundations, item 3, you would say 'fedete'. **If a player has more than one of the cards requested they MUST trade that card**.

To tell your trading partner what you are able to give to them, you use the 'I will give' gesture, tapping your chest and extending your hand, palm up, and name the items you are willing to offer in the same way as before, 'rafa rafa rafa', or 'widi widi widi wi' etc. Not more than one card each can be exchanged at a time, and you cannot trade with the same person twice running.

You have about fifteen minutes to practise the initial gestures, the language and the process of exchange.

Trading session

Once you have learnt the language and understand the rules, the trading session starts and the people start to barter. **Using only the language learnt**, each player has to find out who can supply each type of building material required, and exchange what they have for what they need. Players can do business with only one other player at a time. There is a shortage of certain imported items but there will be enough for many complete houses.

(The facilitator writes the names of all the members of the Pawpaw culture on a blackboard or a sheet of newsprint on the wall, and negotiates with the facilitator from the other culture to see if they are ready to exchange observers).

Meanwhile the rest of the players continue practising the culture and trading to build houses. When they seem to know how to do it, ask for a volunteer to go and observe the other group. After the observers have reported back, groups of visitors from each culture visit the other culture.

These rules must not be shown or explained to visitors.

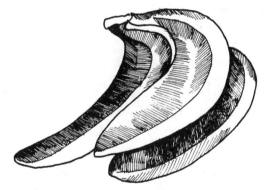

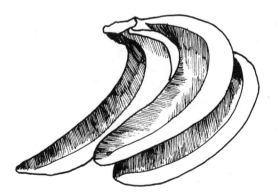

Church

Council or Literacy class

Planting

Band

Youth club

Meetings

Park

Football or Pre-school

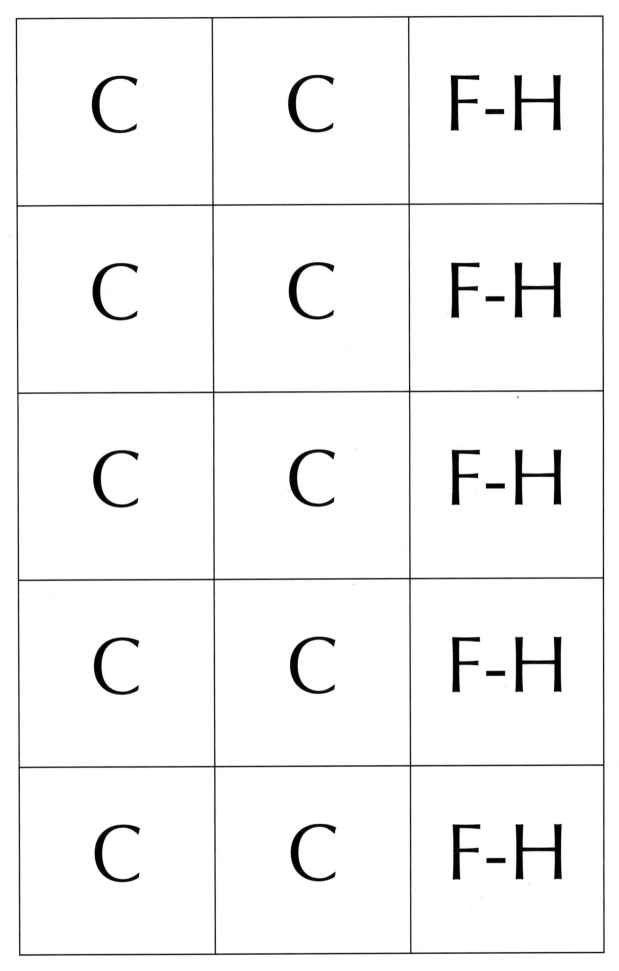

C	C	F-H
C	C	F-H
C	C	F-H
C	C	F-H
C	C	F-H

Rules for BANANA culture

These rules are strictly secret and must never be left around or shown to anybody from another culture.

This is a very gracious culture, more concerned with relationships, traditions, respect, manners, community life, creativity and beauty than with achievement and efficiency. Friendliness, greetings and protocol are extremely important and it is essential to show proper respect to each person, especially those in authority and the opposite sex. Men are considered the head of the family and women the heart. This culture puts a high value on family life. All co-operate to ensure a vibrant community life for all age groups. They aim to build a peaceful and happy community, in which each family gets the kind of home they would like. The most honour is given to the family which contributes most to the well-being of the whole community and the beauty of the neighbourhood.

Envelopes

Each participant is given an envelope containing:

- a Banana badge
- a slip of coloured paper showing which family they are in
- the rules for the Banana culture.

The chief has the cards for accomplishing the community and family tasks. These include:

- community work hour cards (C cards)
- building of family house work cards (F-H cards)
- pictures of community projects
- pictures of completed houses

The aim of this game

The aim for each person in this culture is to be co-operative, work to develop the community as a whole and enjoy people. Each individual aims to work alongside their family and other family groups to enhance the community, and later to work on building their own house. Co-operating with all group members is a key to success in this culture. At the same time, great respect is given to the chief and also to his guards.

Rules and procedures of banana culture

Read these rules aloud together. Participants can ask any questions of clarification of the facilitator. Then start to practise the culture. As soon as the game starts, all communication is done through gestures in complete silence, except for the chief and the guards, who may speak, and after the completion of a community project. All members of the banana culture then sing joyous traditional songs after each project is put on the 'map'. People may reply when they are spoken to by the chief or the guards.

To start, participants all gather to choose the leader or chief, and two guards. They greet one another with the traditional gestures (see Language and communication). They elect a leader by pointing to the candidate of their choice. If they see there is not agreement, voters can change their vote by pointing at someone else, until one person clearly has a two-thirds majority.

The facilitator puts a crown or hat on the chief's head and gives him/her a large newsprint map of the area. The chief then conducts the election of the two guards in the same way and puts caps on their heads. All members of the group accept the authority of the chief and guards and show them great respect, mainly through talking only to them, bowing and giving gifts. It is extremely disrespectful to the chief and guards to talk to anyone else.

To offer gifts to anyone besides the chief is considered corruption, and anyone attempting to do so is taken to the chief and deported from the country.

The chief has control of all land. He divides up the plots on the map, leaving some land free for other use. He puts his own house wherever he wants to on the map. Foreigners and women may not own land or houses.

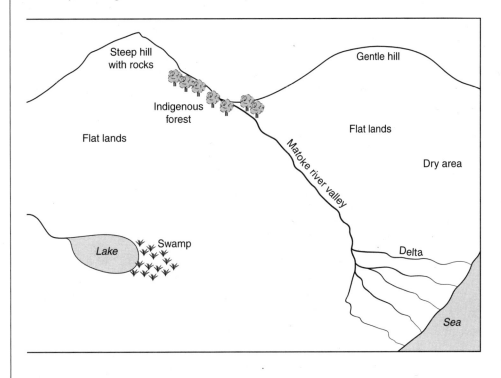

Language and communication

If the group is made up only of women or only of men, divide the group in half and indicate the women and men by wearing scarves or hats. Men and women must be clearly identifiable. The chief and guards are always men.

Bananas try to greet everyone in the group regularly and also greet all visitors. Respect is shown through use of the following gestures:

- Men greet one another by tapping their heads, looking one another in the eye and placing a friendly hand on one another's shoulder.
- Men greet women by tapping their hearts, putting their palms together and bowing. It is rude to look a woman in the eye for too long.
- Women greet one another by holding both hands, smiling into one another's eyes, and gently tapping their right cheek.
- Women greet men by tapping their heads and dropping a light curtsey. It is brazen to look men in the eye for too long, but light flirtatious glances are allowed.
- Men in the group are very sensitive if women are not treated with respect, or if women from other cultures are brazen and speak out.
- If strangers do not show respect Banana men respond by shunning the person. If the offence is more serious they take them to the chief or a guard, who reprimands them and may expel them from the land.

Rules for co-operative work projects

1. Establish your family group. Families play an important role in the Banana culture. Each person has a slip of coloured paper in their envelope. In silence, find other members of your family by finding others who have the same coloured paper: pink, blue, green and yellow, etc. (at least three, preferably four people in each family). Each family chooses an area of the room to represent their home.

2. Showing respect to the chief. The first task of each family is to show their respect to the chief and support of the village by bringing things to the chief. The family finds and takes to the chief the following symbols:

3 small leafy twigs	[planting trees]
3 pebbles	[hauling stones]
3 spoonfuls of earth	[digging]
3 dry sticks	[collecting firewood]
3 spoonfuls of water in a small container	[carrying water]

When the family have brought all these to the chief he gives them a piece of land. He gives them some choice but makes the final decisions about land allocation himself. He then gives each family a total of ten cards marked 'C' meaning community work and each person one card marked 'F-H' meaning family house work. The chief also gives each family two community projects which they joyfully accept. (The chief gives out the same three or four community project 'cards' to each family. This is to ensure that the families begin working together on some common projects.) It is customary to give the chief a gift at this time. The guards should help the chief to make sure people are served promptly and queues do not grow.

3. **Purpose and use of the cards**. Each family now has both community and family-house 'work cards' and community project cards. Each person in

the family is then given several 'C' work cards and one 'F-H' work card. The family then decides which of the community work projects they would like to engage in. Each family could choose one or two projects initially.

Work hours required to do a community project or build a family house. Each community service project requires 200 community hours to complete (or 20 C cards). Each C card is worth 10 community hours. Each F-H card is worth 10 family-house building hours. It takes 50 family-house hours to complete building the house (or 5 F-H cards).

4. **Working on community projects**. Family members now go to other families, greeting them, enjoying their company, and seeing if other families are interested in doing the same community project. This is done by showing the community service cards. Each person finds a team of 3 or 4 people to work together on the same project which will require 200 hours of work (or 20 C cards) to complete. This is a very friendly exchange and people mill around the room, negotiating to get enough people to have 20 C cards working on the same community project (e.g. planting trees or running a literacy class). It is possible to give a F-H work card to a community project. The head of each family will be somewhat concerned if family members do not complete work on their own house. However, he would show a friendly concern.

5. **Completing a community project**. When work teams on one project meet, they see if they have collected 20 C cards for the same purpose. When they have, they take their cards and the community service card with the picture to the chief. The chief is very pleased and he places the picture of the service on the map. Everyone begins singing to celebrate the event. Everyone in the village comes to the chief's house and the singing and dancing begins. Soon the chief asks people to get back to work. He gives those family members who have 'spent' their community hours more C cards and another project picture.

Families meet to decide on another community project. Remember these meetings are conducted in silence but with gestures. The family could decide to spend some work on their own family-house, or have some members do community projects and some work at home. The process continues. Giving gifts to the chief at certain times is considered very courteous.

Building the family house (F-H)

It takes 50 family-house work hours (5 F-H cards) to build a family house. A family will not have enough F-H cards to complete the house (as every family size is about 3–4 members). However, they can give generously of their F-H cards to other families. If they do this, the chief sees that this family member is community spirited and gives that person, who 'worked' on another family's house, another F-H card. But remember that community projects still have priority over family houses and as it only takes 5 F-H cards to build a family house, this can be negotiated rather easily between families. The 5 F-H cards are taken to the chief by the head of the family whose house has been 'built'. Those who helped build his house also go with that family to the chief and they receive one new F-H card from the chief. The head of the family and the chief place a house on the map. Everyone is happy.

Note to the chief If all the community projects are completed and placed on the map within the time frame of the game, continue to give out more community projects and C cards.

Visitors

Each visitor is welcomed in a very friendly way by all Banana members. Someone must explain to each one, using gestures only, that before they receive permission to stay in the place they must help in the village work as all Banana members do. They must therefore bring 1 leafy twig, 1 pebble, 1 teaspoon of earth, 1 dry stick, and 1 teaspoon of water to the chief. He gives them a small white card (residence permit), along with one C card and one F-H card.

Visitors are given a few minutes to understand greeting customs. After this they are expected to be friendly and show respect to all Banana members, especially the chief, the guards and the women, and to communicate as the Bananas do.

The visitors may not buy land or build their own houses. They may be invited to stay with families. Bananas show much appreciation if visitors contribute work-hours to help build the family home or to community service projects. However, visitors are watched carefully by the guards and the whole community, and if they violate the traditional customs [e.g. talking out loud, or offering gifts to anyone but the chief or guards, failing to greet people properly or to do their share of work], they are shunned, people turn their backs on them, they may be reprimanded by the chief, or **deported**, depending on the seriousness of the offence.

These rules must not be shown or explained to visitors.

Exercise 4. Yin/Yang: life-giving and life-restricting aspects of culture

The aim of this exercise is:

- to help people become more aware that all cultures have both positive and negative elements,
- to understand that the same culture may have different life-giving and life-restricting aspects for different groups within it,
- to identify our own sub-cultures and share the life-giving and life-restricting elements within them, and
- to understand how others experience their own sub-cultures.

Procedure

1. Brainstorm with the group: What different groups exist within any one culture which may cause individuals to experience their culture in a similar way?

2. Write their suggestions on newsprint and if the following points have not been mentioned add them, giving examples: age, gender, wealth or poverty, type of education, type of work, rural or urban setting, language, religion, political experiences, contact with other cultures, etc. We call these groups sub-cultures within the wider culture.

3. Ask the participants to form **groups of four or five** from the same culture in which they share at least three of the different factors which have just been mentioned. Ask the participants to look around the room and to identify a group of three to five people with whom they share a similar background in several of the above ways; e.g. one group might be urban Zulu women over 40, another young Afrikaans speaking professional men, another young married Muslim women etc. Ask each group to state what sub-culture they represent. Remind them that one can only really understand a culture from inside it.

4. **Input on Yin/Yang**

   The Yin/Yang diagram is a very ancient Asian symbol showing the balance of opposites in the whole of reality. Prepare a copy of the diagram ahead of time on newsprint, and put it up on the wall to show the Yin/Yang symbol. Explain that some things that are life-giving for some people within a culture may be life-restricting for others; for example, some cultures give more honour to old people and young people feel their opinions are ignored, while in other cultures the youth are given much more attention and old people feel left out.

   Point out that there are green and grey areas, and explain that green is a symbol of life and grey is a symbol of ashes or cement, of lifelessness. Point out that there is a spot of grey in the green area, and a spot of green in the grey area. Ask what they think this means.

5. Each group is asked to discuss which aspects of their own culture are life-giving and which are life-restricting, life-denying, or even at times life-destroying for their own group (such as bride-burning in India, or pressure to remain slim, which causes anorexia in young women in some Western cultures). They will record these aspects of their culture using the Yin/Yang diagram.

207

a. Ask each group: 'In your sub-culture, what aspects of your own culture do you experience as life-giving, and what aspects do you experience as life-restricting?' Suggest they work in silence for a few minutes deciding what are the life-giving and what are the life-denying or life-restricting elements in the culture for them personally.

b. Ask groups to draw the Yin/Yang diagram on newsprint, colouring the life-giving area green, and the life-restricting or life-denying area grey. As they discuss these in the group ask them to record the different points that have been made, by drawing and labelling arrows into the green section of the diagram to show the life-giving elements, and into the grey section to show the life-restricting elements. The facilitator can draw a few arrows on the newsprint diagram to illustrate how this should be done.

c. Encourage them to use the diagram rather than making lists, as the visual image draws out the contrasts in the experience of the different groups during the report-back more clearly.

6. When each group has covered most of the points they can think of, ask each group to choose a spokesperson and then to come together.

7. Give each group an opportunity to put up their picture and explain how they see the life-giving and life-denying elements of their culture for their particular group. It may become very clear that men and women, young people and elders, privileged and diasadvantaged people experience the culture very differently. People may ask questions of clarification but not start a discussion until all the groups have presented their posters. Then open up the discussion for further exchange on the cultures and the effects of gender, age, background etc.

8. At the end sum up, noting again how all cultures have both positive and negative elements which affect different groups of people in different ways.

Time   Approximately 1 to 2 hours

Materials Yin/Yang diagram drawn and coloured green and grey on newsprint; newsprint, markers, tape for all groups.

SECTION THREE

Other cultures

Exercise 5. Hurts and misunderstandings

The purpose of this exercise is to bring out into the open some of the things which frequently cause pain and misunderstanding in intercultural contact. There needs to be a certain level of trust in the group before starting this process or people will be unwilling to share, but if it is well done it can greatly increase the trust between different cultural groups. Pain is often caused unintentionally by people who are unaware of the values and customs, and also of the sensitivities, of those coming from a different culture. This is particularly true of those who belong to the dominant culture, who tend to assume that everybody else thinks and feels exactly as they do.

It is important to recognize real issues of injustice existing in the society which may have affected some members of the group more than others, but it is also important to encourage people to give each other the benefit of the doubt and assume goodwill in those present if possible.

Procedure

1. Ask the participants to form **groups of three**, if possible all coming from different cultures. They should try to choose people whom they may not yet know very well, but with whom they have begun to feel at ease. Each one of the three should be prepared to act as a mediator if any two of the group seem to have difficulty understanding what the other is trying to say.

2. It may be necessary to remind the group that everyone is the expert on their own feelings, so if a person says they feel hurt or humiliated when people say or do certain things, the others must accept the fact of these feelings, try to understand them, and not tell the person she should not feel that way.

3. Questions to discuss in small groups:

   a. When have you personally felt hurt or misunderstood by people in other cultures, who by their words or actions seemed to show lack of respect for you as a person or for the culture and values of your people?

   b. Do you feel your people are sometimes stereotyped in a derogatory way, or treated with lack of respect? (For example, in the past domestic workers were often referred to as 'Boy' or 'Girl', even when they were responsible adults, often with their own children or grandchildren.)

   c. What do you think are the major culture clashes operating in our situation here and now?

   d. What do we need to do to build understanding and respect for all people and for one another's cultures?

4. After 20–30 minutes ask the groups to return to the **whole group**, and give them an opportunity to share some of the insights they have gained. It is important to keep the group informal and to build up as deep a sense of trust as possible. People may recall some very painful memories and the facilitator should be very sensitive in judging when to encourage a person to share these, without putting undue pressure to speak on those who do not wish to do so.

Time   1 to 2 hours, depending on how deeply the group wants to share

Materials None.

Exercise 6. The Great Gariep: appreciation of other cultures

The aim of this exercise is to build an appreciation of diversity and to share ideas about building a common culture, enriched by the values and customs of all the different cultures in a particular area. The exercise was originally used in South Africa, where the need for healing the great divisions caused by apartheid is exceptionally urgent, but it can be adapted for many other situations. A river, growing as each tributary makes its contribution to a great life-giving watercourse, is a beautiful symbol for a process which recognizes the traditions and values of each ethnic or cultural group, but also encourages the growth of a common unifying culture for the whole nation.

The 'Gariep' was the original name of the Orange River, the major river running through Southern Africa from east to west. The use of the original Khoisan name indicates a reverence for the indigenous cultures from which the dominant Western industrialized cultures have much to learn.

Procedure

1. Ask the participants to form **groups of four to six people** from mixed cultural backgrounds and to discuss the following questions:

   a. What values, practices or customs from another culture, not your own, would you like to see included in the common culture of your country in the future?
   [The following examples can be given if the groups have difficulty getting started:
   In one workshop Africans said they would like to include the celebration of birthday parties from Western culture. Celebrating a person's birthday is an opportunity to rejoice in the existence of that person and to express appreciation of all the things that s/he contributes to the community. Whites said they would like to include the attitude of 'ubuntu', valuing a person just because they are a person, and not only because of their productivity. This also includes greater reverence for old people.]
   b. How can we celebrate and build appreciation of all the different cultures in our country?

2. Bring the **whole group** back together to share their insights. If possible encourage the whole group to plan a social evening which includes celebration of the different traditions with items contributed by everybody present. One could also invite some special groups to broaden the diversity if necessary.

Time   30 to 60 minutes

Materials   Large map of a large river and its tributaries.

Reflections. The rainbow story

This story can simply be read. However, it is much more effective if it is acted or danced with clothing or scarves in the different colours. Either one person can read the whole story as the narrator, while different people dance the roles of the different colours and Rain, or each of the eight players can read or learn by heart their own words. It has been done both very informally with minimal preparation, or rehearsed and performed for a larger group.

An informal discussion can be held afterwards using the questions:

1. What struck you particularly about this story?
2. In what way is it related to our discussion on culture?

The rainbow

Ancient people recognized the rainbow as a symbol of peace and harmony, and the ancient Hebrews recognized it as a special sign given by God that he wants all living things to live and to flourish in peace and harmony –

> all clans
> all tribes
> all colours
> all faiths
> all nations

– that between us there should be no division but mutual respect and appreciation of one another's gifts as well as of our differences. In this way we enrich one another by reflecting to one another the beauty and magnificence of God. (Genesis 9:8 – 17)

> And God said:
> 'When the rainbow appears in the clouds,
> I will remember the everlasting promise
> Between me and all living beings on earth.'

THE STORY OF THE RAINBOW (An Indian Legend)

Once upon a time, all the colours in the world started to quarrel; each claimed that she was the best, the most important, the most useful, the favourite.

Green said, 'Clearly I am the most important. I am the sign of life and hope. I was chosen for grass, tree, leaves – without me all the animals would die. Look out over the countryside and you will see that I am the majority.'

Blue interrupted, 'You only think about the Earth, but consider the sky and the sea. It is water that is the basis of life and this is drawn up by the clouds from the blue sea. The sky gives space and peace and serenity. Without my peace you would all be nothing but busybodies.'

Yellow chuckled, 'You are all so serious. I bring laughter, gaiety and warmth into the world. The sun is yellow, and the moon is yellow, the stars are yellow. Every time you look at a sunflower the whole world starts to smile. Without me there would be no fun.'

Orange started next to blow her own trumpet, 'I am the colour of health and strength. I may be scarce, but I am precious for I serve the inner needs of human life. I carry all the most important vitamins – the carrots and pumpkins – but when I fill the sky at sunrise or sunset, my beauty is so striking that no one gives another thought to any of you.'

Red could stand it no longer. He shouted out, 'I am the ruler of you all, blood, life's blood. I am the colour of danger and of bravery. I am willing to fight for a cause. I bring fire in the blood. Without me the earth would be empty as the moon. I am the colour of passion and of love; the red rose, poinsettia and poppy.'

Purple rose up to his full height. He was very tall and he spoke with great pomp, 'I am the colour of royalty and power. Kings, chiefs and bishops have always chosen me, for I am a sign of authority and wisdom. People do not question me – they listen and obey.'

Indigo spoke much more quietly than all the others, but just as determinedly, 'Think of me. I am the colour of silence. You hardly notice me, but without me, you all become superficial. I represent thought, reflection, twilight and deep waters. You need me for balance and contrast, for prayer and inner peace.'

And so the colours want on boasting, each convinced that they were the best. Their quarrelling became louder and louder. Suddenly there was a startling flash of brilliant white lightning; thunder rolled and boomed. Rain started to pour down relentlessly. The colours all crouched in fear, drawing to one another for comfort.

Then Rain spoke: 'You foolish colours, fighting among yourselves, each trying to dominate the rest. Do you not know that God made you all? Each for a special purpose, unique and different. She loves you all. She wants you all. Join hands with one another and come with me.

'She will stretch you across the sky in a great bow of colour, as a reminder that she loves you all, that you can live together in peace,

    – a promise that she is with you

    – a sign of hope for tomorrow.'

Based on an Indian legend,
written by Anne Hope, 1978

CHAPTER 5
Transforming governance

Introduction

Section One: Defining government

Section Two: Key problems for citizens to overcome

Section Three: Budget priorities and redistribution

Section Four: Developing community-government partnerships

Section Five: The fine art of lobbying

Introduction

Many countries are in a process of transition and governing structures are changing. There are many reasons for these changes. In some countries it is because of the conditions imposed by the International Monetary Fund (IMF), in other places there has been a change from military to civilian rule, or a change in the social contract with the poor.

This chapter looks at five areas of governance that are critical to local communities. The five sections follow a certain logic. However, each section stands on its own and can be used as a separate workshop.

Although there is much talk about democracy, there are few examples of an equitable sharing of power with local communities so they are able to shape their own destinies. The following exercises can enable both communities and government personnel to think through and plan the changes needed for empowerment of the people.

This chapter is based on some key assumptions which include:

- A participatory process in itself gives credibility to the outcome for the whole community. At the same time it offers opportunities for 'training' with the key stakeholders in an area.

- Even very poor communities have resources and some power to revitalize themselves. Creative partnerships can boost their level of confidence in themselves and their ability to identify the resources in their area. This in turn can unleash their energy and motivation to act.

- Poverty cannot be eliminated by government alone or by communities waiting for government to act. Government is bureaucratic, slow and cumbersome. Partnerships with pooled resources will enable community-centred, people-driven development. This can occur in coalitions within civil society or partnerships between civil society and government.

- Women are the biggest consumers of resources and are the hardest hit by the lack of facilities in rural areas. This not only impacts further on their participation, but makes them the best consultants regarding community needs. Therefore, women should make up at least 50% of community representatives at workshops and meetings.

- Economic growth will not bring jobs to many of the marginalized in society. Facing the fact that there will continue to be 'jobless growth', new models of self-reliance must become part of the work of development.

- Local government officials and councillors need to clarify their own roles and policies with regard to their future work with communities. A number of agencies are in real difficulty because they have neither clarified their relationships with each other nor established clear public policy positions. This leads to unnecessary organizational conflict and confusion of roles.

- Public policy formation without input by communities is a recipe for failure. The process for input must be carefully designed, not raising false expectations yet at the same time genuinely serving to bring government closer to people.

SECTION ONE

Defining government

> **Governments are public instruments created by, for and with the people of a nation to protect and enhance the well-being of each individual and all communities.**

> **Governance involves the exercise of power to manage the affairs of a nation, organization or group.**

Most people in any country have mixed feelings about government. People may feel positive, negative, proud, fearful, ambivalent, sceptical, apathetic, or distant. But everyone has some opinion about government. One of the tasks of community development programmes is to clarify:

- How we view government;
- Our own mental blocks in working with government;
- An analysis of the financial holds on governments (who 'owns' a government);
- How we can work to form partnerships with government;
- How to 'lobby'.

This section is about linking civil society with government through appropriate structures and functions. Later in this chapter we will define civil society, which includes: non-governmental organizations (NGOs), community based organizations (CBOs), trade unions, religious organizations and popular movements.

Modern society has become so complex that governing bodies (which make up a government) become further and further removed from the everyday lives of the people. Meeting basic needs is a constant necessity, and no government in the world can do this on its own. Some government agencies try to respond to certain needs such as migration from rural to urban areas. Yet we have seen how government bodies can sometimes block rather than serve the interests of the people – even with the best of intentions.

Exercise 1. **A warm-up**

The following exercise is to help a group at the beginning of a workshop to focus on their relationship to government(s) at different levels.

Procedure

1. Ask participants to get into **pairs** and to list the various elements of government that they know or have heard about at all levels. Then brainstorm this list on newsprint in the **whole group**.

2. Now ask participants to think silently about how they feel about:

    - Local government;
    - Provincial government;
    - National government.

    Ask each one to write down a few words about each level of government.

3. Then ask each participant to draw a diagram (or picture). They must first draw themselves and then place the different elements of government in the picture. They start with those elements of government they know best and then move to those parts they know least.

4. Put the participants in **groups of four** and ask them in these small groups to share how they feel about different levels of government and their pictures.

5. When they have all shared their pictures, ask the groups to discuss:

    a. What do your pictures mean to you as a group?
    b. If you are working closely with some part of government, what makes that possible?
    c. Why do you feel 'far away' from some other part of government?
    d. What does this mean for us in our communities?

6. Share responses to these last questions (a–d) in the **whole group** and write up on newsprint those key words that you want to come back to later in the whole workshop.

Time   1 to 1½ hours

Materials   Paper, crayons, newsprint, markers and tape.

Exercise 2. A case study

Procedure

1. Ask participants to get into **groups of five**. Have one person read the case study about government out loud to their small group. The group then discusses the following (or similar) questions which have been written up on newsprint.

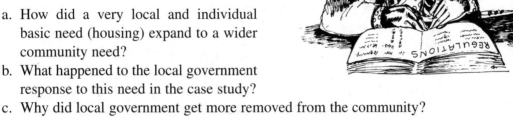

2. Suggested discussion questions:

   a. How did a very local and individual basic need (housing) expand to a wider community need?
   b. What happened to the local government response to this need in the case study?
   c. Why did local government get more removed from the community?
   d. What were the key problems in providing housing in this community?
   e. What resources are needed to solve the housing problem?
   f. What is the role of:

      - Government decision-makers;
      - Government departments;
      - The local community?

   g. Who needs to take initiative in solving the problem?

3. In the **whole group**, share the responses to each question.

Time   1½ hours

Materials   Copies of the case study about government for each participant. Questions on newsprint.

A case study about government

In a country that was hit by a drought and few opportunities for young people, thousands of people fled to a major city in search of employment. The city was overcrowded and most people had to live on the streets or build shacks in open spaces. The voters and taxpayers of that city agreed that something needed to be done. Elected officials became overwhelmed by the task of finding or building houses and creating jobs for more than a half million new residents of the city. Government staff responsible for housing said they did not have the funds to build public housing for so many people and within the safety and health standards regulations.

Some community groups started pushing for different solutions such as temporary electricity or sanitation and water facilities to be built on the land where they had built their own shacks. An experimental programme was agreed in one area by the local government officials for a squatter community to improve their shacks. Government hired people to supervise the construction of water and sanitation systems, and roads in the area. As time went on, new regulations were developed and more staff were hired to ensure that land was used properly and safety and health standards adhered to. New residents had to apply for use of land.

More people continued to flock to the city and were living on the streets and had an endless search for housing. Mothers were seen standing in long queues at the social welfare service centres or housing offices and were told they could not build anything because of regulations. The housing crisis increased and city officials did not know what to do.

Exercise 3. Shape of our reality

This is a very stimulating exercise which helps people to share their perceptions of the most important things happening in the world, or their own world. (The original exercise, called 'Shape of the World' can be found in Chapter 9 of *Training for Transformation* Book III.) It can be adapted to look at a much smaller reality – a neighbourhood, district, city or province in this case. It develops interest in the forces which are changing our world, for better or for worse, and can clarify assumptions which will inform a strategic plan for the future.

It may be advisable to do a listening exercise (see, for example, *Training for Transformation* Book II) before starting, to ensure that people try to understand each other's point of view. If the exercise is done in a spirit of respect for differences, it can lay a basis of trust in a very diverse group and provide a common experience for many types of analysis later in a workshop. If members of the group you are working with come from very different backgrounds, the sharing can stretch people's insights through the variety of perceptions.

If members of the group come from similar backgrounds, besides doing a listening exercise it may be important to include some input on the situation in their area to help ground perceptions in reality. (For example, in one area there could be a perception of 'high crime' when in fact police statistics show the crime rate to be low. Or the group may be using only official data on the housing backlog while community-based groups may have more realistic numbers of houses needed.)

Procedure

Ask the participants to form mixed **groups of five** and then to sit around tables where newsprint, markers, crayons and individual papers are provided. The facilitator explains that there are five steps in the exercise. Each step is explained, one at a time, and the facilitator illustrates each step on newsprint on the wall.

1. Main illustration

    a. Ask each person to draw a circle on a plain piece of paper. Explain that this circle represents the world in which the participants live.
    b. Ask each person to draw a picture, symbol, illustration or diagram of the world (nation, province, district, town or neighbourhood) in the circle. 'What are the main features (main themes) you would emphasize?' Give time for each person to make their own drawing.
    c. Ask participants to share what they were trying to express in their drawing in their small group.
    d. Then ask each group to make a common picture on newsprint including everyone's ideas. Either plan together a new drawing which includes all the ideas or draw different ideas in different parts of the circle. (Warn them not to make the circle on newsprint too large, in order to leave space outside the circle for writing on later.)

2. Future new impacts

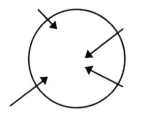

    a. Ask each small group to discuss: 'What do you believe is having an impact on the world (nation, province) now, and will continue to affect it strongly, over the next few years?'
    b. Show this by putting arrows into the circle and labelling them. Arrows going directly into the centre show the most impact, while arrows not reaching the centre describe a more limited impact.

3. Influences dying out

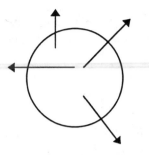

a. When the small groups have finished this task, ask each small group: 'What forces or influences which have been strong are dying out in the world (nation, province) now and will continue to do so in the next few years?'

b. Again, they show this on their group picture by using arrows pointing out of the circle and labelling them. Arrows leaving from the centre represent important influences dying out, while arrows leaving from less central parts of the circle describe weaker influences fading away.

4. Long-range impact

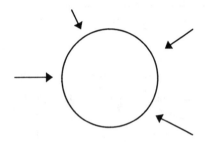

a. When the small groups have finished the above task, ask each group: 'What things do you believe will one day have an impact on the world (nation, province) but are now five or ten years, or more, away?'

b. Show these by arrows next to the circle and label them.

5. Implications

a. When all the above tasks are completed, ask each person to reflect quietly and write on: 'What is the major insight this process has given me?' (Or, what does this mean to me in relation to what I expect from government and from civil society?)

b. After about 5 minutes of quiet time, ask the participants to discuss their points in their small groups and then write on newsprint a summary of the insights and implications they have discussed.

c. Share these implications in the **whole group**. This can be a very useful basis for further work in the group. Each group is asked to put up their newsprint and participants can then walk around looking at each newsprint, asking questions as they go.

Time   About 2½ to 3 hours

Materials   Newsprint, markers, crayons, tape, individual paper, tables for groups to work at.

Input on governance*

(The input on governance can be a summary of issues that participants themselves have brought up after using any of the above exercises.)

Governments are public instruments created by, for and with the people of a nation to protect and enhance the well-being of each individual and all communities. Governance involves the exercise of political power to manage a nation's affairs. Governance can be seen in three ways:

- Governments operate on different 'levels': central, provincial and local;
- Governments operate through public institutions such as parliaments or councils, judiciary, laws, courts and police;
- Civil society can direct the energies of people to meet their own needs, either directly through self-help groups or by pressuring public institutions to respond to their needs.

Governance operates through:

- Formal and informal rules;
- Application of these rules by different social actors and organizations. Important questions in this regard include:
  - Is governance evaluated by outcomes and measurable goals?
  - To whom are individuals and organizations (in and outside government) held accountable?
  - What mechanisms are used to established accountability?
  - Is the accountability structure transparent and open?

Governance depends on:

- The type of political authority and its legitimacy;
- The practice of leadership by example;
- The system of formal and informal rules;
- The interaction between organizations of civil society and political institutions.

Symptoms of non-functional government in society:

(this can be brainstormed by the group)

- Poor services;
- Failure to take decisions and implement policies;
- Poor financial management and lack of control over the budgets;
- Use of public resources by private individuals;
- Arbitrary application of laws and rules;
- Excessive rules and regulations which discourage creativity and community initiatives;
- Excessive rules and regulations which discourage public servants from responding to community needs and can lead to corruption and apathy;
- Non-transparent decision-making;
- Resources allocated to 'special interest groups' rather than being targeted to development needs;
- Ownership and control of decisions not in the hands of the people.

Key elements of good government:

- Political legitimacy and accountability that is transparent;
- Freedom of association and participation of people in key decisions affecting their lives;
- Fair, accessible and reliable judicial systems;
- Public servant accountability, evaluations and transparency;
- Freedom of information and expression;
- Effective and efficient public service management;
- Co-operation with civil society organizations.

---

* This summary is adapted from: *Governance, Public Sector Management and Sustainable Human Development: A UNDP Strategy Paper*, October 1994.

Exercise 4. **Clarifying the purpose of government**

People both within and outside government need to clarify the purpose of government. Different people have very different expectations of government. Some people believe that government intrusion in their lives should be limited as much as possible. Others believe that the government should be active in ensuring fair distribution of resources and services. Businesses often resist regulation by government of how they operate, while workers often want government intervention to protect them from unfair labour practices and arbitrary actions of employers.

This exercise is a warm-up to help groups to think about why government exists.

Procedure

1. Ask participants to discuss the following statement (written on newsprint) in **groups of three**. Ask if they agree or disagree with the statement, and how they would change it.

> **The purpose of government is to protect individual freedom and the rights of all the people in their nation. It is NOT the purpose of government to enhance their economic well-being.**

2. In the whole group, discuss the different alternatives and try to build consensus.

> **Input**
>
> We all make up government. However, different people have different roles to play. Democracy is built on the idea that people should have a voice in the decisions that affect their lives. But how people can express that voice varies. The Western style of democracy has been mainly practised through representation. Elections are held to find the leaders who 'represent' the people from their particular geographic area.

Time   ½ to 1 hour

Materials   Statement written on newsprint.

Exercise 5. Questionnaire: key choices

The questionnaire for this exercise can be duplicated for each participant to use for discussion. You will note that the questionnaire is in two parts. You may wish to hold two separate discussion sessions or have all the questions discussed over a period of one day. This questionnaire has been tested with NGO leaders and government officials. It is designed for all sectors of a society.

Procedure

1. The aim of this session is to clarify for ourselves the purpose of government. Ask everyone to find 4 other people and form **groups of five**. Try not to let any group become larger than 5 people. Ask them to find chairs and be seated. Hand out the Purpose of Government Questionnaire.

2. Read the instructions at the top of the questionnaire.

3. Tell participants they will have about 5 minutes in silence to complete the questionnaire. Explain that they will first complete the questionnaire as individuals and then later as a group.

4. When participants have completed their individual work, go over the instructions for group discussion found at the end of the questionnaire. Remind the small groups that they have 45 minutes to try to come to consensus and to discuss the consequences of their choices.

5. After about 45 minutes, give the group a short break. Ask one person from each group to come to the front during this break to record their 1st and 2nd choices for each question on newsprint.

6. Bring the **whole group** back together. Circle with red pen where there appears to be consensus. With each question, ask the group, 'It seems we agree on this. Do you agree, can we move on?'

7. At the end, summarize where the whole group has been in agreement and where there are areas of difference. Discuss in the whole group those questions where there are differences and **how they could compromise** to come to an agreement. Remind the group that a compromise often means 'I (we) can live with this compromise'.

8. Summarize the 'purpose of government' from what the participants have said and from the inputs found in Exercise 4 and in this exercise.

Time   About 2 hours

Materials   A copy of the questionnaire for each participant, newsprint, markers.

223

Alternative design for a mixed group from civil society and government

If some participants come from government and some from civil society, it can be very instructive to separate them into different small groups (e.g. only NGOs in some small groups and only government personnel in other small groups). Again, use groups of no more than 5 participants. Then when you record their small group answers on newsprint, use different coloured markers for government and civil society. If differences between them are based on whether they are in or outside of government, it will be clear. Discuss what these differences mean and how they could be resolved.

Input on the purpose of government

The purposes of government include the following:

1. Government does that which individuals are not able to do for themselves (like building roads or hospitals, providing defence or schools);

2. Government provides these services from public money (through taxes) and thus there are limits to what it can provide;

3. Citizen input on priorities for the community is critical so that there is a sharing of responsibility for the services which are for the common good;

4. Government is to ensure that services are equitably distributed;

5. Decisions about priorities and services which most affect local communities must be decided with some mechanism of citizen input.

The purpose of government can also be put this way: government should empower people rather than marginalize them. Government structures should provide for people's participation in decisions that affect them. Sustainable human development is pro-poor, pro-jobs, pro-women, and pro-children.*

Suggested discussion questions:

a. Do we agree with these purposes of government? Why or why not?
b. What would we add? What would we change?

---

* UNDP Strategy Paper, October 1994.

SUGGESTED DESIGN FOR A WORKSHOP FOR SECTION ONE

- Introduction to workshop on government
- Warm-up exercise on what is government
- Case study on problems of government responding to needs
- 'Shape of our Reality' to begin defining community needs
- Clarifying purpose of government
- Key choices of government
- Inputs (two of 10 minutes each)

(Breaks and meals would come between exercises.)

Government: Key Choices
Purpose of Government Questionnaire

Public debate about the role of government is critical to the health of a nation. However, these debates are riddled with conflicting values which cannot be resolved by simply reading more or going to school. We all need to wrestle with the 'trade-offs' and come to some resolution. The aim of this questionnaire is to spark discussion, not to give right or wrong answers.

Instructions

For each of the following questions, rank the choices presented to you. Place a number 1 beside your first choice, a number 2 by your second choice, etc.

Example: Because the government has limited money, it is the purpose of government to provide:

Individual ranking		Group ranking
_____	a. free quality primary education for everyone.	_____
_____	b. free quality primary and secondary education for everyone, even if it would mean less hospital care for all of our citizens.	_____
_____	c. free quality education from primary through university or vocational schools for everyone, even if it would mean less hospital care and higher taxes for everyone.	_____

You will have a few minutes by yourself to answer these questions in silence. Put your 1, 2, 3 in the space at the left marked 'Individual Ranking.'

PURPOSE OF GOVERNMENT

1. Which of the following statements comes *closest to your belief* about services to communities? (Put in rank order)

Individual ranking		Group ranking
_____	a. Community services (like water, sanitation, roads, electricity, rubbish collection, parks, public transport, etc.) are the right of every person and it is the role of government to see that all have access to these services, regardless of their ability to pay.	_____
_____	b. Community services should be available to individuals as something to be purchased from private companies with little government regulation.	_____
_____	c. Community services are for people who pay for those services, and government needs to find ways to provide minimum services for those who cannot pay for the services.	_____

2. Creating new jobs and the growth of our economy are both critical to our future. If you were in charge, what would be your rank order of priority?

Individual ranking **Group ranking**

_____ a. Encourage businesses to create more jobs (by having them pay less taxes). _____

_____ b. Create jobs on public programmes (like building roads, collecting rubbish more often, doubling the number of teachers) with our tax money paying for these increased expenses. _____

_____ c. Encourage individuals to start small businesses by offering low interest loans, management training and markets for their products. _____

3. In rank order, what do you see as the main purpose of central government?

Individual ranking **Group ranking**

_____ a. Protecting individual freedom and ensuring everyone has basic human rights. _____

_____ b. Protecting individual property. _____

_____ c. Ensuring that the benefits of the economy are distributed equitably. _____

_____ d. Ensuring that the poor, women, youth and unemployed have more services and opportunities than those with high incomes. _____

REPRESENTATIVE VERSUS PARTICIPATORY GOVERNMENT

4. Education is a key to the future of our country. Rank **who you prefer to make the decisions** about education priorities and direction.

Individual ranking **Group ranking**

_____ a. Provincial and national government officials. _____

_____ b. A board of community representatives made up of parents, students, teachers, experts and government officials. _____

_____ c. Educators and experts in the education field. _____

5. Who do you believe should decide on priorities for services to our community? (Such as housing, roads, water, sanitation, adult basic education.) Put a number 1 next to the statement you most agree with, a number 2 to the next one, and so forth.

Individual ranking   **Group ranking**

_____ a. It is best to leave it up to the experts in universities and the business community who know how to plan and get things done. _____

_____ b. These priorities are of such importance that we cannot leave it only to experts and government officials. People must get organized to make their voices heard. _____

_____ c. Our elected representatives and city planners are informed about community priorities and can be trusted to make the right decisions for us. _____

6. Taxes are the main way for government to receive money. The way in which taxes are collected can affect whether the economy will create jobs and also how fairly different income groups will contribute to government spending. Rank who you prefer to make decisions about who should pay what amount of taxes.

Individual ranking   **Group ranking**

_____ a. Provincial and national government officials. _____

_____ b. A board of community representatives made up of taxpayers at all levels, economists and government officials. _____

_____ c. Experts in the fields of economics and taxes. _____

Instructions for discussion

In your small group, you will now have about 45 minutes to do two tasks:

1. Begin with the first question and move down the list, discussing your choices.

   Try to come to consensus as a group on each question. If in conflict, ask each other 'What can you (we) live with?' If consensus is not possible, record the majority opinion. After you have reached a group decision, mark your group choice in the right-hand column.

2. Stop after each question and ask yourselves, as a group: 'What are the consequences of our choice?' Then move to the next question.

Key problems for citizens to overcome

Communities face particular problems inside themselves when dealing with government. These problems include:

- apathy
- alienation
- dependency
- leadership
- powerlessness

The following exercises are important for groups to work on before attempting to develop partnerships with government.

Exercise 6. Apathy

One of the main behaviour patterns of the oppressed is apathy. 'The way things are now is the way it will always be,' is a common theme of the poorest of the poor. There is little time to think outside the present reality. The following exercise, particularly when combined with the first exercise in Section Four of this chapter, is a helpful tool for moving a group out of apathy.

The Paulo Freire methods of developing critical consciousness are all based on breaking the cycle of silence (see *Training for Transformation*, Book I).

Procedure

1. Give a copy of the Speed bumps case study to each participant.

2. Ask participants to form **groups of four** and have them read this case study out loud to each other and discuss the following questions:

   a. What happened in this community over 10 years?
   b. Why did the community not get speed bumps?
   c. What were the problems within government?
   d. What were the problems within the community?
   e. Why do communities not act on their own behalf?

3. In the whole group ask participants to share their responses to these questions and particularly the responses to the last question. The key to breaking apathy is helping leadership to act on those things about which people have strong feelings. Tell the group that you will come back to their understanding of why 'communities do not act' later.

Time   1 to 1½ hours

Materials   Copies of the case study, questions on newsprint, newsprint, markers and tape.

Speed bumps case study

In a poor area of a major city, low-income people had come to notice that on the main street through the area, cars and trucks were driving very fast. Residents were very concerned about the safety of their children. Some community people complained to the city council but nothing was done. Several years later, some new residents came to the area and they also complained. They suggested to the city council that speed bumps be put on that road. Nothing was done. After 10 years, no speed bumps had been installed. When community members were asked, they complained that you could not get anything out of the city council. That was the way things were in this area.

Exercise 7. Alienation

Book I of *Training for Transformation* (page 95) describes a play called the 'CDO play' which is a useful tool for exploring how different styles of leadership lead to alienation. Another method is to use the two pictures showing different styles of decision-making.

Procedure

1. Ask participants to form **groups of four or five** people.

2. Give each group a copy of the two pictures of different styles of leadership.

3. Ask the groups to look at the two pictures and discuss the questions.

4. Ask the **whole group** to think about who they know in government with whom they could discuss this. Who will set up a meeting with the person and when?

5. Share the diagram and analysis of government decision-making.

6. After exploring the diagram and analysis with the whole group, ask people to get into **groups of five** and complete the following two tasks:

   a. Draw a different diagram to show an alternative way of decision-making which would include local people;
   b. What would be the first step you could take to encourage citizens to give input into decisions affecting their community?

   In the **whole group** ask participants to share responses.

Time   About 1 hour

Materials   Draw the diagram on how government decisions are made and write the analysis of decisions on newsprint before the workshop. Handout with two pictures and questions.

a. What do you see in the first picture? What do you think is the reaction of the people to this leader and what will be the long-term effects on them?

b. What is happening in the second picture? How is the behaviour of the government official different? Who do you think is the official?

c. Does this happen in our situation and, if so, how does it happen? What are the main places where decisions are taken that affect our own community?

d. Make a list of the types of government decisions on which you would like to have community input.

e. Look at those types of decisions. Now, what structures (rules) about how government makes those decisions could be put into law?

HOW DECISIONS ARE USUALLY MADE BY GOVERNMENTS

Cabinet
Ministers/Deputies/Director-Generals
(final authority over policies and programmes)

↓↓↓

Ministries
Civil servants and consultants/experts
(develop the policies and programmes for their ministers)

↓↓↓

Elected officials
Parliaments and committees
(usually ratify plans made by the ministries)

↓↓↓

Implementation
(department civil servants or businesses contracted to do the job)

ANALYSIS OF DECISIONS (example on roads)

It is important that groups and officials step back from decisions and ask themselves:

a. Economic interests

Who gets the roads?
Who gets the contracts to build the roads?
Are public works employees competing for union jobs to build the roads?

b. Political interests

Who decides?
What are the decision-making structures?
Are these structures transparent, open, accessible?

c. Values

What are the public reasons given to justify the decisions taken?

Exercise 8. Dependency (The River Code)

The issue of dependence has been written about at length. The first three books of *Training for Transformation* are mainly on adapting Paulo Freire's work on breaking apathy in a community. However, new layers of dependency have grown in communities. The following play is an adaptation of the River Code found in *Training for Transformation* Book I.

Procedure

1. Ask seven participants who come early to a workshop (or at a tea break) to practise for this play. Read the play to them and then have them practise the play in a place away from the other participants.

Dependency play

This is a mime or a play without words. Two lines fairly wide apart are drawn on the floor in chalk to represent the banks of a river. String can be used instead if one does not want to draw on the floor. Pieces of paper are used to represent stepping stones in the river and an island (a piece of newsprint) is put in the middle of the river.

Seven people are needed for the play.
Each person has a large label:
- a businessman
- an educated privileged person
- a government official
- three community people
- an NGO person

The community people are to one side and are pretending to talk to one another. The businessman goes to the river, sees the stones and confidently walks across the river to the other side and then goes and sits down. The educated person goes to the river and does the same thing. The government official goes to the river and again, does the same thing. The three community people, scratch their heads, talk and point at the river but seem unclear on how to proceed. They try to cross (but not at the stepping stones) and they fail.

The NGO person comes up to them and sees their difficulty. The NGO person leads them to the river and shows them the stepping stones. S/he encourages them to step on the stones but they are afraid, so s/he agrees to take one on her back. By the time she gets to the middle of the river, the person on her back seems very heavy and she has become tired, so she puts the person on the little island.

The NGO person goes back to fetch the other two people who also want to climb on her back. The NGO person refuses. Instead she takes their hands and encourages them to step on the stones themselves. Halfway across these two people start to manage alone. These two community people both cross the river and the NGO person also crosses the river. When they get to the other side, they are very pleased with themselves and they walk off together, completely forgetting about the first person sitting alone on the island. He tries to get their attention, but they do not notice his frantic gestures for help.

End of play.

---

2. Ask the whole group to discuss the following questions:

   a. What happened in the play?
   b. Why could the businessman easily get over the river?
      Why could the educated person get over the river?
      Why could the government official get over the river?
   c. What does the river represent in this play?
   d. What did the community people feel before they tried to cross the river? What did they feel after they tried on their own and failed?
   e. What happened when the NGO person carried one person? When the NGO person helped the other people?

3. Ask people to form **groups of five** and ask them to discuss the following questions (putting the questions on newsprint).

   a. What does all this mean in real life?
   b. What is the problem that this play shows?
   c. Who can solve the problem? What is the role for each person in the play?
   d. Develop a new play to show how each person could act differently, but remembering each has a different role to play in society.

4. Ask **three** of the groups to put on their new play.

5. Discuss in the **whole group** how to build self-reliance.

Input on dependency syndrome

When people have been disempowered, their own self-image is that they are not capable of doing tasks which, in fact, they can do. However, there are different types of dependency.

Dependency means to rely on someone else. It can also mean being subordinate (or under) someone else. When one is subordinate, one's confidence in oneself often turns into a belief that one must rely on others to do things for one.

Counter-dependency means that a person (or group) will always do the opposite of what any authority figure suggests. For example, if your mother suggests you wear a certain type of outfit, you will always do the opposite. You are still dependent on your mother but will counter her 'authority' no matter whether it is reasonable or not.

Independence means not being dependent on authority, not being dependent on something outside oneself to legitimate one's being or actions. An example would be someone acting on her own, maybe taking suggestions from others, but making the decision herself and moving forward.

Interdependence is a recognition and an acting on the knowledge that there is mutual dependence in some areas of life. For example, in order to build a campaign, no single group can do all of the work and so each group is mutually dependent on other groups to co-ordinate actions. On an individual basis, no person can be totally self-sufficient in the modern world. We rely on the telephone system for the phone, or depend on the farmer to grow our food.

(**Note:** After this input, it can be very helpful to discuss in pairs how each person sees their own behaviour and also how their own organization operates with other organizations.)

Time   1½ to 2 hours

Materials   Questions and input written on newsprint before the workshop. Chalk, tape or string to make the river, and paper for the stepping stones and island.

Exercise 9. Leadership

This exercise is an adaptation of the 'CDO Play' found in Book I of *Training for Transformation.*

Procedure

1. Ask five participants who come early to a workshop (or at a tea break) to practise the following play.

Leadership play

Five community people are sitting waiting for a meeting to begin. The leader comes in and greets each person. She asks each person how they are and each speaks of a different problem which they are struggling with: a house falling down, a drunken husband, no water, bad schools. The leader hardly listens to these complaints. She is a busy person wanting to get home to other things. She sits and opens the meeting. She says that their agenda this day is about the need for a clinic in the area that a donor wishes to put in and where it should go. The leader then tells each person what they must do to organise a fund-raising day: one must collect chickens, another must organize a larger meeting on Saturday, and so on.

During this meeting, each member of the group becomes more passive. One gets sleepy, one looks out of the window, one begins to argue but gives up very quickly. Another one walks out of the room.

---

2. After the play, in the **whole group** discuss the following questions:
   a. How did the leader behave?
   b. How did the group react to the leader?
   c. What kept the group from becoming active?
   d. How can the group change the type of meetings that take place?

3. Then ask participants to form **groups of four** and discuss the following two questions:
   a. Does this happen in our situation? If so, how?
   b. Why is this happening now in our society?

4. In the **whole group**, discuss the last questions. You can summarize the discussion with the following input.

Input on national leadership

In most countries, people yearn for a leader who will get them out of their troubles. Some of us have been privileged to live in South Africa and experience the extraordinary leadership of President Nelson Mandela. His authority extends beyond borders and because he appears as if he has nothing to lose, he is able to take very unpopular stands and leads with great integrity. Most political leaders are looking to their political future and often do not have the political courage that emanates from someone like Mandela.

On the other hand, politics is often called the art of compromise. President Bill Clinton in the United States tends to listen to different sides of issues and then develop a compromise position.

Voters in the USA criticize this type of leadership because it makes the president look as if he has no 'backbone', does not stand for anything, and can be easily swayed. As societies become more complex and national economies become dependent on transnational companies who are not accountable to any government, the ability to 'govern' is questioned at all levels.

Strong moral leaders like President Mandela are very rare. Too much reliance on any one leader can have the effect of making local people apathetic and dependent. The development of structures and methods to encourage citizen input and partnerships between government and organizations of civil society needs attention. Is it even possible for countries and local communities to take control over their own destinies?

Time   1½ to 2 hours

Materials   Questions written on newsprint before the workshop.

Exercise 10. Resource empowerment

Communities have many resources. Besides the land and natural resources, community members often have many skills (for example, they may have been the very people who built roads).

Procedure

1. Return to the case study on speed bumps found in Exercise 6 in this chapter. Review the story with the group. (In a rural area you may want to use a different example. Choose a problem or issue that could be tackled if the tasks were divided up.)

2. Ask the group to form **groups of three**. Ask each group to make a list of all of the tasks needed to make 10 speed bumps on your road, including in this list questions to which you may not know the answers.

3. In the **whole group**, newsprint the list of all the tasks. In the whole group now label:

   a. What can we do ourselves? (C)
   b. What do we need from outside the community? (O)
   c. Of the things from outside the community, what do we need from government? (G)
   d. How could we plan with government to get speed bumps?

4. This is a very important discussion. The realization by community people that they themselves have the skills and resources to get what they need is a very important first step. This is not to say that self-reliance is the only way communities can move forward. But it is important to recognize that governments cannot always respond to all the needs of a community.

Time   1½ to 2 hours

Materials   Case study on speed bumps.

Exercise 11. What 'maps' are needed to find government resources?

As communities become clearer about the priorities they wish to tackle, they often discover that some of the work, skills, resources and funds needed are beyond them. If, however, they are determined to get something in their community, their skill in organizing themselves is critical. Chapter 10 in *Training for Transformation* Book 3 has many planning and organizing tools to enable groups to move forward at this stage. But groups also need information on who in government is responsible for what services, or how to access funds for specific things.

In South Africa, Schedule 4 and 5 of the Constitution give the responsibilities of different levels of government. Once one has decided which level of government (local, provincial or national) has the responsibility for a specific function, then the search begins.

Procedure for finding the person who is responsible for a particular area

1. The most important factor in getting what you need is NOT to give up. It may take 15 telephone calls or 100 telephone calls. The point is, never give up.

2. You must have a telephone and one or two telephone numbers of the department you expect to deal with.

3. Before you call, write down what information you are seeking and have a short speech formulated in your mind. For example, 'I am calling for the Sizanani Action Group and we want to apply for a grant to build 20 houses. What is the phone number of the person I need to speak with and what is his/her name?' You may have to say this same speech 20 times before you get to the person you want. Along the way, ask if there is more than one person dealing with this issue, because the first name they give you might be a person who is on leave for four weeks.

4. Once you reach the person you need to speak with, you need to have another speech ready. Introduce yourself and the issue you want addressed. If the response is that there are forms you will need to fill out, or some papers you need, ask where you can personally pick up the forms and who on the staff helps groups to fill out such forms. This is their job. Insist on picking up the forms directly. (You can get the forms posted to you, but often this can mean a delay of months.)

5. Make an appointment with the person who will help your group fill in the forms. If the person is coming to you, have at least three or four community members present. If you must go to the person in the department, take three or four people with you. This is to ensure that you all can understand clearly what is needed.

6. Report back all findings from your contact with different departments to your whole group or organization. Each time you have more information, it is very important to report the information back. This is called accountability.

Note Advice offices can be a very good resource to help your group. Use them to 'find your way' through the bureaucracy.

Time   One week: this is an in-service training programme

Materials   Telephone, paper and pens.

SECTION THREE

Budget priorities and redistribution

'How you spend your money will tell you what your priorities are.' This statement is true both for individuals and for governments. If a government spend most of its budget on the military and the police, we know that it values security and law and order above other human needs. If most of its tax money is spent on job creation, training and education, we know that it places a high value on human and social development.

In South Africa, more than 35% of all spending is done by government. Most of the money that the government gets is from the people through taxes. How it spends the taxpayers' money will affect the economy. For example, in 1999 the government spent about 20% of its budget on education and 1.8% on housing. If the government decided to reverse those spending priorities and put 20% of the money into housing, this would dramatically change the economy of the country. Massive numbers of teachers would have to be retrained as builders, plumbers, or electricians.

The priorities of government spending reveal its values

Governments receive most of their money through taxes. In South Africa, there are six main types of national taxes:

- Individual income tax (Pay As You Earn – PAYE);
- Value Added Tax (VAT);
- Import tax;
- 'Sin tax' (on tobacco, liquor and fuels);
- Corporate tax;
- Property tax.

The tax you pay if you own a house is called 'rates' and that tax is paid directly to the local government for services.

It is important to realize that all the tax money the government receives is our money. Even unemployed people pay taxes through VAT or 'sin taxes'. This means that the government is actually 'owned' by the people. Government workers are our employees. We pay them and they are to be of service to us. They are accountable to all the people.

This section is a brief introduction to a one-day workshop called the Budget Game, developed by Sally Timmel. The workshop is aimed at helping ordinary people understand how the government works, how it sets priorities, how and where it spends its money, how the tax system is set up and how people can try to make inputs into budget priorities.

A. The Budget Game*

The one-day workshop called The Budget Game is a simulation exercise. (A simulation is taking a part of reality or a situation and reducing it into a shorter time and space in order to experience the larger reality.) Participants become a ministry for the day. In groups of about 5 participants, they receive and discuss one-page materials on their ministry, then on taxes, on the public debt, and possible action steps. They attend 'Cabinet' meetings to discuss cutting different budgets or raising taxes. The entire Budget Game is based on real numbers and facts.

More than 3000 people have been through budget workshops in South Africa. The outcomes they report include increased understanding of how government works; much more sympathy about the decisions and hard work that government has to do; and greater understanding of how budgets work. Evaluations done six months after participants attended budget workshops show that the greatest application for many was a better understanding of their own organizational budgets.

The Budget Game has five steps:

1. Understanding how a budget works by exploring a household budget and then examining the national budget for the current year;

2. Focusing on the needs of the country and priorities of key ministries (there are 11 sectors in the game but usually only 5–6 priorities are chosen by the group);

3. Looking at the difficult choices between departments (a summary of national budget which lists all departments and their total budget line);

4. Exploring how the tax structure works, the public debt, and the limits of government money (the six methods of taxation and several pages on the debt);

5. Focusing on the budgeting process and what actions communities can take in the future (an input on the budget process, partnerships and the Action Planning Tool).

What follows are four examples of materials for the Budget Game. All the numbers and calculations have been carefully researched and must be accurate. Information can be gathered directly from the Ministries and national departments. It can take a minimum of three months to collect enough data of the right kind for a Budget Game.

---

* Acknowledgement is given to The Budget Project, UCT, where Sally Timmel first developed the Budget Game.

EXAMPLE:

Housing

THE NEED The estimates of the housing shortfall range from 1.2 million to 3.5 million. New houses needed each year because of migration to cities are 198 000–328 000.

Cost to build:	
• one site and service (toilet and water)	8 000–15 000
• 4 rooms self-built house (without water/toilet)	9 100–10 130
• 4 rooms commercially built house (no water/toilet)	30 000–45 000

The number of people living in squatter communities is estimated at 10–12 million. The number of houses built with subsidies increased at the end of 1996 to 10 000 units per month being approved. By September 1996, 99 227 subsidies were paid out and 317 000 subsidies approved. Most funds have been given to the provinces but only 21% of the 1995/96 budget was spent.

Cost to meet housing backlog with self-built houses	**R 16.0 billion**
(To build 1.2 million self-built houses with sanitation)	
Cost to meet backlog with commercially built houses	**R 36.0 billion**
Amount in 1999/2000 national budget	**R 3.6 billion**

(this includes rollovers (money not spent) from the last two years)

POLICY DIRECTION The housing policy that was developed was for government to give subsidies to first-time homeowners. Subsidies are given after a house (or site and service) is built which means the family needs to have upfront money before building. The amount of subsidy depends on the level of monthly income:

family income of R 800 or less	R 15 000 subsidy
family income of R 1500 or less	R 12 000 subsidy
family income of R 2500 or less	R 7 500 subsidy
family income of R 3500 or less	R 5 000 subsidy

There are three kinds of subsidies:

a. for commercial developers which the government expects will be the main way of building houses;

b. for individuals who must apply for the subsidy through a bank. Banks have declared that anyone may apply for a loan of no less than R10,000, at present interest rate of 18% depending on the size of the loan. People must show that they have saved money each month;

c. for institutions (e.g. housing associations and co-operatives). An institution usually has to prove that each member is able to pay and each person has to complete a 5-page application.

On 27 February 1996, the South African Federation of Homeless People received R10 million to build houses. The federation is made up of 850 saving and credit associations (roughly 60 000 people) who have shown they can save: 98% of their members repaid their loans. They demonstrated to government their ability to save and are now in a position to build houses. (Sources: People's Dialogue, White Paper on Housing, 1999/2000 Budget.)

TASK: What would be the most effective way of providing houses for the homeless as soon as possible? How could this be funded?

EXAMPLE:

Value Added Tax (VAT)

Total amount the government expects to receive from VAT   R40.3 billion
The estimates of money received from VAT (1994/95)

1. Housing   11.4 billion
2. Food   6.0 billion
3. Transport   2.2 billion
4. Recreation   1.9 billion
5. Medical   1.9 billion
6. Clothing   1.8 billion
7. Furniture and equipment   1.5 billion
8. Fuel and power   1.2 billion
9. Insurance   1.0 billion
10. Personal care   0.9 billion

BACKGROUND

VAT is a regressive tax. A regressive tax is where no matter what the size of a person's income, everyone pays the same rate of tax. For example, no matter what your income, everyone pays the same amount of VAT on food or clothes. It is called 'regressive' (or backwards) because it taxes all people at the same rate. This is different from a 'progressive' tax which is where the portion paid increases with one's income. Individual income tax is 'progressive'. The more one earns, the larger proportion of tax one pays.

The poorest people in South Africa, who form 53% of the population, account for less than 10% of all buying of goods and services. This is in contrast to the top 5.8% of the population which accounts for over 40% of all consumption. However, the poor consume more basic goods in relation to their income than high income people (RDP report, 1995). The poorest 20% of the population spend 9% of their income on VAT, while the top 20% spend about 5% of their income on VAT (Women's Budget Initiative, 1996).

INCREASING VAT

VAT was increased dramatically in 1992. At that time it was said it would only be used as a way of taxing for five years. It is now seen as one of the easiest ways of collecting revenue.

Increasing VAT from 14% to 15% would bring in about R500 million.

The government estimates that about R20 billion is not collected each year from all types of taxes and about R5 billion of this is from VAT which is not collected from all businesses in the country.

(Sources: RDP Report, 1995, Unit for Fiscal Analysis, The Budget Review, 1996.)

TASK: Should VAT be increased or decreased? If yes, on which items and why?
If not, why not?

EXAMPLE:

Lower payments on the public debt

	Public Debt	Interest Payments
1997/98	R308 billion	R39.6 billion
1996/97	R288 billion	R41.0 billion
1995/96	R263 billion	R28.4 billion

Major lenders to the South African government are:

* The Public Investment Commission   40%
  (the non-profit institution that administers civil servants' pensions)
* Private insurers, banks, private pension funds   27%
* Reserve Bank   4%
* Overseas lenders   5%
* Others including households, private business and charities   24%

In 1996/97, South Africa received R345 million in loans from the IMF and for 1997/8, South Africa received R1.38 billion.

FUTURE DEBT It is estimated that if the economy grows as expected, interest rates and inflation remain the same, the following could happen to the debt:

Year	Interest Costs	Total Debt
1998	R46.0 billion	R333 billion
1999	R50.3 billion	R359 billion
2000	R54.1 billion	R384 billion

Can the interest payments be changed? Some argue that cancelling the apartheid debt would give South Africa a very poor credit rating and the government would struggle to get loans in the future. They also say that cancelling the debt would hurt pensioners.

However, poor pensioners do not have private pensions. They receive their pension directly from the Ministry of Welfare. Civil service pensioners receive their pensions from the Civil Service Pension Fund, which is guaranteed by the Constitution. The Civil Service Fund receives its money from the individual civil servants themselves and from government (their employer) contributions.

In 1991 the government tripled its contributions to the Civil Service Pension Fund. It invests this money in the Public Investment Commission (PIC) which is chaired by the Minister of Finance and is a government body. The PIC has accumulated over R150 billion which it does not need to pay out pensions. The government is actually borrowing 40% of the money it needs from itself.

If the Public Service Pension Fund was restructured back to a 'Pay As You Go' system, it would release about R15 billion a year, which could be used to meet the RDP goals. Regarding overseas loans, there is precedent from other countries (such as the case of Cuba brought by the USA) where debts of former regimes were cancelled because the past regime oppressed its own people. This type of debt is called an odious (or 'hateful') debt.

TASK: If the government pays less on the debt, who would gain and who would lose? Who should pay for the apartheid debt? Why? How?

EXAMPLE:

Partnerships

THE NEED From the national budget, one can see that government is very limited in what it can do. There is very little money to meet all the needs of the majority of people. We need to look at where government spends the taxpayers' money – defence versus housing, or foreign affairs versus job creation. These are concerns that communities can raise.

One also sees that the number of taxpayers is small (only about 10% of the population). If there were more taxpayers, there would be more public funds to provide services to communities. If there are more jobs, there will be more taxpayers, and so a cycle of doing all things quickly is very important – but there are limits.

An example of how community involvement makes a difference:

Rural tarmac road built by government costs per km	R300,000
Rural tarmac road built by government and community costs per km	R 50,000

PARTNERSHIPS Some people believe that it is important to challenge both the government and private businesses to form partnerships with community people to meet basic needs. A group called Habitat uses one approach. This group works with local communities on the issue of housing and recruits business people to voluntarily give their skills and time to build houses in poor areas. Architects, builders, and other skilled labour is freely given to an area to build houses. Government often supplies the building materials.

ALTERNATIVES Some people believe that neither government (which is big, bureaucratic and slow in delivery) nor businesses (which are mainly in the business of making profits) are able to respond to community needs. They believe the communities must take the initiative themselves.

An example of this is the South African Federation of Homeless People. From 1990 to 1995 the federation grew to 350 community associations whose purpose is savings and credit. Their aim is to save for building houses, though loans were given for other needs. The loan repayment rate has been 98% (most banks would be happy with a 75% return). They demonstrated that they are a good risk and a sound federation. On 26 February 1996, the Housing Ministry gave them a grant of R10 million for houses. Their approach is to develop self-reliance and then government will follow their lead. They demonstrated in 1996–97 that they can build a four-roomed house for less than R9000 and put in water and sewerage for about R1000. However, conflicts can emerge if there is a mix of private contractors, public contractors and community self-help building projects. The specific parts of work need to be defined before any joint ventures are established.

TASK: What can we expect of government? What can we expect from businesses? What can we expect of ourselves in our communities to meet our own needs? What policy would you recommend to government?

B. Facilitator's guide

Aims of the Budget Game

1. To look at priorities within different departments of government
2. To make choices about 'trade-offs' between different departments
3. To explore ways of raising public funds
4. To enable people and organizations to participate in the budget process.

Procedure

This workshop is designed for a group of 25–45 people and takes about six hours. The times shown below are only for illustration. The words in *italics* are suggestions of what the facilitator can say during this part of the workshop. They are a guide and, of course, it is best to use your own words.

9:30 am **Welcome and overview of the programme**
This workshop today is to help us all understand how the government works, how different departments make budgets and some of the difficulties they face. We are doing this workshop with this group so that you can find ways to have input into the budget in the future.

Before we go further, it is helpful to find out more about all of us here in the room. I am [introduce yourself]. An easy way for us to know all of us in the room is to do a short exercise. Could everyone put their papers and pens down? Now, when I say something that is correct for you, I would like you to stand up for a few moments.

Stand Up If . . .
you were born in [city you are in]
you were born in a rural area
you were born in a city
you have worked in a rural area
you have helped someone become literate
you read a newspaper at least three times a week
you do a household budget at home
you stick to your household budget each month
you are left-handed
you sing in a choir
you like maths or numbers
you are a member of a trade union
you work with women's groups
[Use any ideas that will work with your group]

9:50 **What is a budget? Why is a budget so important?**
Could you turn to the person next to you and discuss, for a few minutes, what is a budget and why is a budget so important?
Give the groups 3–4 minutes for discussion and then ask people to give you one idea at a time on what is a budget (put on newsprint) and why budgets are important.

(Your summary. A budget is the income one is expecting and the expenses one is expecting over a certain period of time – one month, one year, etc. The national budget is important because it is a way to plan and to hold the government

244

accountable for what they say they will do. The government is spending our money. The South African government spends more than 35% of all the spending in the country. That is a lot of money.)

Review aims of this workshop.

10:00

Household budget

We all operate on a budget, some of us actually do use budgets in our homes – some of us more than others – but we all have income and expenses.

Let's do a short exercise on a budget first.

Ask participants, **in twos**, to do a household budget for a family of five with a set income. Give them 5 minutes to do this. Did they all end up with the same amount of expenses? If they overspent, what will they do?

Overspending is called a deficit.

Borrowing or cutting other expenses are some ways to find more money. This is exactly like the government.

The local, provincial, and national governments also operate with a budget.

First, *whose money does the government hold? Whose money is it?*

Second, *the amount of money that the national government has comes from all the taxpayers, and so it is a lot of money. When we see the national budget, we will be talking about millions and billions of rand.*

What is a million and what is a billion?

How do we write these numbers? 1000 or 1 000 thousand
                                   1 000 000 million
                                   1 000 000 000 billion

The amount the government expects to receive (revenues) in taxes 1999/2000 is:

R192 billion (R192 000 000 000)

It is expecting to spend R217 billion (R217 000 000 000)

How much will the government overspend? (R25 billion)

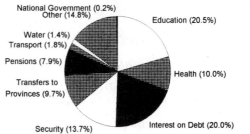

Where does the money come from and how will it be spent? (the budget)

Show Budget PIE CHARTS on newsprint here. Review some definitions of terms.

10:30

PRIORITIES

In fours or fives, *discuss what are the main needs in your community and the whole country. Make one long list of needs.* After about 10 minutes, ask the groups *to come up with the top six priorities.*

(**Note:** If there are only 25 participants in the whole workshop, you may want to ask them to only come up with the top five priorities, because you want five people in each small group [or ministry] in the next session.)

Whole group share (newsprint) – agree on top six priorities.

11:00	**BREAK** (At the break, place the six labels of ministries around the room with tape.)
11:15	**Now everyone will be in a ministry. Ask each person to choose a ministry she would like to be part of.**

(There will be some shifting of people because each group should have no more than five people. Ask people to shift to a second group if needed.)

Give each ministry their green card (health, housing, jobs, etc.).

When everyone has a card, ask that a person in each group reads the card out loud, so they can help one another with difficult words or if they do not understand something.

Have them discuss the priorities of their ministry and decide the amount of money needed to fund each priority. They have 30 minutes.

(**Note:** As the facilitator, you now become the 'Minister of Finance'. Go around to all the groups, introduce yourself and ask them if they have enough money in their ministry. Then announce to the whole group: 'the economy has not grown as much as expected and so cuts will have to be made.' Give each participant a copy of the budgets of other ministries and, if they wish, they can cut other ministries' budgets. Give participants the 'Summary of Budget Expenditures' handout. They now have 15 minutes more to prepare what they believe should be the priorities of the whole country. **What do you value most?**)

12:00	**2-minute break**
12:02	**Whole group** 'cabinet' meeting with deputies, advisers and assistants.

'Now is the time to argue for your priorities and what you think could be cut from other departments.'

Facilitator's role is to keep the group on these two topics:
1. **the priorities for their department and**
2. **the consequences of cutting other departments.**

12:45	**LUNCH BREAK**
1:30	**Let's find the money**

Have people go back to their same groups. Different groups now get two cards. One is a pink card which is taxes and one is a yellow card which are cuts or other methods of getting more money.
*Your task for the next **30 minutes** will be to discuss how to get more income to fund the programmes you want. Discuss the consequences of your choices – what we will gain and what we will lose.*

2:15	**Fishbowl with two empty chairs**

Each group is asked to send their 'deputy minister' to a meeting to discuss where to find more money through taxes, cuts or other means. This group sits in the inner circle of chairs. The other participants sit on the outside of the circle and can speak only if they go to an empty chair in the inner circle. Once they have said their point, they must leave the empty chair.

The facilitator's role here is to act as the Minister of Finance. As different people speak, the facilitator may want to press people about **why they made certain decisions, and the consequences of their choices.**

2:45 **BREAK**

3:00 **OPTIONAL DISCUSSION** (if time)

In 2s and then the whole group:
What are the major problems the government faces?
What does this mean for us in the community (or NGOs)?

3:30 **Input on Budget Process (by the facilitator)**
[The facilitator needs to learn about the budget process in his/her own country and explain it here.]

How can community groups give input on the budget?

Other countries

UK: the local and county political party leaders recommend budget priorities to their national party for debate.

USA: the budget is developed by departments and cabinet, presented to Congress in February, and Congress has public hearings and debates for eight months before voting.

4:00 **Move to new groups according to geographic area or organization**
Hand out the 7 Steps of Planning (*Training for Transformation* Book II) or any other planning tool. The workshop moves from thinking to action.

4:25 **EVALUATION** (one word evaluation)

C. Budget reform guidelines

Socio-economic planning should guide budget allocations. The following guidelines need to be looked at on every level of government. Budgeting processes need to be carried out in collaboration with all key social partners.

1. **Programme based budgeting process.** Governments at all levels need to use what is called 'programme based budgeting' or 'measurable outcome based budgeting'. The principle is that budgeting is linked to direct outcomes. Not only can one measure improvement, but also clear mandates are given and work done by government staff can be evaluated.

2. **Participation.** Communities need to participate in the initial stages of setting budget priorities and planning, rather than simply being informed at the end of the process. Participation would include:

   - Input on naming the problems and developing the framework and vision;
   - Input on setting priorities within a framework;
   - Participating in evaluating each department, programme and sub-programme in terms of this framework and priorities on a regular basis.

The Wheel of Fundamental Human Needs

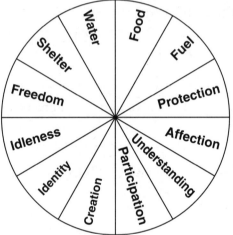

3. **Make public an audit** of all assets in open community meetings.

4. **Do a comparison of budget priorities** over the past ten years and inform the public of the change in priorities.

5. **Change the reporting format** of the budget to reflect a programme based budgeting process. (This would include narratives which state explicitly geographic areas and timetables for delivery, costs of attaining the goals, and a glossary of terms, including all abbreviations.)

6. **The budgeting process should be made transparent** and published for public comment before decisions are made. This would make it necessary for a draft budget to be published three to nine months before voting on the final budget.

How can you have an impact on a government budget in the meantime? See Section Five of this chapter.

SECTION FOUR

Developing community–government partnerships*

Governments, by themselves, are very limited in what they can do. There is very little money to meet all the needs of the majority of their people. We need to look at how the government spends the taxpayers' money, and which areas of spending can be cut in favour of increased spending in other areas. This is called a 'trade-off'.

Some people believe that it is important to challenge both the government and private businesses to form partnerships with community people as they try to meet basic needs. A group called Habitat uses this approach. The group works with a local community on the issue of housing and recruits business people to give their own skills and time (or the time of their workers) to build houses in poor areas. Architects, builders and other skilled workers are loaned without charge by private business while government often supplies the building materials.

Other people believe that neither government (which is big, bureaucratic and slow in delivery) nor business (which is mainly concerned with making profits) is able to respond to community needs. They believe that communities must take the initiative themselves and start local projects.

Some key problems within governments

Some of the key problems that government personnel face include:

- Having limited budgets (or resources) so delivery of services is poor;
- Not having clearly defined and measurable goals by which to accomplish tasks;
- Not having strategic plans to deliver services;
- Unclear roles and areas of responsibility which leads to a lack of flexibility and creativity;
- Over- or under-accountability (UNDP Strategy Paper, 1994).

We suggest that if communities participate in developing a strategic plan, and if there are government personnel responsible for delivery, then limited budgets can stretch like 'loaves and fishes', and dramatic development can be achieved.

---

* This section has been used by Fair Share, Cape Town, South Africa in several communities. Samkhele Marrengane and Elroy Paulus have been important trainers in ensuring the success of these designs.

A. PRELIMINARY WORK WITH A COMMUNITY

It is important that development groups, community groups and NGOs have developed sufficient trust, vision and organization before they enter into a partnership with government. Preliminary work with community groups, councillors, business and officials is essential before a workshop with all stakeholders is possible.

By encouraging communities to take initiative, local leaders can begin a process of developing partnerships with local government. In joint planning between local councils and community groups, budget priorities become clear. Below you will find three models.

Three models for beginning a process of local partnerships

1. **Work with all stakeholders.** The first model is based on the goodwill and more-or-less-equal commitment and political will of all stakeholders. Discussions are held with key players in a specific local area and should include:

   - Leaders in the communities;
   - All local government officials;
   - A number of key local councillors;
   - Business forum leadership.

   The interviews focus on the need for common strategic planning of all stakeholders and finding out if there is common agreement to pursue such an initiative.

2. **Work with community leadership.** If there is a lot of tension or conflict among the four sets of stakeholders, more in-depth work with community leadership is critical. The first workshop or set of meetings can be on how to build co-operation with the other stakeholders. If this fails, the community leadership can develop its own strategic plan for the area, and present the plan to council. This model shifts the power to the community. The community also assumes some responsibility for moving ahead on the plan – with or without local government help.

3. **Work with co-operative local councillors.** If a partnership model is not yet feasible and the local development committee is weak, it is possible to begin by identifying some strong local councillors. A meeting with these local councillors to consider the need for partnerships can be the first step. The next step is to encourage local councillors to organize themselves and motivate the various sectors to come together to do common strategic planning.

Alongside this initial work, workshops can be held with community leaders on any of the following areas:

- Clarifying the group's understanding of development and planning processes;
- Budget workshops to prepare for deciding budget priorities within local government;
- Methods for involving the community as a whole, to get their input into future developmental needs and priorities.

Who participates in the workshop?

A 2–3 day workshop with all stakeholders is required to begin a process of partnerships.

At the beginning of a strategy planning process the involvement of all stakeholders – community leaders, NGOs, CBOs, the business community, town officials and councillors – is critical. If one sector develops a plan without the other, there will continue to be conflict over roles and goals. We therefore strongly suggest that the following people be present for Stage 1 and 2 workshops:

Town officials	10–15 people (heads and deputies)
Town councillors	all councillors
Community representatives	10–15 people
Development forum / NGOs	10–15 people
Private sector	10–15 people
TOTAL	**60–75 people**

The participants at the strategic planning workshop would be as shown in the pie chart.

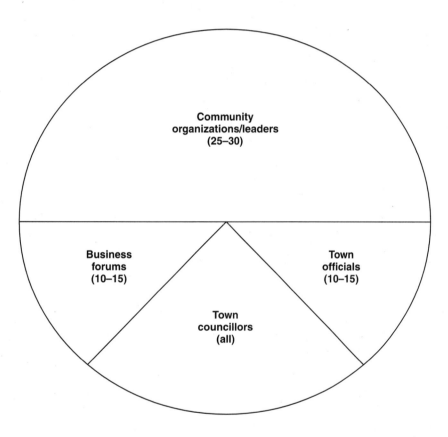

Questions: Who will represent the community?
What process will we use to select these people and our method of accountability?

251

B. WORKSHOPS WITH COMMUNITY LEADERS AND LOCAL GOVERNMENT

Two key aspects of building partnerships between communities and government are:

- Building trust between people; and
- Bridging the planning 'gap' that occurs when the two groups plan separately from each other.

The following workshop model can be used to bridge those gaps.

Exercise 12. Warm-up on expectations

Procedure

1. After introductions and a trust building exercise (see, for example, *Training for Transformation* Book II) ask participants to form **mixed groups of four** – with people they do not normally work with. Ask them to discuss two questions in their small groups:

   - What do we expect from this workshop?
   - What are our hopes and worries about our area?

2. When they have completed this, ask them to come back to the whole group and write up their expectations, hopes and worries on newsprint. Tell the group that this will be the basis of the workshop.

Time   45 minutes

Materials   Newsprint and markers.

Exercise 13. The door exercise – 'Your standpoint is your viewpoint'

This short play is useful to set norms of communications in a workshop, especially if the group comes from very mixed backgrounds. Its purpose is to help those people who consider their way of seeing things as 'the only way things can be'. It can help them to understand that their view comes from where they themselves 'sit' in society. Our views and priorities are profoundly affected by our personal experiences (e.g. our class background).

The door play

Two people sit facing each other with one person facing the door (if there is more than one door, choose an object in the room of which there is only one, for example the blackboard or the window or the table). This is important. The second person sits with his/her back to the door. The third person comes to the two of them, from one side, and asks, 'Where is the door?' They both respond immediately. The one facing the door says 'in front'. The one with his/her back to the door says 'behind'. The third person looks perplexed and asks again 'where? and the responses are: 'in front', 'behind' – each out-shouting the other. The play then ends.

Procedure

1. Ask three people to prepare and then act out the door play for the others to watch.

2. In the whole group, discuss the following questions:

   a. Who was correct? Was anyone correct for the third person? (because the door was at his/her side, not behind or in front).
   b. What does this short play tell us?
   c. What are the factors that affect our different views of reality? (culture, class, education, gender, age, race, etc.).

3. **In twos**, participants then discuss: What do we all need to do in this workshop to ensure good communications between us, so that we can work well together?

4. After about 5 minutes, in the whole group ask participants to give their points for good communication during the workshop. Put these on newsprint, so they can be referred back to during the workshop.

Time   30 minutes

Materials   Newsprint, markers.

Exercise 14. Issue identification through the 'shape of our reality'

Most needs assessments and issue identifications are done through a study of numbers (called a quantitative needs survey). These will show how many houses, roads, or water taps are needed in an area. These needs assessments are important because they can show what and where needs are. This information is measurable and accurate and called scientific knowledge.

However, such information says nothing about how the community views these needs. Understanding what people have strong feelings about and how they perceive their problems is another form of knowledge. This is called social knowledge. Paulo Freire found that emotion is linked to motivation and both words have at their stem the word 'moti' – to be moved, to act.

It is therefore critical to link scientific and social knowledge together, and this gives us transformative knowledge.

Stage 1: 'Shape of our reality' exercise

A very good reason for using this exercise for a combined community and government partnership workshop is that it puts all the participants on a level playing field. No group will have all the answers because you begin with perceptions. We highly recommend using the exercise and it is easy and fun to run.

The procedure for this exercise appears in Exercise 3 of this chapter.

Stage 2: Vision statement

Everyone, especially officials and councillors, needs to understand the difference between a vision and a mission statement. The definitions in the box can be used as an input.

- **The vision is our ultimate aim:** 'a disease-free community', 'a society where women are accepted as full human beings', ' full employment for all who can work, at a living wage'

- **A mission statement** defines the task of an agent or body. It is the purpose for which the agent or body exists. 'The mission of our department is to ensure we meet our goals promptly and communicate with local communities on a regular basis.'

---

1. After the groups have finished the five steps of the 'Shape of our reality' exercise, ask each person to write a vision statement for the town. It is one sentence, and should begin, 'My vision for (name of town) is . . . '. Also ask them to write, 'My hope for (name of town) is . . . '.

2. When each person has completed this task, ask each small group to write a common vision statement for their town. It must be one sentence and they need to incorporate everyone's ideas and come to consensus. Each group writes its vision statement on newsprint.

3. When each group has finished writing its statement, these are shared with the whole group. The group discusses the similarities and differences. A small team is asked to write a common vision statement during a break and presents this back to the whole group for ratification.

Stage 3: Priority setting

1. Ask the participants to go back to their small groups of five to list the issues that emerged during their discussion. Then ask the small groups to rank the top 5 or 6 priorities for their town in order of importance.

2. Bring everyone back to the whole group. Ask each group to read out ONE of their priorities and then ask one person from all of the other groups to raise their hand if they also had that as a priority (in their top 6 list). Go around the room asking for one priority from a group at a time. Soon you will identify the top priorities for the town.

When all of the top six priorities have been listed, with a tally of the number of small groups who had that priority, take another colour marker and circle the top priorities for the whole group.
Ask the whole group whether these priorities seem to be the top priorities for the community at the moment. Get confirmation on priorities.

Time   2 hours (besides the Shape of Reality exercise)

Materials   Newsprint, markers, crayons, and tape.

Exercise 15. **Setting measurable goals**

Procedure

1. Write on separate sheets of paper the topics that have emerged from the priority setting session. With tape, put these different priorities up around the room. Then ask all the participants to think about which two issues they would most like to work on, their first and second choice.

2. Ask participants to stand under the paper with the priority they want to work on. At this stage there will be confusion. Help participants to sort themselves into groups of no more than 5 to 6 people in each group. (The reason to keep all the small groups to about the same size is so they will conclude their work at approximately the same time.)

3. Give each participant a copy of the handout 'Goal setting for strategic planning'. Ask each group to choose one person to read the handout aloud to them. Their task will then be to answer all the questions, writing their plan on paper.

4. When the small groups have completed this task, the whole group reassembles. Each group is asked to share its goal statements and time lines, but NOT the details. Tell participants that there will be another session to refine the details which will also go into the final report.

Time   2 hours

Materials   Handout on 'Goal Setting for Strategic Planning', paper for each group.

Goal setting for strategic planning

Task

1. Look again at the vision statement agreed to earlier. In your group, take that priority you are working on and **make a need statement**. Do this by finishing this sentence:

   'There is a need for _____'

   You may have more than one need statement.

2. Now, take these need statements and **make a goal statement**. Goals are the situation we hope to have reached by a specific date. Goals are long range **destinations**, but destinations that it is possible to achieve. Example: by the end of 1999, we plan to have clean water supplies in every house in Mbekweni.

   Goals are points of arrival, not actions to be taken.

3. If you have more than one need statement, you may well have more than one goal statement. Each goal statement may have a different time frame. For our purposes there are three different time frames to use:

   a. Immediate goals (within six months);
   b. Medium-term goals (between six months and 2 years);
   c. Long-term goals (between 2 and 5 years).

   After writing your goal statements, give each one a time frame.

4. When you have finished writing your goals, check with a facilitator to ensure that the goals are measurable and that you are on the right track. Write all the goals and time frames on newsprint.

5. Be prepared to report this back to the whole group.

Exercise 16. Role clarification

Once the group has agreed on goals, it is very important to clarify *roles* in meeting those *goals*. We often have unspoken assumptions about what others will do to accomplish goals. All assumptions about what we expect of ourselves or others in achieving the goals must be clear and open.

Procedure

1. Ask the participants to go into homogeneous groups (groups with members in similar positions, for example, government officials, councillors, NGO leadership, women's leaders, business representatives or community leaders, etc.)

2. Ask each group to discuss these questions:

   - What do we expect of ourselves to achieve the goals we have agreed on?
   - What do we expect each one of the other groups that are here to do to meet the goals?

   Ask each group to write on separate sheets of newsprint:

   - Its expectations of itself;
   - Its expectations of each other group.

3. It is most helpful if each homogeneous group can be in a separate room. This gives them the freedom to speak very openly and frankly with each other. This task will take them at least 1½ to 2 hours.

4. In the whole group, each small group then reports back their expectations of themselves and their expectations of other groups. In this session, participants can ask questions of clarification but no discussion on the points is allowed. It is wise to have a break after this session. It can be helpful if all the items applying to each group are now written on to one sheet (the group's own expectations of itself and all the other groups' expectations of it). Otherwise, each group (e.g. councillors, officials, community) can just take its own expectations sheet and the expectations sheets written for them by other groups.

5. Each small group goes back to their homogeneous group, and with its written list (or the newsprint) of all of the expectations, each group reviews the expectations of all the other groups and decides what is possible and what they are able to take responsibility for.

6. In the whole group, each small group reports back about each of its own expectations of itself and what it agrees to and disagrees from the expectations from all of the other groups. The facilitator checks with the whole group to see if all the expectations are fully accepted by the groups concerned.

Time   6 to 7 hours

Materials   Newsprint, markers, tape for all groups.

Exercise 17. Home group planning

With goals having been formulated by mixed groups, and the roles of each sector somewhat defined, the next step is to get down to practical planning on the priorities.

Procedure

1. Before this session (preferably the night before) make copies for each participant of the following:

   - Vision statement;
   - Priorities;
   - All the goal statements.

2. The whole group is now divided into the following small groups:

   - Several **groups of five to six** participants, mixing councillors and officials;
   - 'Home' groups in specific communities (geographic areas);
   - Business;
   - Development forum (optional as these people could go to their own community groups).

3. The councillors/officials group is asked to split up into smaller groups, with each taking responsibility for planning in relation to 3–5 goals. They are given the Home group planning tool (see handout), but may want to adapt it.

4. The community and business groups are asked to use the planning tool. All groups are to write their plans and timelines on paper ready to be handed in for a final report.

5. After about 2 hours, ask all the groups to come back to the whole group to report on the main plans they have developed, but not all the details.

Time   3+ hours

Materials   Copies for each participant of the vision statement, priorities and goals. Planning tool handout for each participant.

Home group planning tool

1. Review all of the goals developed earlier and **choose those goals** that are of most importance to your area.

2. Now begin developing a plan:
   - **What are the stages needed to get to our goal?** (These are sometimes called objectives.)
   - Brainstorm a list of all the activities, resources, materials, money, tools, labour, kinds of skills needed to do this (everything you would need to get to the goal).
   - Put these lists on newsprint.

3. Now review this list, and look at each item and do an inventory of:

   a. What and who in the community itself could do these things?

   (For example, some people in the community may have built roads or houses and therefore have these skills. Others may have a way to get discounted materials for the project. Others may be good at organizing.) Name the people (for yourselves only).

   b. What is needed from outside the community?

   At the end of this task, you will have two lists: the things the community can do to achieve the goal, and what resources are needed from outside the community.

4. **Develop a timeline** – plan when it would be realistic to start and how long each step towards the goal will take.

5. Next to each task, write **who, where,** and **how.**

6. Have your plan(s) on paper and be prepared for someone in your group to report back to the whole group.

Exercise 18. **Follow-up structures and plans**

This workshop is too short to make complete plans and it may not be appropriate that every stakeholder be involved in all of the planning. But structures are needed to ensure accountability and continued communication among stakeholders. The following is a useful planning tool.

Procedure

1. Make enough copies of the follow-up plans form for each small group. It is best to do them on newsprint with lots of space for writing.

2. Ask participants to get into **mixed groups of five** people and discuss: What tasks need to be followed up? Give them about 5 minutes to discuss this.

3. Participants then report back to the whole group and a list of follow-up tasks is written up on newsprint.

4. If the list is long, take a 5-minute break to categorize the list with a small team of participants. If the list is short, the whole group can quickly define the follow-up tasks. One task that MUST be on the list is an ongoing stakeholders' co-ordinating committee.

5. Now, with the tasks consolidated, ask participants to divide up into task teams. Those who wish to deal with one task should go to one area of the room; other participants who wish to deal with another task go to another area of the room, etc. The whole group is now divided up into task teams. Give each task team a copy of the follow-up plans form. They are to fill in the form on the newsprint.

6. When the groups have finished, each group reports back to the whole group. Make sure that the whole group agrees with the follow-up plans.

Follow-up plans form

Task	Process (how?)	Who	Time frame	Outcomes	Evaluation	Recommend to whom?

Time   1+ hour

Materials   Newsprint, markers, handout (or pre-prepared newsprint).

Exercise 19. Final evaluation

To conclude the workshop, ask all participants to write on paper their responses to the following questions:

a. What has been most helpful about this workshop?
b. What has been least helpful about this workshop?
c. In future workshops of this nature in other places, what would you recommend changing?

Procedure

1. Give participants about 15 minutes to answer these questions.

2. If you have time, you could then ask for some feedback on each question. In all cases, get the written responses so that you, as the facilitator, can get some feedback about the workshop.

Time   15 to 45 minutes

Materials   Pens and paper.

Facilitator's notes

The following is the process used by Fair Share in South Africa to develop local partnerships

1. Contact several key activists in an area.

   Explain the purpose of developing partnerships – that without community input into strategic plans, some problems will emerge in the future:

   - community needs can be overlooked;
   - communities feel alienated from the process and do not 'own' the delivery 'dumped' on them;
   - Masakhane (payment for services) will not succeed;
   - the dependency on government to deliver will continue;
   - access to local/provincial budgets by communities can be lost.

2. After explaining the aim, suggest the following:
   a. could they set up interviews with local town officials and councillors (over a period of one day, e.g. half-hour interviews with individuals or 1 – 2 hour group meetings.)
   b. a second day in the area doing a community leadership workshop on:

      - provincial budget or
      - need clarification to approach local government to do strategic planning together and a process of identifying who from the community should be part of common strategic planning 2–3 day workshops.

      These workshops may have to be on a weekend.

3. Develop a schedule –   2 days in one community
   2 days in another community
   2 days in a third community

Example:

Friday   Upington (interviews/meetings with local officials and councillors)

Saturday   Upington (community workshop)

Sunday   De Aar (community workshop)

Monday   De Aar (interviews/meetings with local officials and councillors)

STRATEGIC PLANNING WORKSHOP PROCESS

The workshop used by Fair Share is aimed at enabling the different sectors of civil society and government to interact in order to build trust, understanding and a common plan for the municipality. Because the methodology is participatory, coming to understand viewpoints from different perspectives takes much more time than in groups which have a common experience or common language. We recognize that the time was not sufficient for detailed plans to be completed. It is our hope that a spirit of mutual respect and co-operation has been established and that the on-going process of planning will continue.

The following processes were used in the workshop.

Aims of workshop and communication norms

In order to establish exactly what the group hoped to accomplish and encourage communication between people, the workshop started with small groups identifying the elements of the aims of the workshop they most wanted emphasized. A small play was used to illustrate how everyone speaks from their own standpoint – from their own experiences. This led to the group setting up its own norms of communication between each other for the three days.

Identifying key issues of the town

Groups of five from mixed backgrounds were formed. Each person was asked to illustrate how they saw their town at this time – its main theme or illustration. The small group then discussed what they were trying to show and made a common picture on newsprint. Then groups illustrated what would have an impact on their town in the coming years and what would be dying out in the near future.

Consensus on a common vision for the town

All the participants then looked at the work of all the other small groups. From a rough understanding of the whole group, individuals wrote what this meant for the future of their town and what they hoped for their town. Each of the small groups then wrote a vision statement. These statements were shared in the whole group. At the end of the evening programme, a task team from different groups took the statements and wrote a new statement for the whole group. Definitions of 'vision' and 'mission' were clarified before this task was taken on.

Setting priorities

The same small groups took the issues that had emerged in the previous discussions and added other issues that might not have been discussed and decided on the top six priorities for their town. Each small group shared a priority, with other small groups indicating if that priority was also on their list of priorities. Thirteen priorities were identified in this initial round of priority setting.

Cont. ▶

Goal formation

The following day, the thirteen priorities were put on separate sheets of paper around the room. People chose a priority that they either had most interest in or which was their responsibility for the municipality. In these interest groups, they decided on the various needs for that priority and formulated measurable goal statements. These goal statements could have different time frames: immediate, medium-term and long-term.

Role clarification

Until a group is clear on its goals, the roles and functions of the different sectors of society cannot be clarified. The participants were asked to go into their sectoral groups: councillors, officials, business and community groups.

Each group was then asked to clarify what they expected of their own group and each of the other groups to meet the goals for their town. Each group reported back these expectations. Then the homogeneous groups took all the expectations from the other groups and responded to those expectations – did they agree, disagree or did that expectation need to be modified? Some of the differences that emerged needed much longer discussion and negotiations. These were put aside for follow-up sessions after the workshop.

Initial steps to plan implementation of goals

Participants were asked to move into 'home' groups that could carry the goals forward. There were three groups of officials and councillors which tackled about three of the goals each. Each area met separately. Each person was given a copy of all the goals they had formulated the previous day. The municipality groups began an initial planning process. Each community group chose the goal that was most important to them. They looked at the resources that they themselves could provide and the resources they needed from outside the community to reach the goal. These plans were briefly shared in the whole group.

Mechanisms for follow-up of this workshop

The whole group brainstormed the issues they felt needed to be followed up after this workshop. After the tasks were identified, small groups were formed to develop a plan, including who would take responsibility to follow up on this task, how it needed to be carried forward, time frame, expected outcomes and, if needed, who would make the final decisions.

Some best practices

During the workshop, several examples were given of projects that have been very successful. Their success was in their actual achievement and partnership between civil society and government.

South African Federation of Homeless People

The South African Federation of Homeless People began with community people developing saving and credit societies, for the purpose of saving for a house. The federation is made up of more than 350 saving and credit associations. They have shown they can save and their repayment on loans is 98%, a rate most banks would envy.

They found the process of securing government subsidies for homes very complicated and slow. They approached government as a group which had demonstrated their seriousness and ability to work together. They made a group application for housing subsidies and in February 1997 were granted R10 million.

They make their own bricks, design their own homes, build the houses and work with government to install the infrastructure.

They believe in self-reliance and getting the work done themselves. They became convinced that waiting for government would not meet their needs. They took the initiative, and government followed their lead.

Masakhane – co-operative home building (Habitat)

Many studies have shown that social stability, health and crime prevention are enormously improved where people own their homes. An international group called Habitat is a non-profit organization which helps people either build their own homes or renovate slum dwellings.

Communities are identified that are organized and want to build their own homes. A partnership is arranged between the community and Habitat. Habitat organizes more well-off people in the town or city to volunteer their time and expertise. These include architects, engineers, plumbers, electricians and also regular folk who can contribute towards the building as unskilled labour. Former President Carter in the USA gives one day a month to helping to build houses in poor communities.

In South Africa, the Masakhane campaign has been focused on people paying for their services. If we believe in 'leadership by example', another part of the campaign could be a reciprocal arrangement of corporate executives, professors, managers, housewives, secretaries – people from all walks of life – to freely give of their energy and time to help build houses. Construction companies could be asked to give one day a month of their labour force to help build houses.

A partnership case study

People in Chief Sibongile Zungu's Madlebe area outside Empangeni, KwaZulu-Natal, realizing their plight, and understanding that lack of jobs in the nearby towns of Empangeni and Richards Bay was not going to improve, worked with their chief, Community Development workers in their area, and business, to devise a plan that would lead to income generation.

The community saw a gardens project as the best way out of their difficulty. Scores of trucks ferried vegetables from far away Pongola and Jozini (four and three hours respectively), so there was a good chance that what they grew would find a good market right on their doorstep. *There was only one problem: there was no road linking their area to the nearest town, Empangeni. So how would their produce get to potential market areas?*

The chief and the development workers sought funding from the Southern African Development Bank, which they obtained. They asked business to loan the project whatever machinery they could, as well as provide the necessary expertise. The community pledged their free labour, knowing that when the road was completed and the gardens were running, they would be able to make money from selling vegetables to businesses in Empangeni and the harbour town of Richards Bay, to people in the two sprawling townships, as well as former KwaZulu homeland areas surrounding the two towns.

The community is into its second year of success. Not only is there income for the industrious ones, there will probably never again be cases of malnutrition. There is reason to believe that more people in other areas would benefit from this partnership model.

Primary health care partnerships

A church-based development and health care programme in Kenya was able within two years to wipe out four major diseases within one district: kwashiorkor, scabies, worms and dysentery. The church development programme initiated community development work in the district for five years prior to the health care programme. From these communities' discussions, the need for primary health care in the area emerged as a priority. Fifteen women were to become their health care workers and were chosen by communities themselves.

The government was invited to give two rooms for the three-month residential course. The church-based health care programme provided two primary health care trainers. The fifteen women and trainers lived, worked and studied together for three months. At the end of the participatory and experiential learning course, the primary health care workers returned to their areas.

Because the communities had a high stake in this programme, they contributed to the stipend of their newly trained primary health care worker. This model of training and community initiative has now been applied in many countries in Africa through the Flyer Doctor service and government public health departments.

Partnership workshop design

Warm-up exercise
The door exercise
Shape of our reality
Vision and priority statements
Setting measurable goals
Role clarification
Home group planning
Follow-up structures of accountability
Evaluation

Note: This is actually a 3-day workshop allowing time for meals, teas, recreation and breaks. The facilitator and town clerk should negotiate prior to the workshop who will write the final report.

> 'If you have come to help me, you are wasting your time. But if you have come because your liberation is bound up with mine, then let us work together.'
>
> Lila Watson
> *(Australian aboriginal woman leader)*

SECTION FIVE

The fine art of lobbying

Sometimes government policies are very clear that co-operation between government and communities is essential, for example community policing. Government staff look for ways to work with communities. However, sometimes the actual practices of government do not include opportunities for citizen inputs and exclude communities in the planning and implementing processes. When one encounters such obstacles, a group may need to 'lobby'.

What does the word lobby mean? The word lobby comes from the word used to describe an entrance hall outside other rooms in a parliament building or council chamber. People wanting to speak to Members of Parliament or other officials would wait in the lobby and approach them as they came out of meetings or their offices. Then they would try to persuade the Member of Parliament about how s/he should vote on a particular bill. Because this interaction took place in a lobby, the verb, to lobby, came into being.

To lobby means to advocate or push for a cause or a point of view on legislation that is coming up for a vote in parliament. People who 'lobby' are called lobbyists.

We all lobby every day of our lives. We try to persuade people who are about to make decisions on a certain issue. This first exercise is to help participants understand different ways in which they already lobby.

Exercise 20. What is lobbying?

Introduce this session with a short explanation of what lobbying is (see above).

Procedure

1. Ask participants to go into **groups of three** and complete the following two tasks:

   a. Make a list of the ways you have pressured government departments or officials, when you or a group have felt an injustice has happened or they were wrong on a certain issue.

   b. Make a list of the ways you have tried to persuade members of your family or friends about an issue you feel strongly about.

2. When groups have completed both tasks (about 10 minutes) ask them to share their ideas. Put their ideas on two different pieces of newsprint, one labelled 'government' and one labelled 'friends'.

Time   1 hour

Materials   Two pieces of newsprint, markers and tape.

268

Input on lobbying

These lists show different ways in which we try to persuade others to see our point of view. Some ways are more gentle than others. In fact, lobbying is really 'gentle persuasion', offering facts to back up a position.

In looking at the lists the group has made, you can see that they represent a continuum of actions from very gentle methods to perhaps strikes and boycotts. The strongest actions are withholding something that the other party needs, like one's labour, buying power, or votes in an election. However, these actions are not always the first steps to take, because then if that action fails to produce the results your group wants, additional threats are not as easy to organize.

A few principles for advocacy

- Advocacy assumes that people have rights and those rights are enforceable.
- Advocacy works best when it is focused.
- Advocacy is mainly concerned with rights, benefits and values.
- Advocacy is usually about policy to ensure that institutions respond to and work in the interests of the people most affected (Amidei, *So You Want to Make a Difference*).

Exercise 21. **Clarifying your purpose**

It is critical for those who lobby to be clear about what they expect of government and also what they see as the role of citizen groups in society. Before developing strategies, it is important to clarify these questions.

Use Exercise 4 of this chapter, on the purpose of government.

Role of elected officials and civil servants

It is very important for those who lobby to understand the particular functions of elected representatives and appointed officials in government.

For example, in a parliamentary system, the national cabinet (or elected council in local government) makes most policy decisions. We can liken them to the centre of the flower.

The roots of the flower are the grassroots, or the voters who put the elected officials into power. The role of advocacy and lobbying is to strengthen the stem between the flower and the roots. Often this stem is neglected. We have discussed how to build partnerships (or a very strong stem) in the previous section.

But to really understand the political process, one must look at each petal in the flower. It is very important to understand the functions of each petal or section.

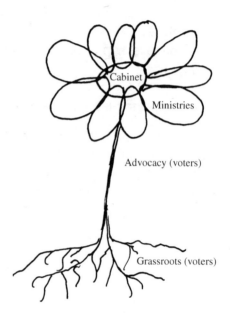

Cabinet minister ⟶

Deputy minister ⟶

Cabinet staff ⟶

Parliamentary committee and chair ⟶

Director-general of department ⟶

Civil service staff ⟶

Procedure

1. Ask people to get into interest groups and fill in the names of people in each of the areas of the flower in the diagram. Ask them to fill in the civil service staff functions and names of the people who are responsible for each section.

2. In the areas participants do not know, ask them to state how they could get this information.

3. These diagrams can be shared with the whole group if the group is interested in all the areas of government that have been discussed.

Time   1½ to 2 hours

Materials   The diagrams on newsprint, paper, pens for each small group.

Exercise 22. **How political parties work**

Procedure

1. Introduce this session with some input on political parties.

2. Hand out copies of the 'Questions for political parties'.

3. Ask participants to go into **groups of four** to discuss the following questions.

   a. Why are party politics important?
   b. How can we find out what each party stands for (vision, direction and policy goals for the future)?
   c. Politics is often built around trust. What makes us trust one party more than another party? List the elements that give us confidence that a political party is trustworthy.
   d. In what ways can we let political parties know what we expect of them?

4. After about 30 minutes, bring the groups together for a **whole group** discussion.

Time   1 to 1½ hours

Materials   Photocopies of the 'Questions for Political Parties' for each participant and discussion questions written on newsprint.

INPUT: How do political parties work?

Most of us who work in communities see many issues affecting the daily lives of people. One of the problems with governments is that they usually respond to these concerns department by department. If it is an educational problem, the education department handles it. If it is a problem of roads or water, the transport and water affairs departments handle it. So the problems that ordinary people face are not addressed as a whole, but in functions or categories.

Role of political parties

Usually it is the political parties who should have a holistic view of the nation. If they are effective, they have set priorities, decided how to address the problems, and offer a vision of the direction they want to see the country take. Political parties offer the voters:

- **a vision** of how they would like to see the nation in the future;
- **a direction** that the country should take;
- **specific policies** that they would implement if they were in power to ensure that their vision is put into practice;
- how they expect government to run and be **accountable** to the people.

Many Western-style 'democracies' break down at this juncture. The United States is often held up as a democratic country. However, the following facts speak otherwise:

- less than half of the eligible voters vote;
- almost all legislators supplement their public salaries from private sources in order to stay in power;
- wealthy individuals and corporations are the main contributors to political campaigns;
- political advertisements on television and radio reduce the political debate about vision and direction to 'tricks';
- members of the US Congress are individually elected and therefore are not necessarily accountable to their political party, but to their campaign contributors;
- campaigns to run for a US Senate seat now cost between $5 million and $40 million, while a campaign for the presidency costs up to $50 million. The candidates must raise most of this money themselves.

'Free and fair' elections in Western democracies mean one's ballot is secret and voters are not physically harassed, punished or rewarded for how they vote. But elections are not 'free' because campaigns are very expensive and the voices of those without money are seldom heard. 'He who pays the piper, calls the tune.'

Questions for political parties

1. From whom does the party receive its money?

2. What is the system for electing party leaders?

3. How long can party leaders be in power?

4. How often do local chapters of the party meet and what is their role in decision-making on the vision and direction of the party?

5. How is input from local chapters given to and discussed at regional and national levels of the party?

6. Does the party have a code of conduct for its leaders?

7. What are the rights and responsibilities at each level of the party?

8. Are the goals realistic or does the party offer campaign promises which may not be kept?

Exercise 23. How public policy is made – reading a Bill

Democratic countries have a representative form of government, with elected officials (e.g. members of parliament) deciding on the policies of the country. Members of parliament are chosen by their parties to stand for election.

During elections, the people may vote for a party and seats in parliament may be allocated to parties according to the number of votes they receive. Parties then give those seats to the candidates on their 'party list', with the first seat going to the first person on the list, the second to the second person on the list, and so on. This method is called the 'party list' method.

Another method is for individuals to be elected from a constituency or geographic area, usually standing within a particular party.

There is much debate about which method to use. Some suggest a combination of the 'list' and constituency systems. In the list method, the elected officials usually have first loyalty to their party. Debates about policies are held within the party more than in parliament. In the constituency election method, elected officials usually have first loyalty to their constituents. This can have a negative side of building up personal loyalties from 'rich' people in that area, with the elected official voting according to the wishes of those who have most personal influence.

In many countries, the Constitution and Bill of Rights are the supreme law. They are the broad framework within which policy must be made. However, parliament has the authority and power to enact laws that determine how the government works, its priorities and direction.

The priorities of a country are often decided through debates on the budget. (See Section Three of this chapter for a one-day workshop on the budget.)

There are other issues besides the budget which regulate social interactions between people. Do labour unions have the right to strike and, if so, for how long? Are there regulations about how disputes between groups of people will be resolved? What kinds of laws are in place to protect property owners? What laws protect prisoners from abuse? Women from violence? Children from abuse? Minority groups from discrimination by the majority? Are there economic rights? Civil rights? Is there protection of nature – clean water, air, the earth?

However, laws protecting the marginal and most vulnerable in society are only as good as the ability to enforce them. Therefore, how can we 'read public policy' to ensure that it is good law?

Procedure

1. As the facilitator, get copies of a short piece of legislation or a policy document which is currently being debated, making sure you have enough copies for all participants. Also make copies of the 'Criteria for reading public policy' handout.

2. Ask participants to go into **pairs** and read the document out loud to each other. Then they use the criteria to judge the legislation. Participants should also add any other criteria they think are important.

3. Participants write down any questions or areas where more information is needed to help them understand the law. (It is most helpful to have a friendly law-maker you can call on for advice or help in finding information you may be lacking.)

4. In the **whole group**, ask participants what is the result of their investigation? Do they favour the proposed law? Oppose it? Want it changed and, if so in what ways?

Time   2 hours

Materials   Copies of a simple Bill being discussed in parliament and the 'Criteria for reading public policy' handout.

Criteria for reading public policy

1. Who benefits from this law?

2. Who loses?

3. How does this law affect women and marginalized people?

4. What will be the consequences five years from now, if this is enforced?

5. Is this something ordinary people will understand?

6. Who is demanding this law and why?

7. How did this issue come to the notice of legislators?

8. How much will it cost?

9. Can it be enforced? If so, by whom and how?

10. What will be the penalty if you do not obey this law?

11. Does the law violate the United Nations Declaration of Human Rights or any other conventions signed by your country?

12. Is the law consistent with your own country's Bills of Rights and/or Constitution?

Exercise 24. **Understanding how a Bill becomes a law***

Procedure

1. Your local, provincial or national representative most probably has a copy of the process by which a Bill becomes a law. The process will differ at different levels of government. As facilitator, ask for a written copy of this process. Make photocopies for all participants.

2. Summarize the key points of this process and give an input, using newsprint.

3. Discuss in the whole group, 'When is the best time for citizens to have input into making legislation?' Hand out the copies of the legislative process.

Time   45 minutes

Materials   Copies of the legislative process.

* Processes and timing of how Bills become laws are different at each level of government. It is important for the facilitator to choose the process which suits the needs (national, provincial or local) of those attending the workshop.

An input on how a Bill becomes law

In some countries, thousands of proposed laws (called Bills) are introduced in parliament, and in the USA, only about 10 to 15 per cent actually become laws. In other countries, where the ruling party has strict control over parliament, the success rate is much higher. Whether a parliament wants to have a large number of proposals before it is a question of judgement and capacity. However, there are a number of factors that can help citizen groups to lobby to turn a Bill into law.

Early introduction If your country allows Bills to be introduced before the parliamentary session begins, it can be helpful to have the Bill written ahead of time. This gives legislators time to study the Bill. It gives citizen groups time to build local support. It means that the legislator can hold public hearings and get media attention.

Multiple sponsors Countries that are run on a parliamentary system usually rely on their party leadership to bring forward legislation. If all legislation must be initiated by the party leadership, this may be asking too much from them. If a legislator has the backing of her or his constituency and at least 10 to 20 other members of the party, s/he needs to put the proposed legislation before the leadership of the party and ask for their support. In negotiating for leadership endorsement, it is important that the leadership not only agrees to the content of the proposal, but also knows that the legislators who endorse the Bill will work for its passage on the floor.

Multi-party sponsorship The ruling party usually has a majority of votes in parliament. However, it is still wise to seek support from legislators from other political parties. This gives the Bill credibility and more chance of being understood and accepted within parties and grassroots.

276

Support from officials Depending on the area covered in the legislation, it is helpful to have the support of the relevant government departments. These departments have both information and expertise in the field. Finding supportive non-elected government personnel is very important. If the Bill is controversial and unsupported by non-elected officials, the next best thing is to seek their neutrality.

Influential sponsors If the Bill has to go through a particular committee, it is much easier if the chair of that committee and a few other high-ranking senior members support it. Even senior members from other parties or other relevant committees can be helpful allies.

Open hearings Calling for an open hearing on a Bill brings the issue before the public and allows for a transparent debate. It gives the public a chance to air their opinions and puts the issues into the public record. Although the general public is often unaware of these hearings, it is possible for legislators to work with organizations of civil society to make the issues known through the public hearings and the information that is brought forward during the hearings.

Amendments Some people think that their proposals must be put into law exactly as they were written. But in order to build wide support, it is often wise to allow others to 'own' the proposal through adding or changing part of it. Encouraging amendments can increase the chance of passage of a Bill and may result in an improved piece of legislation.

(Adapted from Amidei, *So you want to make a difference, 1995,* p 19–20).

Exercise 25. How to lobby – a role play

During Exercise 20, participants will often realize that they lobby others all the time. This is not a new activity. But there is a difference when working on legislation. We need to know the facts and feel confident to discuss the issue.

Procedure

1. Decide with the group before the workshop on one issue which they are wanting to lobby on. Lobbying on many issues at one time is not very effective. Legislators will know you are deeply concerned, but may have trouble remembering all the points you might be trying to make.

2. Ask participants to form **pairs** and discuss the following questions:

   a. What is the main problem that grassroots people are facing regarding this issue?
   b. What are the long-term concerns for local communities (or a specific group) regarding this issue?
   c. Who is suffering and how?
   d. What are some alternative solutions to this problem?

3. After about 10 minutes, ask the small groups to share their main points in the **whole group**.

4. At this stage, input on the Bill is given. This will build on the discussion the participants have just had. The facilitator needs to have a summary of the Bill and motivation for the reasons to support either the Bill or the changes that would be most helpful. It is best to have the summary and the motivation on two separate handouts.

5. Ask participants to go into **groups of four** to discuss the summary of the Bill and the motivation for support or changes. Given them at least 20 minutes.

6. In the **whole group**, ask for questions of clarification and debate. This is a critical session so that participants begin to feel confident with the facts surrounding the issue. This session can take 45 minutes or more.

7. The facilitator and another person now demonstrate a lobby visit. One person plays the lobbyist and the other plays the member of parliament (MP). Act out a lobby visit. This can be for about 5 minutes. Then ask participants what they think the lobbyist was doing. Write these things on newsprint. Compare what the lobbyist did with the list the participants made during the first exercise (on how they tried to persuade a friend). There should be many similarities. Add any of the following points on the newsprint if they did not notice these in the demonstration.

Keys things the lobbyist needs to remember to do

- Introduce oneself as a member of a group.
- Be friendly and warm.
- Give authentic praise for the work the MP is doing.
- Introduce your concern by linking it to a concern of the MP.
- Be clear about the message you want the other person to hear. Use the same phrase at least two or three times (e.g. we are concerned about the apartheid debt and believe there is a solution).
- Give two or three facts about why this issue is so important and why it will help people at grassroots level.
- Have a handout that is no longer than two pages to leave with the MP.
- Thank the MP for his/her time and say that you will get back to them for a response.

278

8. Now ask participants to find a partner to do a practice session. Give participants about 10 minutes to individually read through their materials and write down some notes for themselves on what they will say in the practice lobby session. Ask one person now to be the lobbyist and the other person to play a friendly MP. Give them about 10 minutes for the lobby practice session. After 10 minutes stop the session.

9. Have the participants remain in their pairs and ask them what they have learnt so far. After a few people have shared their experiences and difficulties, ask the pairs to switch. The person who played the MP now becomes the lobbyist and the lobbyist becomes the MP. Give them another 10 minutes to practise.

10. Bring the whole group back together and ask people to share what they have learnt and what they feel they need more clarity on. This can be another session on the issue and clarifying on the Bill. Give this plenty of time.

11. If the lobby practice session is linked to an actual visit to parliament, the group can be organized for the actual lobby visits. Ask those who feel confident about going to lobby on this issue to stand. (If the group has about 30 participants and about eight to ten participants stand, you now have small team leaders.) Now ask other participants to join those who are standing to form **teams of three or four** people. These teams will go together to lobby MPs.

Preparation for lobby visits

One of the best methods of helping participants to learn about lobbying is actually doing a lobby visit. If possible, facilitators should make appointments with MPs (or other legislators) for the participants to visit at a time after the participants have finished the above session. The preparation session might take a morning and the appointments could be made in the afternoon.

Teams are then assigned to the appointment schedule. It usually works best if one can arrange the appointment schedule for three to four visits in the same building and offices that are close to each other. Teams are asked which of the sets of appointments they would like to take. (Some people in the teams might know the legislators and wish to take this opportunity to lobby them.) Ask each team to discuss:

a. What do we know about these legislators?
b. Who will be the main spokesperson?
c. How will we organize ourselves during each visit?
d. Who will keep notes and fill in the lobby form?

Send the teams out to do their lobby visits but be clear about when they are to return to the workshop room for debriefing and evaluation.

Debriefing and evaluation session

1. The participants return from their lobby visits. Ask them to fill in their lobby form in detail. Ask them to discuss:

   a. What did we learn from the MPs we have lobbied?

   b. What follow-up do we need to do as a group on this issue?

2. Give the teams about 20 minutes for this discussion. Ask the teams to come back to the whole group and share their information on each question. Write follow-up suggestions on newsprint.

3. When all of the points have been given, use the follow-up planning tool with the group (found in Exercise 18 of this chapter) to consolidate future plans.

4. The final step in this session is to ask participants to find someone they have not been with during the lobby visits to discuss:

   a. What have we learnt about lobbying?

   b. If we had this day to do over again, what changes would we make in the programme?

   Ask participants to come back into the whole group to share their insights.

Time   One day

Materials   One-page summary of Bill the group will lobby on.
One-page fact sheet to motivate support or changes on the Bill.
Appointments with legislators made prior to lobby visits.
Lobby visit schedule with clusters of visits for teams to take.
Lobby form.

Lobby Form

Name of person you lobbied _____

Committees this MP sits on _____

_____

Response to your lobby visit:

_____ 1. HOT, yes s/he will take it up with full energy and will use her/his leadership to convince others

_____ 2. Yes, interested and convinced but will only follow others on the issue

_____ 3. Perhaps interested, but was rushed, too busy, not clear. This person needs more follow-up by someone else

_____ 4. Perhaps interested, but seemed against the issue.

_____ 5. MP argued with us and against this.

Other comments:

Your names: _____

_____

Your telephone number: _____

_____

Return this form to _____ by _____[date]

Exercise 26. Models of lobbying

Organizations that have decided they will use lobbying as the main focus of their work, or organizations, trade unions, or religious groups that have a 'legislative office', need to make some fundamental decisions.

Procedure

1. Ask participants to discuss these questions:

> **a. Will we do lobbying ourselves or is our main focus to help members in our organization to become empowered to lobby?**
>
> **b. How will the organization be shaped by our lobbying efforts? Will the organization become known on one issue or many issues?** If the organization has many functions (providing direct services, educational programmes and lobbying) how are these approaches integrated?

2. The Advocacy models diagram can be used for discussion with boards of management to help clarify the issues in order to make decisions.

Time   1 to 2 hours

Materials   A copy of the diagrams for each participant.

Advocacy models

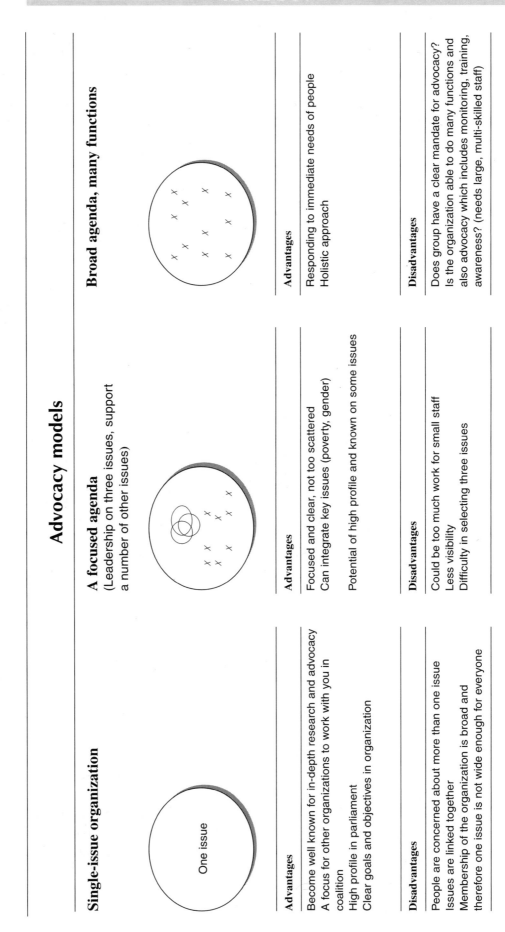

Single-issue organization

One issue

Advantages

Become well known for in-depth research and advocacy
A focus for other organizations to work with you in coalition
High profile in parliament
Clear goals and objectives in organization

Disadvantages

People are concerned about more than one issue
Issues are linked together
Membership of the organization is broad and therefore one issue is not wide enough for everyone

A focused agenda
(Leadership on three issues, support a number of other issues)

Advantages

Focused and clear, not too scattered
Can integrate key issues (poverty, gender)
Potential of high profile and known on some issues

Disadvantages

Could be too much work for small staff
Less visibility
Difficulty in selecting three issues

Broad agenda, many functions

Advantages

Responding to immediate needs of people
Holistic approach

Disadvantages

Does group have a clear mandate for advocacy?
Is the organization able to do many functions and also advocacy which includes monitoring, training, awareness? (needs large, multi-skilled staff)

Different styles of lobbying

There are many different ways an organization can decide to lobby. Three options are described here.

Option 1. Expertise in certain fields

The organization has a staff who are experts in a particular field. The staff (or person) has experience and a breadth of knowledge in a field (health care, labour laws). They work with legislators to frame laws and work in a co-operative relationship with committees and civil servants. This type of lobbying may require an organization to have a large budget to acquire the level of expertise needed.

An example of this style is an office with a staff that includes a lawyer, a health expert and someone knowledgeable about budgets to work with parliament. They would be very well known in their field, have credibility with legislators and, over time, would have developed a co-operative relationship with those committees responsible for framing the legislation.

Option 2. Monitoring legislation

This style of lobbying aims at ensuring that legislators know that their work is being monitored. Lobbyists (as well as volunteers) first find out on a weekly basis the times and agendas of the committees they are particularly needing to monitor. The lobbyist (or team) then attends the committee meetings, taking notes on all the relevant points made during the meetings. They use their notes in weekly meetings to learn what are the key issues that need to be followed up with letters or submissions to the committee. Monitoring can be a basis for building future relations with legislators through informal conversations during breaks.

An example of this is that if a team of people monitor a council or parliament, the legislators know they must be much more careful about what they say and whom they appear to support. If a legislator does seem to be very biased or say things that could violate regulations or the Constitution, the people monitoring should take the matter to the press or lodge a complaint to the chair of the committee in writing. This can help legislators to be accountable and transparent, but only if the monitors do critical follow-up work.

Option 3. Grassroots lobbying

Some people are concerned that the above two methods of lobbying can become individualistic. The knowledge about legislation stays with the lobbyist and it is only through the lobbyist's relation with legislators that changes can be made. This critique is quite valid. The grassroots lobbying style has as its aim to keep constituents informed about the issues that are being discussed which are relevant to the organization. The amount of information gathered initially is less deep than in option 1, but enough to have the facts that are needed to be able to formulate alternative legislation or amendments.

Grassroots lobbyists then spend most of their time on educational programmes, writing fact sheets or Action Alerts to their constituents, or telephoning constituency groups to mobilize actions (writing, calling, making visits to legislators, sending delegations to legislators, etc.). The focus of their work is empowering the base of their organization.

TASK: Discuss which of these options seems most suitable for your organization. Do you have the resources to carry out the option? Do you have a mandate to carry out the option? Note that these three options are not mutually exclusive and large organizations may have the capacity for all three styles. Another model could emerge from discussing these three models.

Exercise 27. Planning tool to gain support for legislation

Procedure

1. In a workshop setting, ask people to form a group around a common issue (e.g. minimum wage law or child abuse).

2. Give them copies of the checklist to gain support for legislation.

3. Ask participants to go into interest groups around the issue for which they seek support.

4. Ask each group to work through the questions on the checklist and develop a plan.

5. When groups have finished their planning, in the whole group ask for a summary of their plans.

Time   2 to 3 hours

Materials   Photocopies of the checklist and planning tool for each participant.

Checklist on gaining support for legislation

Planning to lobby follows common sense.

What are we lobbying for?	(Do we have a clear goal?)
Why are we lobbying?	(What criteria are we using to measure our success and what is our motivation?)
Who are we lobbying?	(Who has responsibility and authority for what – are we lobbying the 'right' people?)
When and how to lobby?	(What is the best timing? While the Bill is in committee?)
Where to lobby?	(In the home area or at parliament/council chambers?)

1. What are we lobbying for?

The group must be clear on what specifically they are lobbying for. It is not good enough to say 'eliminating poverty'. They must come up with a specific piece of legislation, for example 'a minimum wage bill which ensures that all employers pay their workers no less than a minimum wage of R800 a month and that there are enforcement rules to guide the punishment for those who do not abide by the law'.

TASK: Write a clear statement about what you are lobbying for.

2. Why are we lobbying?

It is important in lobbying to use facts. You need facts to support your argument and facts that counter the argument of people who do not support you. These can be written on two to four pages for the lobbyist to use in discussion with the MPs and to leave with the person with whom you are having discussions.

TASK: What are the facts about this issue?

The facts need to be about:

- why this particular Bill is so important;
- how this Bill will help (or hinder) certain people;
- how it will be a contributing factor to help reduce poverty;
- how the Bill will reduce problems in other areas of life;
- how the Bill will affect the country as a whole.

3. Who are we lobbying?

If you are lobbying to get a service implemented, you will most likely need to lobby local civil servants. Most local councils have produced a brochure on who sits on council and who are the heads of every department. Provincial governments also have a brochure about who are the heads of every department.

Targeting If you are lobbying about changing a policy, you need to develop a different strategy. Let us say that you want more regular garbage collection. On the city council in your area, there are 50 councillors. Let us say that you only need a simple majority (or 26 votes) to win a vote. You need to get a list of city councillors and visit or telephone them to ask them if they are in favour of this new law, leaning towards favouring the law, leaning against the law, or firmly against the law.

After you gather this information, you can then list the names of every councillor in one of these five columns:

1	2	3	4	5
favour	leaning to favour	undecided	leaning against	against

Do you now go and visit, telephone, or call all of the councillors to a meeting? Or do you decide to just visit those in columns 2 and 3? It will depend on how many resources and people you have, the amount of time you have and how many people you need to convince to get your 26 votes.

TASK: Who has a list of councillors? If you have a list at the workshop, go down the list and decide who will find out where each councillor stands on this issue. Decide a deadline on when you will report back your information.

4. When to lobby and how?

It is important to know when a vote is taking place on the issue for which you are lobbying. You need to find out who decides on the schedule for the council (or parliament). You will need to visit or telephone that person and ask when that vote will come up.

In many systems, most of the important decisions are taken in committees, as the larger council has too many decisions to take to become 'expert' on all things. The political compromises are made in committee. Often, much lobbying is done with specific committee members. Attending committee meetings and discussing your concerns before and after those meetings is a good time for lobbying.

However, if the vote on your issue is not for a long time to come, it is possible to get community groups to ask for meetings with the person concerned to discuss the issues.

TASK: When is the Bill coming up for a vote? When is the most strategic time to lobby?

5. Where to lobby?

Often people feel that they need to live near where the council or parliament meets in order to lobby. However, councillors all have homes (and sometimes offices) in a particular ward, district or province. Lobbying the person in their own home area can be more relaxed and the person may have more time to listen than when they are busy with committee meetings and other work.

6. Being organized

If you are not organized and ready to work on legislation for a long period of time, your efforts can become 'disempowering'. Some key steps in getting organized include:

- Form a group of at least 10 people to work with a sympathetic legislator in formulating a Bill on your concern.
- Know that you will need to work on this Bill for a long period of time so be sure you are all prepared for this.
- Have regular meetings (every week or every two weeks) to plan strategies and check in to see what has worked and not worked.

Plan ahead Find out when the council (parliament) is in recess. Find out if the councillor has an office or a place to meet during her/his 'free time'. Set up a friendly meeting that is informal so that the councillor does not have to defend a position.

TASK: Decide how you will organize yourselves for at least the first three months.

Exercise 28. Building coalitions – the 3 Cs

This model is extremely useful when a practical goal has been decided on, more support is needed, and it becomes clear that certain people or groups are blocking the achievement of this goal. It is also helpful when there is debate about different approaches to change (for example, if some people think that only one type of action can be useful when in fact many different approaches are needed). This analysis can help unite people using different tactics to achieve a common goal.

When an individual or a small group of poor or powerless people makes a request, they are often ignored. It is as if a mouse were squeaking at a lion. Those in control stand on a solid platform of power.

Very often the only power which the poor have is that of their numbers. But numbers of people are not powerful unless they are united and organized. In the diagram there are three different tactics: building *co-operation* among those who are in agreement, having a *campaign* for awareness amongst the apathetic, and building a platform of power that gives the oppressed equal standing with those who have assumed they have full power (*confrontation*).

Procedure

1. Give the input on the 3 Cs model.

2. Ask participants to form interest groups on the issue they are trying to address.

3. Give the following tasks to the whole group.

   a. The first step is to list, on the left, all the individuals and groups who agree on the importance of the goal. Plan how to get these actively involved in a process of co-operation.

   b. List, in the middle, the names of individuals and groups who are at present apathetic and passive, but who would have much to gain if the goal was achieved. Plan a campaign for awareness for these people and groups, co-operating with those who already agree on the need for change. The campaign aims to draw those who are at present apathetic across to the side of those who agree and co-operate.

   c. List, on the right, the names of those who disagree with the change, paying particular attention to people or groups who are in a position to block the change and prevent the group reaching its goal.

   It will be necessary to challenge or confront those groups and individuals. The first challenge may be in the form of a dialogue. It this does not succeed, those working for the change may have to consider other forms of confrontation or pressure.

   Confrontation can take the form of withholding money or labour. 'We will not contribute any more money until . . .' or 'We will strike on Monday unless . . .'. It can also make use of publicity, newspaper articles, etc., and seek to arouse public opinion.

Time   2 to 3 hours

Materials   Newsprint, markers, tape.

The 3 Cs

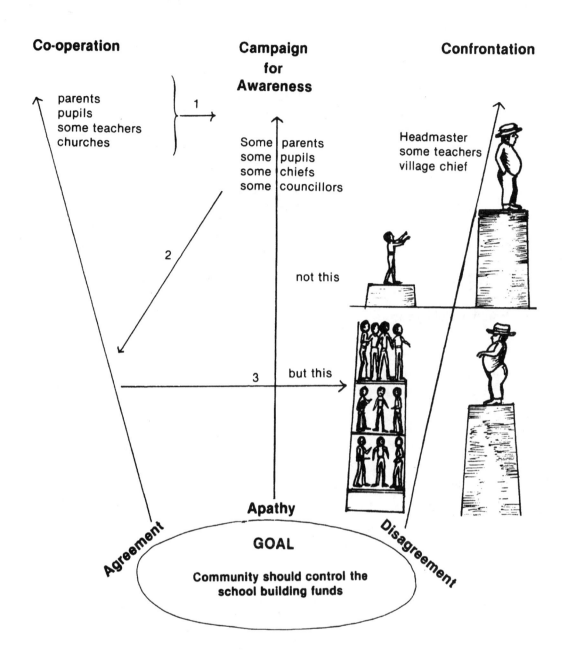

1. List on the left all the individuals and groups who agree on the importance of the goal. Plan how to get these actively involved in a **process of co-operation**.

2. List in the middle the individuals and groups which are at present apathetic and passive, but who would have much to gain if the goal was achieved. Plan a **campaign of awareness** for these people and groups.

3. List on the right those who disagree with the change, paying particular attention to people or groups that are in a position to block the change and prevent the group reaching its goal. It will be necessary to **challenge or confront** those groups and individuals.

> **When spider webs unite, they can tie up a lion**
>
> (Ethiopian proverb)

> Freedom doesn't come like a bird on a wing,
> doesn't come down like the summer's rain,
> Freedom, Freedom is a hard-won thing,
> You've got to work for it,
> Fight for it,
> Day and night for it,
> And every generation's got to do it again.
>
> (*Old trade union song*)

Workshop design on lobbying

What is lobbying?

Clarifying your purpose for lobbying

How public policy is developed

How a Bill becomes law

How to 'read' a Bill

Gaining support for legislation

How to lobby

Planning support

Building coalitions

BIBLIOGRAPHY

Environment

Berry, Thomas, *The Dream of the Earth*, Sierra Club, 730 Polk Street, San Francisco, CA 94109, USA, 1988

Berry, Wendell, *Cross Currents*. Summer 1993. Capital City Press Inc., Airport Drive Box 546A, Montpelier, Vt 05602, USA

de Graft, Joe, *Muntu*, Heinemann Educational Books, Box 45314, Nairobi, Kenya, 1977

Dorr, Donal, *Integral Spirituality*, Gill and Macmillan Ltf. Goldenbridge Dublin 8, Ireland, 1990

Ekins, Paul, Mayer Hillman and Robert Hutchison, *Wealth Beyond Measure: An atlas of new economics*. Gaia Books Limited, 66 Charlotte Street, London W1P 1LR, UK, 1992

Keating, Michael, *The Earth Summit's Agenda for Change: A plain language version of Agenda 21 and the other Rio Agreements*, Centre for Our Common Future, 52 rue des Paquis, 1201 Geneva, Switzerland, 1993

Komai, Felicia (after the novel by Alan Paton), *Cry, the Beloved Country: A Verse Drama*, Friendship Press, 475 Riverside Drive, New York, NY 10115, USA, 1948

Lappé, Frances Moore and Joseph Collins, *Food First: The myth of scarcity*, Souvenir Press Ltd, 43 Great Russell Street, London WC1B 3PA, UK, 1977

Plant, Judith (ed.), *Healing the Wounds: The Promise of Ecofeminism*, The Merlin Press, 10 Malden Road, London NW5 3HR, UK, 1989

Roberts, Elizabeth and Elias Amidon, *Earth Prayers from Around the World*, HarperCollins Publishers, 10 East 53rd Street, New York, NY 10022, USA, 1991

Sitarz, Daniel, editor, *Agenda 21: The Earth Summit Strategy to Save Our Planet*, EarthPress, 1103 West College Street, Carbondale, IL 62901, USA, 1994

Swimme, Brian, *The Universe is a Green Dragon: A Cosmic Creation Story*, Bear & Company Books, PO Drawer 2860, Santa Fe, New Mexico 87504, USA, 1985

Swimme, Brian and Thomas Berry, *The Universe Story: From the Primordial Flaring Forth to the Ecozoic Era*, Arkana, Penguin Books Ltd, 27 Wrights Lane, London W8 5TZ, UK, 1994

The Tribune: A women and development quarterly. International Women's Tribune Center, 777 United Nations Plaza, New York, NY 10017, USA

United Nations Environment Programme and WorldWIDE Network, Inc. Washington DC, 'Success Stories of Women and the Environment', A Preliminary Presentation in Anticipation of the Global Assembly, 1991

Gender

Eisler, Riane, *The Chalice & The Blade*. Harper & Row, Publishers, Inc., 10 East 53rd Street, New York, NY 10022, USA, 1987

Gilman, Charlotte Perkins: *Herland*, Pantheon Books, New York, USA,1979

Johnson, Elizabeth A., *She Who Is: The Mystery of God in Feminist Theological Discourse*, The Crossroads Publishing Company, 370 Lexinton Avenue, New York, NY 10017, USA, 1994

Mackenzie, Liz, *On Our Feet: Taking Steps to Challenge Women's Oppression*, CACE Publications, University of the Western Cape, Private Bag X17, Bellvile 7535, South Africa, 1992

Oduyoye, Mercy Amba and Musimbi R.A. Kanyoro, *The Will To Rise: Women, Tradition, and the Church in Africa*, Orbis Books, Maryknoll, NY 10545, USA, 1992

Ruether, Rosemary Radford: *Gaia & God: An Ecofeminist Theology of Earth Healing*, HarperCollins Publications, 10 East 53rd Street, New York, NY 10022, USA, 1992

Sen Gita & Grown Caren: *Development Crises and Alternative Visions*

Third World Women's Perspectives, Monthly Review Press, 122 West 27th Street, New York, NY 10001, USA, 1987

Walker, Alice, *The Color Purple*, Harcourt Brace Jovanovich, Publishers, 757 Third Avenue, New York, NY 10017, USA, 1982

Williams, Suzanne, with Janet Seed and Adeline Murau, *The Oxfam Gender Training Manual*, Oxfam UK & Ireland, 274 Banbury Road, Oxford, OX2 7DZ, UK, 1994

Racism

Jones, James M., 'Racism: A Cultural Analysis of the Problem', in Dovidio, John. F. and Samuel L. Gaetner (Ed.) *Prejudice, Discrimination and Racism*, Orlando: Academic Press, Harcourt Brace & Co. 1986

Jordan, Wintrop, *White Over Black*, Baltimore: Penguin, 1969

Kovel, Joel, *White Racism: A Psychohistory*, New York: Pantheon, 1970

Marx, Anthony W., *Making Race and Nation: A Comparison of the United States, South Africa and Brazil*, Cambridge University Press, 1997

Terry, Robert, *For Whites Only*, Detroit: Eerdmans, 1970

Culture

Carter, Forrest, *The Education of Little Tree*, University of New Mexico Press and Cherokees Carter Corp, 1976

Koyama, Kosuke, *Mount Fuji and Mount Sinai: A Critique of Idols*, Orbis Books, Maryknoll, NY 10545, 1985

Nyerere, Julius K. *Man and Development*, Oxford University Press, 1974

Shiva, Vandana, *Staying Alive*, Zed Books Ltd, 57 Caledonian Road, London N1 9BU, UK, 1989

Thich Nhat Hanh, *The Heart of Understanding*, Parallax Press, Box 7355, Berkeley, California, 94707, 1988.

Verhelst, Thierry G., *No Life Without Roots: Culture and Development*, Zed Books Ltd, 57 Caledonian Road, London N1 9BU, UK, 1990

Governance

Cheru, Fantu, *The Silent Revolution in Africa: Debt, Development and Democracy*, Zed Books, 7 Cynthia Street, London Nl 9JF, UK, 1993

Corten, David, *When Corporations Rule the World*, Berrett-Koehler Publishers, 14 Oakwood Ave, West Hartford, CT 06119, USA, 1995

Giddens, Anthony, *Beyond Left and Right*, Stanford University Press, Stanford, CA, USA, 1994

Mihevc, John, *The Market Tells Them So: The World Bank and Economic Fundamentalism in Africa*, Zed Books, 7 Cynthia Street, London Nl 9JF, UK, 1995

Rifkin, Jeremy, *The End of Work: The Decline of the Global Labor Force and the Dawn of the Post-Market Era*, A Tarcher/Putnam Book, G.P. Putnam's Sons, 200 Madison Avenue, New York, NY 10016, 1995

Robertson, James, *Future Wealth: A New Economics for the 21st Century*, Artillery House, Artillery Row, London SW1P 1RT, England, 1989

Yankelovich, Daniel, *Coming to Public Judgment: Making Democracy Work in a Complex World*, Syracuse University Press, Syracuse, NY 13244, 1991

Music and Liturgies

Cry of Ramah, Collen Fulmer, Loretto Spirituality Network, 725 Calhoun Street, Albany, CA 94706. Audio Tape

Woman Prayer – Woman Song: Resources for Ritual: Miriam Therese Winter, Meyer Stone Books, 714 South Humphrey, Oak Park, IL 60304, 1987

Women's Prayer Services (edited by Iben Gjerding and Katherine Kinnamon), Twenty-Third Publications, Box 180, Mystic, Connecticut 06355, 1988

The Best of Struggles, This Ancient Love; Spirit of Life; We're Coming Home; Rain on Dry Ground, This Tough Spun Web; and I come of my People. Women's music audio tapes by Carolyn McDade, Box 510 Wellfleet, MA 02667.

Fair Share

For more information about Fair Share, write to them at School of Government, UWC, 1 Scott Road, Observatory 7925, Cape Town, South Africa. E-mail: fairshar@netactive.co.za